D0359649

GROWING UP
NATIVE
AMERICAN

GROWING UP NATIVE AMERICAN

An Anthology

Edited and with an Introduction by
PATRICIA RILEY

Foreword by
INÉS HERNANDEZ

WILLIAM MORROW AND COMPANY, INC.
New York

E98
C5G76

Copyright © 1993 by Bill Adler Books

Foreword © 1993 by Inés Hernandez

Additional copyright notices appear on pages 335 and 336, which serve as an extension of this copyright page.

All rights reserved. No part of this book may be reproduced or utilized in any form or by any means, electronic or mechanical, including photocopying, recording, or by any information storage or retrieval system, without permission in writing from the Publisher. Inquiries should be addressed to Permissions Department, William Morrow and Company, Inc., 1350 Avenue of the Americas, New York, N.Y. 10019.

It is the policy of William Morrow and Company, Inc., and its imprints and affiliates, recognizing the importance of preserving what has been written, to print the books we publish on acid-free paper, and we exert our best efforts to that end.

Library of Congress Cataloging-in-Publication Data

Growing up Native American : an anthology / edited with an
    introduction by Patricia Riley : foreword by Inés Hernandez.
        p.   cm.
    ISBN 0-688-11850-X
    1. Indians of North America—Children.   2. Indians of North
America—Ethnic identity.   3. American literature—Indian authors.
I. Riley, Patricia, 1950–
E98.C5G76   1993
810.8'03520397—dc20   92-46484
                                                               CIP

Printed in the United States of America

First Edition

1 2 3 4 5 6 7 8 9 10

BOOK DESIGN BY RUTH KOLBERT

*This book is dedicated
to the Native American children
of the past, present, and future*

FOREWORD: REFLECTIONS ON IDENTITY AND CULTURE

[My grandfather] and the grandmothers and grandfathers before him thought about us as they lived, confirmed in their belief of a continuing life. . . . [T]hey brought our present beings into existence by the beliefs they held (Simon Ortiz).★

I am a Nimipu (Nez Perce) woman on my mom's side, and a woman of Mexican Indian descent on my dad's. As an educator, a scholar, a poet, and a human being, I identify as a native woman of this hemisphere. I am honored to write an introduction to this collection. I begin with the words of Acoma writer Simon Ortiz because the passage raises questions that I believe are addressed throughout the selections in this book. To begin with, what does Ortiz mean when he says that the grandmothers and grandfathers "thought about us"? How did they think about us? What is "a continuing life"? How did they bring us into existence by their beliefs? Is what Ortiz says common to all peoples? Maybe so, maybe not. The answer reveals itself as the selections herein shed light on the distinctiveness of Native American belief systems, and Native American cultural responses to historical experience. Given the current interest in "diversity" and "multiculturalism," as well as the changing demographics of this nation, it may very well be that many people of many ethnicities, including recent immigrants from

★Passages cited within this introduction may be found in the selections in this anthology.

7

throughout the Americas as well as other parts of the world, will find something in this collection that will speak to them with respect to issues of identity, culture, community, and representation.

I cannot assume, however, nor should anyone, that the readership of this book will be completely non-Indian. I would hope that this book falls into the hands of many Native American readers who will see the text as a respectful opening into the multilayered and intricate worlds from which they (we) come. I sense that they will find themselves in some selections more than others (which is not a judgment on the selections but a comment on the heterogeneity of "the" Native American experience in relation to U.S. society), depending upon what their own personal experience has been, and what they have been told, if anything, about the experience of their families and their people. There are stories told with the certainty of being brought up as an "Indian." There are other stories where the contours and distinctions have become fuzzy, sometimes through outright denial of a heritage. As Joe Bruchac says:

> *In the face of those denials I felt, at times, like one who looks into a mirror and sees a blur over part of his own face. No matter how he shifts, changes the light, cleans the glass, that area which cannot be clearly seen remains. And its very uncertainty becomes more important than that which is clear and defined in his vision.*

And yet, in Bruchac's very writing of these lines, *he* provides a mirror for those who have undergone the same experience. His words, like the words of the other native people represented here, form the mirrors by which the images, of native people come into sharper focus for all of us.

Native people know that the term "Indian" is a misnomer, but we have made it our own, just as we have made "American Indian" and more recently "Native American" our own, even though in our original languages, each of our peoples had (and have) their own name for themselves and for this part of the earth that is now known as "America." We refer to each other by the tribe or nation that we are from—that is one of the first questions we ask each other, "Who are your people?" and

"Where are you from?" I am Nimipu; in my mother's language Nimipu means "We, the people." It is our name for ourselves as human beings. This is so for most other native peoples, as is evidenced by the recent exhibit (August 26–October 19, 1992) of contemporary Native American art at the College of Wooster Art Museum in Wooster, Ohio, which was entitled "We, the Human Beings." The labels "Native American" or "American Indian" are in the end simplistic generalizations, generic terms, that at best acknowledge the fact that indeed indigenous peoples in this hemisphere did and do have something in common. This book serves to demonstrate some of the ways that we come together, in variation, around themes that are central to our experience.

What we have most in common today might be called the two major components of our identity. One is our identification with this hemisphere as our original land base, articulated through the oral tradition in the sacred stories of our beginnings, as well as in the stories (or "teachings") about our sacred principles, our relationship to the earth and all of life. One of the beliefs that all the writers convey is the importance of memory. Ortiz says, "I can't remember a world without memory. Memory, immediate and far away in the past, something in the sinew, blood, ageless cell." In remembrance we find continuance; native peoples know this. And as N. Scott Momaday says, the spirit informs the memory* and the one memory is of the land.†
Ortiz writes of "the ageless mother pueblo of Acoma." Ignatia Broker tells us of the "grandfathers and grandmothers who were the dust of the forests." My own grandfather Ukshanat (Thomas Andrews) used to say that at one time we were all one people, from the north to the south of this hemisphere, which is not to say that we all spoke the same language or practiced exactly the same "culture." What he meant was that we were (and I would say we are still) all related in our *relationship* to this

---

*N. Scott Momaday, "The Magic of Words," in *Survival This Way: Interviews with American Indian Poets*, ed. Joseph Bruchac (Tucson: Sun Tracks and University of Arizona Press, 1987).
†N. Scott Momaday, "Man Made of Words," in *Literature of the American Indians: Views and Interpretations*, ed. Abraham Chapman (New York: New American Library, 1975).

9

particular land base that has always been our homeland. Each distinct "culture" learned (and learns) its form and expression from the particular sacred places or land base that its people are from. And so we have desert peoples, mountain peoples, coastal peoples, plains peoples, lake peoples. These peoples traveled and knew each other; they had established trade routes and complex networks of communication and social relations. That is not to say they did not sometimes go to war with each other, but they also made peace with each other.

The other common denominator is the historical experience of colonization that began to be imposed on us over five hundred years ago, and that is marked by the arrival on the shores of this hemisphere of a man named Columbus who was lost. Columbus, under orders of the Spanish Crown, quickly turned his "mistake" into a colossal feat of Empire, paving the way as he and his men did for what has come to be known as the "Conquest" of the Americas. Simon Ortiz's essay properly frames this collection, because in it he reminds us to place his own and the other narratives within the context of both the colonial experience, and the resistance movements that were (and are) seeking "decolonization," including those of "present-day Indians in Central and South America with whom we must identify." In the main, these selections remember what the guiding principles of the original cultures were as they interrogate and oppose the "right of conquest," genocide, colonialism, "Manifest Destiny," the missionization campaigns, cultural genocide, imperialism, stereotyping, and the imposition on ourselves of who we are from the "conqueror's" perspective. The infamous "Conquest" is not a fait accompli; many native peoples have designated the arrival of Europeans—call them colonizers, agents of colonial (and imperial) rule, settlers, or immigrants— as the "Invasion." The experience of indigenous peoples at the hands of those who came and "conquered" in this hemisphere is regarded as the "continuing Invasion." I cannot say this strongly enough. What we have in this collection, in many cases, are stories by or about "prisoners of war"—this is not a statement meant to alarm anyone, or to arouse feelings of guilt in anyone. It is simply a matter of fact.

We were the enemy. It is one thing to read about this interchange from the perspective of the "victors," quite another to read about it from the perspective of those who were defeated militarily and then subjected to indoctrination programs that were meant to "defeat" them in every other way as well. The United States in its westward expansion, justified by the notion of a "Manifest Destiny," defeated Native American peoples with its superior military technology and seemingly limitless armies. For indigenous people of the U.S. Southwest, Mexico had previously played out its own role as "conqueror" and colonizer. But as Ortiz says, "Aacquu did not die in 1598 when it was burned and razed by European conquerors, nor did the people become hopeless when their children were taken away to U.S. schools far from home and new ways were imposed upon them." "Forced acculturation"—"brainwashing"—"re-programming"—whatever the process is called that was imposed at Indian schools, they were, in Lame Deer's words, "like jails and run along military lines." But he, like many other Indian youth, refused "to cooperate in the remaking of [him]-self." I would venture to say that he and all of the rest of us who have survived have called on every ounce of our originality to give us the strength and inspiration for what Ortiz calls our "fightback." This originality is found in the original cultural teachings that honor our humanity, our dignity, and our spirits as necessary components of our identity.

Momaday says that "[n]otions of the past and future are esentially notions of the present. In the same way an idea of one's ancestry and posterity is really an idea of the self." I have heard many elders say that we that walk the earth now are the link between our ancestors and our unborn generations—the past and the future come together in us. Is this idea particularly and only Native American? Of course not, and yet perhaps its particular manifestation is. I know that I am not the only Native American person who relates to the story of Waterlily's being given the gift of her own personal history. When I read how her memory is nurtured by the "recitals of her early doings and sayings" (Deloria), how indeed her very being in the world is of significance for others as well as for her, I am reminded of my own mother, and of how she was (and is) with me, with my sons, and with my grandchildren. I understand how "having one's senses" means growing in awareness and responsibility for one's self and one's words and actions in relation to all things. For those native people who have been fortunate enough to receive some or all of their cultural understandings, I believe that we would agree that children are sacred and honored members of our communities, as are the good grandmothers and the good grandfathers. There is an intimate, special bond between the youngest and the oldest members of the community. It is common among Indian people to hear children being referred to as "little grammas and little grampas." When you call a child a "little gramma" you give her a sense of the importance of her place over the generations, just as you acknowledge her ability to teach you right now from the wisdom of her little person's perspective. Children learn to be attentive because we are attentive to them, as several of the selections in this collection demonstrate so beautifully.

There are other stories, too, however, that show us the consequences of war, capture, surrender, relocation, and conversion. In Sarah Winnemucca's story, we see the terror of the children as the whites approach. From the game of "playing buried" in Waterlily's story, we move to the reality of being "buried alive" in Sarah's story. And in most cases the transition was just that quick. From the family's "planting sage bushes over [the] faces [of the children]" (Winnemucca) to hide them from the usurpers, we come to "Joe" being brutally beaten in Francis La Flesche's story of the Omaha children in boarding school. We also see that even in the midst of their own despair, and their own infrequent but joyous reunions with their families, the young boys know when to be quiet and show respect, as when they come upon the woman who is in mourning. It is a delicate balance that they are keeping, negotiating for their lives in an alien setting that was meant to bring them into line and to destroy every shred of self-esteem that their own culture had given them. These are the stories of subversion and insubordination—what would today be praised as admirable and even heroic if any U.S. soldiers were to become prisoners of war. Boarding schools were (and are) simultaneously sites of indoctrination and resistance. As Lame Deer said, "I came out more Indian than when I went in." There is something to be said for determination and the ability to be creative in the most repressive of situations. Lame Deer learns "some good fox songs" in the basement that is a place of solitary confinement. In the same manner, just this last year, in 1992, Paiute/Pit River artist Jean LaMarr created a piece entitled *We Danced and Sang Until the Matrons Came,* which is her own commentary on the subversiveness of children who are placed in boarding schools.

What is crucial to remember regarding Native American peoples who live within the United States is that in over three hundred cases, the U.S. government entered into treaty agreements with Indian peoples on a nation-to-nation basis. The fact that all of these treaties have been broken and dishonored by the U.S. government is directly related to the fact that the "unfortunately ordinary" problems that Ortiz speaks of—poverty, battered self-esteem, alcoholism, and personal and cultural disintegration—are still with us. These problems do not constitute Native American "culture." It is not the fault of our "culture" that our communities are suffering as they are today. Our communities are still contending with and contesting the intentional and systematic pattern of unjust treatment that is at the core of our historical relationship with the U.S. government. Worst of all, Native Americans are still denied religious freedom in this society, and for native people, spirituality and culture are inextricably interwoven, so the denial of religious freedom is a direct attack on the culture. Knowing how "to live beautifully from day to day" (Walters) and how to ensure a "continuing life" (Ortiz) have as much to do with spirituality as they have to do with culture. They both have to do with ethical understandings of how to be in the world in relation to all that lives, to all that is.

What part does language play in the formulation of the idea of the self? Everything. We always come back to language. N. Scott Momaday won the Pulitzer Prize for literature in 1969, for his novel *House Made of Dawn* demonstrating his command of the English language in all its beauty. In 1992, Rigoberta Menchú, a thirty-three-year-old Mayan woman and revolutionary leader, won the Nobel Peace Prize for her dedicated work toward a peaceful ending of the repression against indigenous people in Guatemala, and for her conscious articulation of the struggle her people are waging. Menchú, in her own autobiography, states that she learned how to speak Spanish in order to defend her people. The voices in this collection come to us in English, in one of the invaders' languages. Sometimes, the command of English has cost the very high price of the original native language. And yet, learning the system that is oppressing us, Ortiz reminds us, gives us "the motive of a fightback," and a major aspect of the system is the language. After all, language has been used against us—the language that ridiculed our naming of the world. The language that has misrepresented us and distorted our faces so that we would not recognize ourselves— the racist language that called (and calls) us "savage," "heathen," "drunkard," "squaw," or "chief." The duplicitous language that betrays us in the courts, and tries to keep us fighting among ourselves along bloodlines. The entitled "conquerors' " languages that even tried to erase from us the memory of our own names, replacing them with names in English, French, Spanish, and Portuguese. In many Native American communities our languages are being resuscitated (many were never completely lost). As they are revived, we are revived. This does not mean that we will no longer speak "the invaders' languages." We have made them our own, too, and in that sense, we are, like Bruchac, "able to understand the language of both [or all] sides, to help them understand each other."

Patricia Riley has carefully selected and woven together these "growing up" stories, which give us a sense of the commonality and diversity of experience (in terms of historical moment, gender, full or mixed bloodness, reservation or urban background) within the Native American community. I hope readers of this book will understand the fallacy of trying to use only "a few ill-chosen words . . . to encapsulate an entire human life!" (Bruchac) In matters of identity, labels are generally imprecise and problematic in their "lumping together" of peoples who do identify with each other culturally and by ethnicity. Often, unfortunately, people can become quite rigid in their notions, especially if they have unquestioningly accepted restrictive (and prescriptive) stereotyping. Recently I had a non-Indian student in a Native American literature class become indignant when a guest speaker (who curates Native American art exhibits) showed us images by contemporary Native American artists that made use of irony, highlighted contradiction, and otherwise manifested "Indian humor." In response to the presentation, the student wrote furiously (and with an assumed authority that was quite startling) that the "true" images of Indians are those that depict still and solemn faces. He insisted that the artists were catering to and appeasing non-Indian audiences. There were just too many smiles, and the subjects (and the artists) were just having too much fun! *That* couldn't be "Indian." Indeed, humor is very much a part of living and "fighting back" as an Indian in today's world.

I hope readers will get a sense also of the "strong positive view of our collective Indianness" (Ortiz), and "the integrity and dignity of an Indian identity" (Ortiz), as well as the intense struggle that is involved in "being human" from a Native American perspective in contemporary society. I am happy that Patricia Riley has dedicated this book to young Native Americans; they deserve to come first in a collection that is about growing up Native American. If they come to read these stories that are about people like them, maybe they won't feel as "distant as the stars" (Johnston) from their own people, wherever they might be. Maybe the question and declaration from the little girl in Anna Lee Walters's story will ring true for them, too, "You Indian, ain't you? We your people!" And in the end this book is also for all young people everywhere, for their just hearts and spirits, and for their own "belief in a continuing life."

Inés Hernandez

NOTE

For those readers who would like more information on Native American literature, here are a few titles of the many available: *Studies in American Indian Literature: Critical Essays and Course Designs*, ed. Paula Gunn Allen (New York: Modern Language Association of America, 1983); *Narrative Chance: Postmodern Discourse on Native American Indian Literature*, ed. Gerald Vizenor; and *Survival This Way: Interviews with American Indian Poets*, ed. Joseph Bruchac. For a focus on the diversity of Native American Women writers, Beth Brant's *A Gathering of Spirit* and Rayna Green's *That's What She Said: Contemporary Poetry and Fiction by Native American Women* are good introductions. *The Rights of Indians and Tribes*, by Stephen L. Pevar, and *American Indian Federal Policy*, ed. Vine Deloria, Jr., are important for providing the legal, legislative, and political explanations of the status of Native Americans in the United States. *The American Indian in Western Legal Thought: The Discourses of Conquest*, by Robert A. Williams, Jr., and *The State of Native America: Genocide, Colonization and Resistance*, ed. Annette Jaimes, both provide a hemispheric and global perspective to the status and struggles of indigenous peoples today. *The Sacred: Paths of Knowledge/Sources of Life*, Anna Lee Waters, Peggy Beck, and Nia Francisco, which is published by Navajo Community College Press, focuses on Native American spiritual foundations, and the journal *Wicazo Sa [Red Pencil]Review*, ed. Elizabeth Cook-Lynn, offers perspectives on Native American Studies as a discipline, and on issues of critical importance to the Native American community today, such as the current struggles for Native American religious freedom.

ACKNOWLEDGMENTS

I would like to thank Inés Hernandez, Terry Wilson, Clifford Trafzer, John Purdy, and Jana Sequoya for their excellent scholarship, constant support, and helpful suggestions. I would also like to thank Gerald Vizenor for making me aware of this project and for his important work in the field, and Will Schwalbe for his patient editorial assistance.

CONTENTS

Contents

INTRODUCTION

What does it mean to grow up Native American? There are as many answers to that question as there are Native American people. Certainly, there are as many stories. Stories of oppression and survival, of people who grew up surrounded by tradition, and people who did not. Stories of the pressures of forced assimilation and stories of resistance, of heritage denied and of heritage reclaimed. A multiplicity of stories. When I began to choose narratives to exemplify both the commonality and diversity of Native American experience, I also began a backward journey through my childhood to examine my own growing up Native American.

I remembered a conversation that took place between my mother and my great-aunt Avorilla one hot and humid summer afternoon during a visit to my father's family in Jackson, Tennessee. My mother mentioned that my paternal grandmother had always attributed the black hair and brown skin that she and her sister shared as coming from their Black Irish ancestors. My great-aunt got a real look on her face and said, "Oh, she did, did she? So that's what she tells people." I was a young girl then, maybe seven or eight years old, and did not yet understand the practice of "passing" or the historical factors and racial prejudice that brought it into being. Nor did I understand the internal conflict and anguish of those who attempted to be what they were not.

This same grandmother, who took such pains to disguise her Cherokee blood, woke me up very early one morning that summer. The dew had been heavy the night before and still

21

glistened on the grass as she led me by the hand into the piney woods to show me the place where the little people danced at night. She said she often heard their music and their voices. I thought she was talking about leprechauns, though she never once said that was who they were. Leprechauns were Irish and I knew all about them from my mother's side of the family. Many years later, after I had searched out and reclaimed my Cherokee heritage, I came to understand who my grandmother had been really talking about: the Cherokee little people, the Yunwi Tsunsdi. Especially fond of lost children, these protective guides helped them to find their way home again. My grandmother, this woman who had lived her entire life in denial of her Indianness, blessed me in the only way she knew how, with a memory and a story that would eventually enable me to find my way home again to my Cherokee roots. I can't help· but wonder if that was what she had intended all along.

I also thought about the fact that, as a child growing up in the 1950s and 1960s, I was completely unaware that books written about Native American people by Native American people existed. I never got a chance to read John Joseph Mathews's *Sundown* or Sara Winnemuca Hopkins's *Life Among the Piutes* until I was a grown woman because they were shelved in the anthropology section of the downtown library. I would never have thought to look there. At the time I didn't know about anthropology or the way that tribal people were objectified. It was an inappropriate place to house Native American literature and it continues to amaze me that Native American autobiographies and novels are still shelved in the anthropology sections of many bookstores today.

As I thought back on what I had missed, I also contemplated the history books I studied in school and the numerous books about Indians that did line the shelves of the bookmobile that serviced the eastern edge of Fort Worth, Texas, where I grew up. Most of those books had been written by men and women who, for the most part, had never even seen an Indian, much less known one. As a child, I didn't pause to think about that. I think a great deal about it today because the lives depicted in the books I read then bore absolutely no resemblance to the lives of my neighbors or friends. I was a ten-book-a-week bookmobile reader, but I never came across an account of a Cherokee family that ran a small grocery store in the black part of town—like the people who lived in the big white house on the hill next to where I lived. I never saw a novel about an Osage boy who tended his mother's goats and knew how to make cheese, as well as number one, grade A slingshots out of old tree branches and pieces of inner tube—like the boy who lived in the woods across the street from me. I never read a short story about a teenage Cheyenne girl, adopted by Mormons, taught to despise herself and her tribal religion, but promised that if she were good and followed all the rules she would be white when she died. I went to school with a girl who had experienced these things.

In the books available to me as a child, Native Americans were usually exotic, cultural artifacts from the past, the stereotypical "Vanishing Americans," sometimes portrayed as romantic or noble, but always backward savages on their way out, and soon to be no more. The truth is, we have not vanished, though we have often "disappeared" from the minds and hearts of America, even as we continue to be romanticized and exploited by various "New Age" philosophers who appropriate and distort Native American spiritual traditions, but never look for nourishment in their own ancient European tribal traditions.

Thinking about all these things, I decided to use the opportunity of putting together this anthology as a chance to rectify, in some small way, the situation of my childhood, not only for myself and my own children, but for anyone, Indian or non-Indian, interested in the real-life experiences of Native American people. One of the most enjoyable aspects of this task is being able to include some of my favorite authors, such as Leslie Silko, Louise Erdrich, Michael Dorris, N. Scott Momaday, and Simon Ortiz. These writers have had an enormous impact on the way I have come to see myself and the world around me.

Many of the stories I have chosen resonate for me on a deeply personal level as well. Joe Bruchac's telling about his Abenaki grandfather who claimed to be French reminds me very much of my own grandmother. I'm especially fond of Geary Hobson's "The Talking That Trees Does." Each time I read it, I find myself transported all the way home to the moist southern air, the pungent earth smells, and the people that I still dream about almost every night. The young female protagonist in Vicki Sears's story, "Grace," brings to mind the Cheyenne girl I mentioned earlier, and makes me wonder if she was ever able to find her own personal "grace" to make it through. I hope she did and that she has been able to find her way home again as I have.

Growing Up Native American is made up of the works of twenty-two Native American writers, women and men, from fifteen nations across the United States and Canada. I have included selections from Canada because the imaginary boundaries laid down between these two countries are nonexistent in the minds and hearts of tribal peoples.

The anthology is divided into four sections with a brief introduction to each section. The stories in the first three sections are in chronological order. In most cases, I have enclosed the author's tribal affiliation in parentheses. In the instances where I have not done this, references to tribal affiliation can be found either in the title or the biographical information preceding the story. Authors listed as Ojibway or Chippewa are members of the same nation. I have used whichever name the author herself or himself has chosen to use as a means of identification.

GROWING UP
NATIVE
AMERICAN

Going Forward, Looking Back

The languages and oral traditions of Native American peoples have carried the thoughts and beliefs of their ancestors forward to their descendants in contemporary America. Passed from generation to generation through storytelling, oral traditions represent living libraries containing thousands of years of knowledge and history about the world and how to be in it.

From their first intervention, the United States government and Christian missionaries worked together to create a system of tribal education. This new system was designed to eradicate by force the use of native languages and to replace tribal stories with those drawn from Christianity in an effort to remake Native American people in the Euroamerican image.

The cultural extirpation these policies inflicted has had a devastating effect on many Native Americans. However, there has always been resistance. Though numerous languages are no longer spoken, many do still remain in use, and others are experiencing a revival as more and more young people are moving to reclaim them. Countless oral traditions still flourish and continue to evolve as new Native American storytellers add their voices to those of their ancestors, making the transition from the spoken word to the printed page.

THE LANGUAGE WE KNOW
Simon Ortiz

I*n this autobiographical essay, Simon Ortiz addresses the relationship between language and culture. He examines how the Acoma language and oral tradition he learned as a child nurtured him and shaped him into a poet and a writer.*

One of the finest contemporary Native American poets, Simon Ortiz (Acoma) was born in 1941 at Acoma Pueblo in New Mexico. He is a prolific writer whose book From Sand Creek *won the Pushcart Prize for Poetry. His most recent publication is a collection of three of his earlier works entitled* Woven Stone.

I DON'T REMEMBER A WORLD WITHOUT LANGUAGE. FROM THE TIME of my earliest childhood, there was language. Always language, and imagination, speculation, utters of sound. Words, beginnings of words. What would I be without language? My existence has been determined by language, not only the spoken but the unspoken, the language of speech and the language of motion. I can't remember a world without memory. Memory, immediate and far away in the past, something in the sinew, blood, ageless cell. Although I don't recall the exact moment I spoke or tried to speak, I know the feeling of something tugging at the core of the mind, something unutterable uttered into existence. It is language that brings us into being in order to know life.

My childhood was the oral tradition of the Acoma Pueblo people—Aaquumeh hano—which included my immediate family of three older sisters, two younger sisters, two younger brothers, and my mother and father. My world was our world of the Aaquumeh in McCartys, one of the two villages descended from the ageless mother pueblo of Acoma. My world was our Eagle clan–people among other clans. I grew up in Deetziyamah, which is the Aaquumeh name for McCartys, which is posted at the exit off the present interstate highway in western New Mexico. I grew up within a people who farmed small garden plots and fields, who were mostly poor and not well schooled in the American system's education. The language I spoke was that of a struggling people who held ferociously to a heritage, culture, language, and land despite the odds posed them by the forces surrounding them since 1540 A.D., the advent of Euro-American colonization. When I began school in 1948 at the BIA (Bureau of Indian Affairs) day school in our village, I was armed with the basic ABC's and the phrases "Good morning, Miss Oleman" and "May I please be excused to go to the bathroom," but it was an older language that was my fundamental strength.

In my childhood, the language we all spoke was Acoma, and it was a struggle to maintain it against the outright threats of corporal punishment, ostracism, and the invocation that it would impede our progress towards Americanization. Children in school were punished and looked upon with disdain if they did not speak and learn English quickly and smoothly, and so I learned it. It has occurred to me that I learned English simply because I was forced to, as so many other Indian children were. But I know, also, there was another reason, and this was that I loved language, the sound, meaning, and magic of language. Language opened up vistas of the world around me, and it allowed me to discover knowledge that would not be possible for me to know without the use of language. Later, when I began to experiment with and explore language in poetry and fiction, I allowed that a portion of that impetus was because I had come to know English through forceful acculturation. Nevertheless, the underlying force was the beauty and poetic power of language in its many forms that instilled in me the desire to become a user of language as a writer, singer, and storyteller. Significantly, it was the Acoma language, which I don't use enough of today, that inspired me to become a writer. The concepts, values, and philosophy contained in my original language and the struggle it has faced have determined my life and vision as a writer.

In Deetziyamah, I discovered the world of the Acoma land and people firsthand through my parents, sisters and brothers, and my own perceptions, voiced through all that encompasses the oral tradition, which is ageless for any culture. It is a small village, even smaller years ago, and like other Indian communities it is wealthy with its knowledge of daily event, history, and social system, all that make up a people who have a many-dimensioned heritage. Our family lived in a two-room home (built by my grandfather some years after he and my grandmother moved with their daughters from Old Acoma), which my father added rooms to later. I remember my father's work at enlarging our home for our growing family. He was a skilled stoneworker, like many other men of an older Pueblo generation who worked with sandstone and mud mortar to build their homes and pueblos. It takes time, persistence, patience, and the belief that the walls that come to stand will do so for a long, long time, perhaps even forever. I like to think that by helping to mix mud and carry stone for my father and other elders I managed to bring that influence into my consciousness as a writer.

Both my mother and my father were good storytellers and singers (as my mother is to this day—my father died in 1978), and for their generation, which was born soon after the turn of the century, they were relatively educated in the American system. Catholic missionaries had taken both of them as children to a parochial boarding school far from Acoma, and they imparted their discipline for study and quest for education to us children when we started school. But it was their indigenous sense of gaining knowledge that was most meaningful to me. Acquiring knowledge about life was above all the most important item; it was a value that one had to have in order to be fulfilled personally and on behalf of his community. And this they insisted upon imparting through the oral tradition as they told their children about our native history and our community and culture and our "stories." These stories were common knowledge of act, event, and behavior in a close-knit pueblo. It was knowledge about how one was to make a living through work that benefited his family and everyone else.

Because we were a subsistence farming people, or at least tried to be, I learned to plant, hoe weeds, irrigate and cultivate corn, chili, pumpkins, beans. Through counsel and advice I came to know that the rain which provided water was a blessing, gift, and symbol and that it was the land which provided for our lives. It was the stories and songs which provided the knowledge that I was woven into the intricate web that was my Acoma life. In our garden and our cornfields I learned about the seasons, growth cycles of cultivated plants, what one had to think and feel about the land; and at home I became aware of how we must care for each other: all of this was encompassed in an intricate relationship which had to be maintained in order that life continue. After supper on many occasions my father would bring out his drum and sing as we, the children, danced to themes about the rain, hunting, land, and people. It was all that is contained within the language of oral tradition that made me explicitly aware of a yet unarticulated urge to write, to tell what I had learned and was learning and what it all meant to me.

My grandfather was old already when I came to know him. I was only one of his many grandchildren, but I would go with him to get wood for our households, to the garden to chop weeds, and to his sheep camp to help care for his sheep. I don't remember his exact words, but I know they were about how we must sacredly concern ourselves with the people and the holy earth. I know his words were about how we must regard ourselves and others with compassion and love; I know that his knowledge was vast, as a medicine man and an elder of his kiva, and I listened as a boy should. My grandfather represented for me a link to the past that is important for me to hold in my memory because it is not only memory but knowledge that substantiates my present existence. He and the grandmothers and grandfathers before him thought about us as they lived, confirmed in their belief of a continuing life, and they brought our present beings into existence by the beliefs they held. The consciousness of that belief is what informs my present concerns with language, poetry, and fiction.

My first poem was for Mother's Day when I was in the fifth grade, and it was the first poem that was ever published, too, in the Skull Valley School newsletter. Of course I don't remember how the juvenile poem went, but it must have been certain in its expression of love and reverence for the woman who was the most important person in my young life. The poem didn't signal any prophecy of my future as a poet, but it must have come from the forming idea that there were things one could do with language and writing. My mother, years later, remembers how I was a child who always told stories—that is, tall tales— who always had explanations for things probably better left unspoken, and she says that I also liked to perform in school plays. In remembering, I do know that I was coming to that age when the emotions and thoughts in me began to moil to the surface. There was much to experience and express in that age when youth has a precociousness that is broken easily or made to flourish. We were a poor family, always on the verge of financial disaster, though our parents always managed to feed us and keep us in clothing. We had the problems, unfortunately ordinary, of many Indian families who face poverty on a daily basis, never enough of anything, the feeling of a denigrating self-consciousness, alcoholism in the family and community, the feeling that something was falling apart though we tried desperately to hold it all together.

My father worked for the railroad for many years as a laborer and later as a welder. We moved to Skull Valley, Arizona, for one year in the early 1950s, and it was then that I first came in touch with a non-Indian, non-Acoma world. Skull Valley was a farming and ranching community, and my younger brothers and sisters and I went to a one-room school. I had never really had much contact with white people except from a careful and suspicious distance, but now here I was, totally surrounded by them, and there was nothing to do but bear the experience and learn from it. Although I perceived there was not much

33

difference between *them* and *us* in certain respects, there was a distinct feeling that we were not the same either. This thought had been inculcated in me, especially by an Acoma expression—*Gaimuu Mericano*—that spoke of the "fortune" of being an American. In later years as a social activist and committed writer, I would try to offer a strong positive view of our collective Indianness through my writing. Nevertheless, my father was an inadequately paid laborer, and we were far from our home land for economic-social reasons, and my feelings and thoughts about that experience during that time would become a part of how I became a writer.

Soon after, I went away from my home and family to go to boarding school, first in Santa Fe and then in Albuquerque. This was in the 1950s, and this had been the case for the past half-century for Indians: we had to leave home in order to become truly American by joining the mainstream, which was deemed to be the proper course of our lives. On top of this was termination, a U.S. government policy which dictated that Indians sever their relationship to the federal government and remove themselves from their lands and go to American cities for jobs and education. It was an era which bespoke the intent of U.S. public policy that Indians were no longer to be Indians. Naturally, I did not perceive this in any analytical or purposeful sense; rather, I felt an unspoken anxiety and resentment against unseen forces that determined our destiny to be un-Indian, embarrassed and uncomfortable with our grandparents' customs and strictly held values. We were to set our goals as American working men and women, singlemindedly industrious, patriotic, and unquestioning, building for a future which ensured that the U.S. was the greatest nation in the world. I felt fearfully uneasy with this, for by then I felt the loneliness, alienation, and isolation imposed upon me by the separation from my family, home, and community.

Something was happening; I could see that in my years at Catholic school and the U.S. Indian school. I remembered my grandparents' and parents' words: educate yourself in order to help your people. In that era and the generation who had the same experience I had, there was an unspoken vow: we were caught in a system inexorably, and we had to learn that system well in order to fight back. Without the motive of a fight-back we would not be able to survive as the people our heritage had lovingly bequeathed us. My diaries and notebooks began then, and though none have survived to the present, I know they contained the varied moods of a youth filled with loneliness, anger, and discomfort that seemed to have unknown causes. Yet at the same time, I realize now, I was coming to know myself clearly in a way that I would later articulate in writing. My love of language, which allowed me to deal with the world, to delve into it, to experiment and discover, held for me a vision of awe and wonder, and by then grammar teachers had noticed I was a good speller, used verbs and tenses correctly, and wrote complete sentences. Although I imagine that they might have surmised this as unusual for an Indian student whose original language was not English, I am grateful for their perception and attention.

During the latter part of that era in the 1950s of Indian termination and the Cold War, a portion of which still exists today, there were the beginnings of a bolder and more vocalized resistance against the current U.S. public policies of repression, racism, and cultural ethnocide. It seemed to be inspired by the civil rights movement led by black people in the U.S. and by decolonization and liberation struggles worldwide. Indian people were being relocated from their rural homelands at an astonishingly devastating rate, yet at the same time they resisted the U.S. effort by maintaining determined ties with their heritage, returning often to their native communities and establishing Indian centers in the cities they were removed to. Indian rural communities, such as Acoma Pueblo, insisted on their land claims and began to initiate legal battles in the areas of natural and social, political and economic human rights. By the retention and the inspiration of our native heritage, values, philosophies, and language, we would know ourselves as a strong and enduring people. Having a modest and latent consciousness of this as a teenager, I began to write about the experience of being Indian in America. Although I had only a romanticized image of what a writer was, which came from the pulp rendered by

American popular literature, and I really didn't know anything about writing, I sincerely felt a need to say things, to speak, to release the energy of the impulse to help my people.

My writing in my late teens and early adulthood was fashioned after the American short stories and poetry taught in the high schools of the 1940s and 1950s, but by the 1960s, after I had gone to college and dropped out and served in the military, I began to develop topics and themes from my Indian background. The experience in my village of Deetziyamah and Acoma Pueblo was readily accessible. I had grown up within the oral tradition of speech, social and religious ritual, elders' counsel and advice, countless and endless stories, everyday event, and the visual art that was symbolically representative of life all around. My mother was a potter of the well-known Acoma clayware, a traditional art form that had been passed to her from her mother and the generations of mothers before. My father carved figures from wood and did beadwork. This was not unusual, as Indian people know; there was always some kind of artistic endeavor that people set themselves to, although they did not necessarily articulate it as "Art" in the sense of Western civilization. One lived and expressed an artful life, whether it was in ceremonial singing and dancing, architecture, painting, speaking, or in the way one's social-cultural life was structured. When I turned my attention to my own heritage, I did so because this was my identity, the substance of who I was, and I wanted to write about what that meant. My desire was to write about the integrity and dignity of an Indian identity, and at the same time I wanted to look at what this was within the context of an America that had too often denied its Indian heritage.

To a great extent my writing has a natural political-cultural bent simply because I was nurtured intellectually and emotionally within an atmosphere of Indian resistance. Aacquu did not die in 1598 when it was burned and razed by European conquerors, nor did the people become hopeless when their children were taken away to U.S. schools far from home and new ways were imposed upon them. The Aaquumeh hano, despite losing much of their land and surrounded by a foreign civilization, have not lost sight of their native heritage. This is the factual case with most other Indian peoples, and the clear explanation for this has been the fight-back we have found it necessary to wage. At times, in the past, it was outright armed struggle, like that of present-day Indians in Central and South America with whom we must identify; currently, it is often in the legal arena, and it is in the field of literature. In 1981, when I was invited to the White House for an event celebrating American poets and poetry, I did not immediately accept the invitation. I questioned myself about the possibility that I was merely being exploited as an Indian, and I hedged against accepting. But then I recalled the elders going among our people in the poor days of the 1950s, asking for donations—a dollar here and there, a sheep, perhaps a piece of pottery—in order to finance a trip to the nation's capital. They were to make another countless appeal on behalf of our people, to demand justice, to reclaim lost land even though there was only spare hope they would be successful. I went to the White House realizing that I was to do no less than they and those who had fought in the Pueblo Revolt of 1680, and I read my poems and sang songs that were later described as "guttural" by a Washington, D.C., newspaper. I suppose it is more or less understandable why such a view of Indian literature is held by many, and it is also clear why there should be a political stand taken in my writing and those of my sister and brother Indian writers.

The 1960s and afterward have been an invigorating and liberating period for Indian people. It has been only a little more than twenty years since Indian writers began to write and publish extensively, but we are writing and publishing more and more; we can only go forward. We come from an ageless, continuing oral tradition that informs us of our values, concepts, and notions as native people, and it is amazing how much of this tradition is ingrained so deeply in our contemporary writing, considering the brutal efforts of cultural repression that was not long ago outright U.S. policy. We were not to speak our languages, practice our spiritual beliefs, or accept the values of our past generations; and we were discouraged from pressing for our natural rights as Indian human beings. In spite of the fact that there is to some extent the same repression today, we persist and insist in living, believing, hoping, loving, speaking, and writing as Indians. This is embodied in the language we know and share in our writing. We have always had this language, and it is the language, spoken and unspoken, that determines our existence, that brought our grandmothers and grandfathers and ourselves into being in order that there be a continuing life.

THE WARRIORS
Anna Lee Walters

O ne of the most acute difficulties for Native Americans today
is trying to maintain a sense of balance and live with cultural
integrity in a society that places a high value on assimilation and
devalues tribal cultures.

Anna Lee Walters's thoughtful short story, "The Warriors,"
chronicles the struggle of Uncle Ralph, a contemporary cultural
warrior, as he strives to keep beauty alive in a world that seems to
have ceased believing in it. His love and steadfast instruction in the
traditions of the Pawnee people inspire his two nieces to carry on,
giving them the strength and courage they need to make a way for
themselves in contemporary America.

Anna Lee Walters (Pawnee-Otoe-Missouria), is the director of
the Navajo Community College Press in Tsaile, Arizona. She is
the author of The Sun Is Not Merciful, a collection of short
stories, Ghost Singer, a novel, and the co-author of The Sacred:
Ways of Knowledge, Sources of Life.

IN OUR YOUTH, WE SAW HOBOS COME AND GO, SLIDING BY OUR
faded white house like wary cats who did not want us too close.
Sister and I waved at the strange procession of passing men and
women hobos. Just between ourselves, Sister and I talked of
that hobo parade. We guessed at and imagined the places and
towns we thought the hobos might have come from or had
been. Mostly they were White or Black people. But there were

Indian hobos too. It never occurred to Sister and me that this would be Uncle Ralph's end.

Sister and I were little and Uncle Ralph came to visit us. He lifted us over his head and shook us around him like gourd rattles. He was Momma's younger brother and he could have disciplined us if he so desired. That was part of our custom. But he never did. Instead, he taught us Pawnee words. "*Pari'* is Pawnee and *pita* is man," he said. Between the words, he tapped out drumbeats with his fingers on the table top, ghost dance and round dance songs that he suddenly remembered and sang. His melodic voice lilted over us and hung around the corners of the house for days. His stories of life and death were fierce and gentle. Warriors dangled in delicate balance.

He told us his version of the story of *Pahukatawa*, a Skidi Pawnee warrior. He was killed by the Sioux but the animals, feeling compassion for him, brought *Pahukatawa* to life again. "The Evening Star and the Morning Star bore children and some people say that these offspring are who we are," he often said. At times he pointed to those stars and greeted them by their Pawnee names. He liked to pray. He prayed for Sister and me and for everyone and every tiny thing in the world, but we never heard him ask for anything for himself from *Atius, the Father.*

"For beauty is why we live," Uncle Ralph said when he talked of precious things only the Pawnees know. "We die for it too." He called himself an ancient Pawnee warrior when he was quite young. He told us that warriors must brave all storms and odds and stand their ground. He knew intimate details of every battle the Pawnees ever fought since Pawnee time began, and Sister and I knew even then that Uncle Ralph had a great battlefield of his own.

As a child I thought that Uncle Ralph had been born into the wrong time. The Pawnees had been ravaged so often by then. The tribe of several thousand at its peak over a century before were then a few hundred people who had been closely confined for over a century. The warrior life was gone. Uncle Ralph was trapped in a transparent bubble of a new time. The bubble bound him tight as it blew around us.

Uncle Ralph talked obsessively of warriors, painted proud warriors who shrieked poignant battle cries at the top of their lungs and died with honor. Sister and I were very little then, lost from him in the world of children who saw everything with children's eyes. And though we saw with wide eyes the painted warriors that he fantasized and heard their fierce and haunting battle cries, we did not hear his. Now that we are old and Uncle Ralph has been gone for a long time, Sister and I know that when he died, he was tired and alone. But he was a warrior.

The hobos were always around in our youth. Sister and I were curious about them and this curiosity claimed much of our time. They crept by the house at all hours of the day and night, dressed in rags and odd clothing. They wandered to us from the railroad tracks where they had leaped from slow-moving box cars onto the flatland. They hid in high clumps of weeds and brush that ran along the fence near the tracks. The hobos usually travelled alone, but Sister and I saw them come together, like poor families, to share a tin of beans or sardines they ate with sticks or twigs. Uncle Ralph watched them from a distance too.

One early morning, Sister and I crossed the tracks on our way to school and collided with a tall haggard whiteman. He wore a very old-fashioned pin-striped black jacket covered with lint and soot. There was fright in his eyes when they met ours. He scurried around us, quickening his pace. The pole over his shoulder where his possessions hung in a bundle at the end bounced as he nearly ran from us.

"Looks just like a scared jackrabbit," Sister said as she watched him dart away.

That evening we told Momma about the scared man. She warned us about the dangers of hobos as our father threw us a stern look. Uncle Ralph was visiting but he didn't say anything. He stayed the night and Sister asked him, "Hey, Uncle Ralph, why do you suppose they's hobos?"

Uncle Ralph was a large man. He took Sister and put her on one knee. "You see, Sister," he said, "hobos are a different kind. They see things in a different way. Them hobos are kind of like us. We're not like other people in some ways and yet we are. It has to do with what you see and feel when you look at this old world."

His answer satisfied Sister for a while and he taught us some more Pawnee words that night.

Not long after Uncle Ralph's explanation, Sister and I surprised a Black man with white whiskers and fuzzy hair. He was climbing through the barbed wire fence that marked our property line. He wore faded blue over-alls with pockets stuffed full of handkerchiefs. He wiped sweat from his face and when it dried he looked up and saw us. I remembered what Uncle Ralph had said and wondered what the Black man saw when he looked at us standing there.

"We might scare him," Sister said softly to me, remembering the whiteman who had scampered away.

Sister whispered, "Hi," to the Black man. Her voice was barely audible.

"Boy, it's shore hot," he said. His voice was big and he smiled.

"Where are you going?" Sister asked.

"Me? Nowheres, I guess," he muttered.

"Then what you doing here?" Sister went on. She was bold for a seven-year-old kid. I was a year older but I was also more quiet. "This here place is ours," she said.

He looked around and saw our house with its flowering mimosa trees and rich green, mowed lawn stretching out before him. Other houses sat around ours.

"I reckon I'm lost," he said.

Sister pointed to the weeds and brush further up the road. "That's where you want to go. That's where they all go, the hobos."

I tried to quiet Sister but she didn't hush. "The hobos stay up there," she said. "You a hobo?"

He ignored her question and asked his own, "Say, what is you all? You not Black, you not White. What is you all?"

Sister looked at me. She put one hand on her chest and the other hand on me, "We Indians!" Sister said.

He stared at us and smiled again. "Is that a fact?" he said.

"Know what kind of Indians we are?" Sister asked him.

He shook his fuzzy head. "Indians is Indians, I guess," he said.

Sister wrinkled her forehead and retorted, "Not us! We not like others. We see things different. We're Pawnees. We're warriors!"

I pushed my elbow into Sister's side. She quieted.

The man was looking down the road and he shuffled his feet. "I'd best go," he said.

Sister pointed to the brush and weeds one more time. "That way," she said.

He climbed back through the fence and brush as Sister yelled, "Bye now!" She waved a damp handkerchief.

Sister and I didn't tell Momma and Dad about the Black man. But much later Sister told Uncle Ralph every word that had been exchanged with the Black man. Uncle Ralph listened and smiled.

Months later when the warm weather had cooled and Uncle Ralph came to stay with us for a couple of weeks, Sister and I went to the hobo place. We had planned it for a long time. That afternoon when we pushed away the weeds, not a hobo was in sight.

The ground was packed down tight in the clearing among the high weeds. We walked around the encircling brush and found folded cardboards stacked together. Burned cans in assorted sizes were stashed under the cardboards and there were remains of old fires. Rags were tied to the brush, snapping in the hard wind.

Sister said, "Maybe they're all in the box cars now. It's starting to get cold."

She was right. The November wind had a bite to it and the cold stung our hands and froze our breaths as we spoke.

"You want to go over to them box cars?" she asked. We looked at the Railroad Crossing sign where the box cars stood.

I was prepared to answer when a voice roared from somewhere behind us.

"Now, you young ones, you git on home! Go on! Git!"

A man crawled out of the weeds and looked angrily at us. His eyes were red and his face was unshaven. He wore a red plaid shirt with striped gray and black pants too large for him. His face was swollen and bruised. An old woolen pink scarf hid some of the bruise marks around his neck and his top coat was splattered with mud.

Sister looked at him. She stood close to me and told him defiantly, "You can't tell us what to do! You don't know us!"

He didn't answer Sister but tried to stand. He couldn't. Sister ran to him and took his arm and pulled on it. "You need help?" she questioned.

He frowned at her but let us help him. He was tall. He seemed to be embarrassed by our help.

"You Indian, ain't you?" I dared to ask him.

He didn't answer me but looked at his feet as if they could talk so he wouldn't have to. His feet were in big brown overshoes.

"Who's your people?" Sister asked. He looked to be about Uncle Ralph's age when he finally lifted his face and met mine. He didn't respond for a minute. Then he sighed. "I ain't got no people," he told us as he tenderly stroked his swollen jaw.

"Sure you got people. Our folks says a man's always got people," I said softly. The wind blew our clothes and covered the words.

But he heard. He exploded like a firecracker. "Well, I don't! I ain't got no people! I ain't got nobody!"

"What you doing out here anyway?" Sister asked. "You hurt? You want to come over to our house?"

"Naw," he said. "Now you little ones, go on home. Don't be walking round out here. Didn't nobody tell you little girls ain't supposed to be going round by themselves. You might git hurt."

"We just wanted to talk to hobos," Sister said.

"Naw, you don't. Just go on home. Your folks is probably looking for you and worrying bout you."

I took Sister's arm and told her we were going home. Then we said "Bye" to the man. But Sister couldn't resist a few last words, "You Indian, ain't you?"

He nodded his head like it was a painful thing to do. "Yeah, I'm Indian."

"You ought to go on home yourself," Sister said. "Your folks probably looking for you and worrying bout you."

His voice rose again as Sister and I walked away from him.

"I told you kids, I don't have any people!" There was exasperation in his voice.

Sister would not be outdone. She turned and yelled, "Oh yeah? You Indian, ain't you? Ain't you?" she screamed, "We your people!"

His top-coat and pink scarf flapped in the wind as we turned away from him.

We went home to Momma and Dad and Uncle Ralph then. Uncle Ralph met us at the front door. "Where you all been?" he asked and looked toward the railroad tracks. Momma and Dad were talking in the kitchen.

"Just playing, Uncle," Sister and I said simultaneously.

Uncle Ralph grabbed both Sister and I by our hands and yanked us out the door. "*Awkuh!*" he said, using the Pawnee expression to show his dissatisfaction.

Outside, we sat on the cement porch. Uncle Ralph was quiet for a long time and neither Sister or I knew what to expect.

"I want to tell you all a story," he finally said. "Once, there were these two rats who ran around everywhere and got into everything all the time. Everything they were told not to do, well, they went right out and did. They'd get into one mess and then another. It seems that they never could learn."

At that point Uncle Ralph cleared his throat. He looked at me and said, "Sister, do you understand this story? Is it too hard for you? You're older."

I nodded my head up and down and said, "I understand."

Then Uncle Ralph looked at Sister. He said to her, "Sister, do I need to go on with this story?"

Sister shook her head from side to side. "Naw, Uncle Ralph," she said.

"So you both know how this story ends?" he said gruffly. Sister and I bobbed our heads up and down again.

We followed at his heels the rest of the day. When he tightened the loose hide on top of his drum, we watched him and held it in place as he laced the wet hide down. He got his drumsticks down from the top shelf of the closet and began to pound the drum slowly.

"Where you going, Uncle Ralph?" I asked. Sister and I knew

45

that when he took his drum out, he was always gone shortly after.

"I have to be a drummer at some doings tomorrow," he said.

"You a good singer, Uncle Ralph," Sister said. "You know all them old songs."

"The young people nowadays, it seems they don't care bout nothing that's old. They just want to go to the Moon." He was drumming low as he spoke.

"We care, Uncle Ralph," Sister said.

"Why?" Uncle Ralph asked in a hard challenging tone that he seldom used on us.

Sister thought for a minute and then said, "I guess because you care so much, Uncle Ralph."

His eyes softened and he said, "I'll sing you an *Eruska* song, a song for the warriors."

The song he sang was a war dance song. At first Sister and I listened attentively but then Sister began to dance the man's dance. She had never danced before and she tried to imitate what she had seen. Her chubby body whirled and jumped the way she'd seen the men dance. Her head tilted from side to side the way the men moved theirs. I laughed aloud at her clumsy effort and Uncle Ralph laughed heartily too.

Uncle Ralph went in and out of our lives after that. We heard that he sang at one place and then another, and people came to Momma to find him. They said that he was only one of a few who knew the old ways and the songs.

When he came to visit us, he always brought something to eat. The Pawnee custom was that the man, the warrior, should bring food, preferably meat. Then whatever food was brought to the host was prepared and served to the man, the warrior, along with the host's family. Many times Momma and I, or Sister and I, came home to an empty house to find a sack of food on the table. I or Momma cooked it for the next meal and Uncle Ralph showed up to eat.

As Sister and I grew older, our fascination with the hobos decreased. Other things took our time, and Uncle Ralph did not appear as frequently as he did before.

Once while I was home alone, I picked up Momma's old

photo album. Inside was a gray photo of Uncle Ralph in an army uniform. Behind him were tents on a flat terrain. Other photos showed other poses but in only one picture did he smile. All the photos were written over in black ink in Momma's handwriting. "Ralphie in Korea," the writing said.

Other photos in the album showed our Pawnee relatives. Dad was from another tribe. Momma's momma was in the album, a tiny gray-haired woman who no longer lived. And Momma's momma's Dad was in the album; he wore old Pawnee leggings and the long feathers of a dark bird sat upon his head. I closed the album when Momma, Dad, and Sister came home.

Momma went into the kitchen to cook. She called me and Sister to help. As she put on a bibbed apron, she said, "We just came from town, and we saw someone from home there." She meant someone from her tribal community.

"This man told me that Ralphie's been drinking hard," she said sadly. "He used to do that quite a bit a long time ago but we thought that it had stopped. He seemed to be alright for a few years." We cooked and then ate in silence.

Washing the dishes, I asked Momma, "How come Uncle Ralph never did marry?"

Momma looked up at me but was not surprised by my question. She answered, "I don't know, Sister. It would have been better if he had. There was one woman who I thought he really loved. I think he still does. I think it had something to do with Mom. She wanted him to wait."

"Wait for what?" I asked.

"I don't know," Momma said and sank into a chair.

After that we heard unsettling rumors of Uncle Ralph drinking here and there.

He finally came to the house once when only I happened to be home. He was haggard and tired. His appearance was much like that of the whiteman that Sister and I met on the railroad tracks years before.

I opened the door when he tapped on it. Uncle Ralph looked years older than his age. He brought food in his arms. "*Nowa*, Sister," he said in greeting. "Where's the other one?" He meant Sister.

"She's gone now, Uncle Ralph. School in Kansas," I answered. "Where you been, Uncle Ralph? We been worrying about you."

He ignored my question and said, "I bring food. The warrior brings home food. To his family, to his people." His face was lined and had not been cleaned for days. He smelled of cheap wine.

I asked again, "Where you been, Uncle Ralph?"

He forced himself to smile. "Pumpkin Flower," he said, using the Pawnee name, "I've been out with my warriors all this time."

He put one arm around me as we went to the kitchen table with the food. "That's what your Pawnee name is. Now don't forget it."

"Did somebody bring you here, Uncle Ralph, or are you on foot?" I asked him.

"I'm on foot," he answered. "Where's your Momma?"

I told him that she and Dad would be back soon, I started to prepare the food he brought.

Then I heard Uncle Ralph say, "Life is sure hard sometimes. Sometimes it seems I just can't go on."

"What's wrong, Uncle Ralph?" I asked.

Uncle Ralph let out a bitter little laugh. "What's wrong?" he repeated. "What's wrong? All my life, I've tried to live what I've been taught but, Pumpkin Flower, some things are all wrong!"

He took a folded pack of Camel cigarettes from his coat pocket. His hand shook as he pulled one from the pack and lit the end. "Too much drink," he said sadly. "That stuff is bad for us."

"What are you trying to do, Uncle Ralph?" I then asked.

"Live," he said.

He puffed on the shaking cigarette awhile and said, "The old people said to live beautifully with prayers and song. Some died for beauty too."

"How do we do that, Uncle Ralph, live for beauty?" I asked.

"It's simple, Pumpkin Flower," he said. "Believe!"

"Believe what?" I asked.

He looked at me hard. "*Aw-kuh!*" he said, "that's one of the things that is wrong. Everyone questions. Everyone doubts. No one believes in the old ways anymore. They want to believe when it's convenient, when it doesn't cost them anything and when they get something in return. There are no more believers. There are no more warriors. They are all gone. Those who are left only want to go to the Moon."

A car drove up outside. It was Momma and Dad. Uncle Ralph heard it too. He slumped in the chair, resigned to whatever Momma would say to him.

Momma came in first. Dad then greeted Uncle Ralph and disappeared into the back of the house. Custom and etiquette required that Dad, who was not a member of Momma's tribe, allow Momma to handle her brother's problems.

She hugged Uncle Ralph. Her eyes filled with tears when she saw how thin he was and how his hands shook.

"Ralphie," she said, "you look awful but I am glad to see you."

She then spoke to him of everyday things, how the car failed to start and the latest gossip. He was silent, tolerant of the passing of time in this way. His eyes sent me a pleading look while his hands shook and he tried to hold them still.

When supper was ready, Uncle Ralph went to wash himself for the meal. When he returned to the table, he was calm. His hands didn't shake so much.

At first he ate without many words, but in the course of the meal he left the table twice. Each time he came back, he was more talkative than before, answering Momma's questions in Pawnee. He left the table a third time and Dad rose.

Dad said to Momma, "He's drinking again. Can't you tell?" Dad left the table and went outside.

Momma frowned. A determined look grew on her face.

When Uncle Ralph sat down to the table once more, Momma told him, "Ralphie, you're my brother but I want you to leave now. Come back when you are sober."

He held a tarnished spoon in mid-air and he put it down slowly. He hadn't finished eating but he didn't seem to mind leaving. He stood, looked at me with his red eyes and went to the door. Momma followed him. In a low voice, she said, "Ralphie, you've got to stop drinking and wandering—or don't come to see us again."

He pulled himself to his full height then. His frame filled the doorway. He leaned over Momma and yelled, "Who are you? Are you God that you will say what will be or will not be?"

Momma met his angry eyes. She stood firm and did not back down.

His eyes finally dropped from her face to the linoleum floor. A cough came from deep in his throat.

"I'll leave here," he said. "But I'll get all my warriors and come back! I have thousands of warriors and they'll ride with me. We'll get our bows and arrows. Then we'll come back!" He staggered out the door.

In the years that followed, Uncle Ralph saw us only when he was sober. He visited less and less. When he did show up, he did a tapping ritual on our front door. We welcomed the rare visits. Occasionally he stayed at our house for a few days at a time when he was not drinking. He slept on the floor.

He did odd jobs for minimum pay but never complained about the work or money. He'd acquired a vacant look in his eyes. It was the same look that Sister and I had seen in the hobos when we were children. He wore a similar careless array of clothing and carried no property with him at all.

The last time he came to the house, he called me by my English name and asked if I remembered anything of all that he'd taught me. His hair had turned pure white. He looked older than anyone I knew. I marvelled at his appearance and said, "I remember everything." That night I pointed out his stars for him and told him how *Pahukatawa* lived and died and lived again through another's dreams. I'd grown and Uncle Ralph could not hold me on his knee anymore. His arm circled my waist while we sat on the grass.

He was moved by my recitation and clutched my hand tightly. He said, "It's more than this. It's more than just repeating words. You know that, don't you?"

I nodded my head. "Yes, I know. The recitation is the easiest part but it's more than this, Uncle Ralph."

He was quiet but after a few minutes his hand touched my

shoulder. He said, "I couldn't make it work. I tried to fit the pieces."

"I know," I said.

"Now before I go," he said, "do you know who you are?"

The question took me by surprise. I thought very hard. I cleared my throat and told him, "I know that I am fourteen. I know that it's too young."

"Do you know that you are a Pawnee?" he asked in a choked whisper.

"Yes, Uncle," I said.

"Good," he said with a long sigh that was swallowed by the night.

Then he stood and said, "Well, Sister, I have to go. Have to move on."

"Where are you going?" I asked. "Where all the warriors go?" I teased.

He managed a smile and a soft laugh. "Yeah, wherever the warriors are, I'll find them."

"Before you go," I asked, "Uncle Ralph, can women be warriors too?"

He laughed again and hugged me merrily. "Don't tell me you want to be one of the warriors too?"

"No, Uncle," I said, "Just one of yours." I hated to let him go because I knew that I would not see him again.

He pulled away. His last words were, "Don't forget what I've told you all these years. It's the only chance not to become what everyone else is. Do you understand?"

I nodded and he left. I never saw him again.

The years passed quickly. I moved away from Momma and Dad and married. Sister left them before I did.

Years later in another town, hundreds of miles away, I awoke in a terrible gloom, a sense that something was gone from the world the Pawnees knew. The despair filled days though the reason for the sense of loss went unexplained. Finally, the telephone rang. Momma was on the line. She said, "Sister came home for a few days not too long ago. While she was here and alone, someone came and tapped on the door, like Ralphie always does. Sister yelled, 'Is that you, Uncle Ralph? Come on in.' But no one entered."

Then I understood, Uncle Ralph was dead. Momma probably knew too. She wept softly into the phone.

Later Momma received an official call that confirmed Uncle Ralph's death. He had died from exposure in a hobo shanty, near the railroad tracks outside a tiny Oklahoma town. He'd been dead for several days and nobody knew but Momma, Sister and me.

The funeral was well attended by the Pawnee people, Momma reported to me as I did not attend. Uncle Ralph and I had said our farewells years earlier. Momma told me that someone there had spoken well of Uncle Ralph before they put him in the ground. It was said that "Ralph came from a fine family, an old line of warriors."

Ten years later, Sister and I visited briefly at Momma's and Dad's home. We had been separated by hundreds of miles for all that time. As we sat under Momma's flowering mimosa trees, I made a confession to Sister. I said, "Sometimes I wish that Uncle Ralph were here. I'm a grown woman but I still miss him after all these years."

Sister nodded her head in agreement. I continued. "He knew so many things. He knew why the sun pours its liquid all over us and why it must do just that. He knew why babes and insects crawl. He knew that we must live beautifully or not live at all."

Sister's eyes were thoughtful but she waited to speak while I went on. "To live beautifully from day to day is a battle that warriors have to plot for as long as they can. It's a battle all the way. The things that he knew are so beautiful. And to feel and know that kind of beauty is the reason that we should live at all. Uncle Ralph said so. But now, there is no one who knows what that beauty is or any of the other things that he knew."

Sister pushed back smoky gray wisps of her dark hair. "You do," she pronounced. "And I do too."

"Why do you suppose he left us like that?" I asked.

"It couldn't be helped," Sister said. "There was a battle on."

"I wanted to be one of his warriors," I said with an embarrassed half-smile.

She leaned over and patted my hand. "You are," she said. Then she stood and placed one hand on her bosom and one hand on my arm. "We'll carry on," she said.

I touched her hand resting on my arm. I said, "Sister, tell me again. What is the battle for?"

She looked down toward the fence where a hobo was coming through. We waved at him.

"Beauty," she said to me. "Our battle is for beauty. It's what Uncle Ralph fought for too. He often said that everyone else just wanted to go to the Moon. But remember, Sister, you and I done been there. Don't forget that, after all, we're children of the stars."

THE
NINETEENTH
CENTURY

By the beginning of the nineteenth century, Native American tribes in the east and southwest had been engaged in a struggle for their lives and lands for more than 260 years. The arrival of the 1800s with its thrust of western expansion brought further chaos and upheaval to tribal peoples across North America.

The United States' expansion west marked the end of a life of self-governing freedom and the beginning of a life of enforced constraint. Reservations were established. The policy of allotment, which broke up commonly held lands into individual homestead parcels, was imposed to divest Native Americans of their communal traditions and pave the way for assimilation. Treaty making was abolished. Many Native American spiritual practices and ceremonies were outlawed. And tribes were reduced to colonial subject status and declared wards of the federal government.

During this period, the American thirst for land resulted in the forced removal to Oklahoma of the Southeastern tribes as well as the tribes from the Great Lakes. Their journey is known as the Trial of Tears and it resulted in thousands of deaths. Tribes that were allowed to remain in their homelands found their lands reduced to mere remnants of the territories they had once inhabited. Other tribal groups fled farther and farther away from ancestral homelands in a desperate attempt to avoid the onslaught of settlers and soldiers and to regain some control over their own lives.

from *WATERLILY*
Ella Cara Deloria

Set in the mid-nineteenth century and rich in cultural detail, Ella
Cara Deloria's novel Waterlily *tells the story of what life was like
for a traditional Dakota woman from infancy to early adulthood.
This selection reveals the warmth of family life, the intricate web of
reciprocity and responsibility that is kinship, and the depth of what
it means to be honored as a* hunka, *a child-beloved.*

*Ella Cara Deloria (Dakota/Sioux) was born in 1889 on the
Yankton Sioux Reservation in South Dakota. Considered an
authority on the language and lifeways of her Dakota people, she
worked closely with the American anthropologist, Franz Boas.
During her lifetime, she produced several books, including*
Speaking of Indians *and a bilingual collection of her people's
mythology entitled* Dakota Texts. *Ella Cara Deloria died in 1971.*

WHEN TETON CHILDREN COULD BE REASONED WITH THEY WERE
then said to have their senses. Waterlily was past six winters
and going on her seventh when this could be truly said of her.
Before that time, many things that happened were known to
her, but not always because she remembered them in sequence.
Rather, she knew them from repeated accounts of them. And
how she loved those recitals of her early doings and sayings—
so much that she came to think she remembered them as they
had occurred.

"Mother, what was that I did before I was even two winters
old?" she would insist, while Blue Bird pretended to forget the

story she especially liked to hear over and over. "Let me think
. . . You did so many things, I hardly know . . ." And then,
finally, "Oh, yes, for one thing, you once forecast the weather."

"Did I really, Mother?" she would ask, surprised all over
again. "What did I say?"

"You said nothing. You were too small to talk yet. But you
toddled into our tipi with two sticks for the fire. We did not
need a fire, for it was summer, and very warm. We did not ask
for fuel."

"Oh! And then?"

"Well, then"—Blue Bird always had to smile into the eager
upturned face at this point—"And then you seated yourself by
the fireplace and warmed your hands."

Waterlily would laugh merrily. "And what did Grandmother-
killed-by-the-tree say to that?" Blue Bird's old grandmother
who was killed by a falling limb was of course unknown to
Waterlily, but because her way of dying was a familiar story,
Waterlily had so named her.

"She said, 'Hina! This means we are going to have a hard
winter, sure! Children do not pretend cold weather for nothing.'"

This was the place for a long, thoughtful pause, always. And
then Waterlily asked, much impressed with her power, "And
did we have a hard winter, Mother?" She knew the answer very
well, but it was good to hear it again. "Very hard. One of the
worst our people could remember. There was snow and more
snow. Men could not hunt and no buffalo came near, and our
food gave out and many people died. A very hard winter indeed;
may we never know another like the one you predicted."

"Oh, my!" Waterlily would say with awe, her amazement
renewed with each telling. "How did I know that, Mother?"
And Blue Bird would say, "Well, how did you?" and they
would laugh, and the interview would end very satisfactorily
to Waterlily.

She liked to go over her past with Gloku, too. "Grandmother,
what did I do when you carried me on your back?"

"You were such a lively little girl—never quiet. You used to
take my two braids for reins as if you were on horseback, and
pull first this way and then that way until you had my eyelids

stretched back so far that it is a wonder I did not fall into a gopher hole with you on my back!" This was very amusing. Waterlily would clap her hands and laugh, and ask, "Did it hurt, Grandmother?" But Gloku would say, "I forget if it hurt. I only remember how you enjoyed yourself."

Then Blue Bird would cut in, defending her mother-in-law, who was always too indulgent of her grandchildren, Waterlily included. "It was not funny, Waterlily. You were naughty to hurt your grandmother. How would you like your two braids pulled?"

Waterlily would not like it at all. But those had been days when she did not know any better and nothing she did could be held against her. Now, going on seven, she was growing more and more accountable and able to remember past experiences and to be guided by them. And that was because she had her senses at last—her senses and her memory; it was all one.

The autumn day was raw and overcast when Gloku took her dogs and went after fuel, leaving Waterlily and her grandfather in the tipi. "You are a big girl, now, grandchild. Remember to hand water to your grandfather when he is thirsty. That is why your mother wants you to stay with him while I am gone."

The energetic Gloku set her tipi to rights while she said this. She hung all the food high up on the tipi poles, beyond the reach of dogs that might stray in. Then she made her old man comfortable. His sight, which had been failing for years, was now practically gone and he had to have things handed to him that were not close by. So before leaving him alone, Gloku always seated him exactly right, where he could blow the ashes from his pipe into the fire. He was able to fill and light his pipe and to clean it out when he finished, having developed the habit during the last few years by sitting with eyes shut and doing things by feel, as though preparing for total blindness. At least he was already well able to take care of his smoking needs.

The old man sat silently, with thoughts of his past activities. Waterlily threw back the fur rug and set up her play tipi on the ground for a pleasant time with her little dolls. She assigned them different roles and invented simple situations such as came up in the family. She carried on a spirited conversation as though the dolls were talking. After a long time she remembered her duty. "Grandfather! Grandfather! Water!" She held some water out to him. He groped for the dipper, saying "*Hao*, grandchild," by ways of thanks, and drank noisily.

Soon he was back into his reverie, and Waterlily played on until she felt hungry. Opening out the container of food her grandmother had left for them, she offered some to the old man and then started to eat. But the food did not taste as good as that sweetened cake of pemmican hanging high up on the tipi pole. Suddenly she wanted some of it, so badly that she piled up many rawhide cases full of dried meat until she could reach it by standing on them.

It was of a pemmican base, filled with wild fruits and held together in a hard cake by rich oils derived from bones. A little of it was enough, for it was the richest delicacy there was. But Waterlily ate and ate and could not leave off, until she began to feel miserable in her stomach. She was lying very still when Gloku returned. She could hear her outside feeding and thanking her dogs as she unhitched them.

The old man called out, "Are you back?" He knew she was, but this was their way of saying hello. "Yes," she replied. "I am back." As she entered, he said, "You better see what the child has been up to. For a long time she played very nicely with her dolls. But since we ate our meal, she has been very still, and for a child to be that still is a bad sign. It seemed to me she was moving heavy things about and reaching upward— to judge by her grunting efforts. For a time she was all over the place and then she became very silent. I called to her, but she did not answer. See if something is wrong."

Very soon Gloku discovered the half-eaten pemmican cake and let out a cry of distress that brought her daughters and Waterlily's mother running. "My grandchild has sickened herself! Oh, what is to be done?" Her only concern was for the child; that the pemmican cake was largely a loss was something she had no time to think of. But she did turn on the old man. "And you! Here you sit placid while terrible things go on! You might have called out to the others—our tipis all but touch!" Not a word from him.

Waterlily's aunts and mother tried to force medicine down her throat, but it seemed to Waterlily that the tipi was turning round and round. The tipi poles meeting overhead were a great spider web spinning rapidly; the anxious faces of the women whirled with the web until they were all of a piece, slowly fading into darkness.

Fainting was considered the opening step in the dying process. To give in was to surrender to death. If the one fainting were allowed to recline and lose consciousness, permanent death could ensue. With such beliefs, the women shook the ailing girl and kept her in a sitting position though she toppled this way and that. They continually dashed water in her face. Gloku kept saying as she rubbed Waterlily's cold wrists and temples, "Do not forget, grandchild. Keep remembering, or you will die." Remembering also meant being conscious. But Waterlily was not frightened by the threat of dying; it was not important. "Let me alone. I just want to lie still," she moaned.

The medicine eased her enough that she finally slept normally while her relatives sat around her all night. Early next morning the first person she saw was her stepfather, Rainbow. Never had he spoken directly to her till now; always at a distance had he provided her wants dutifully. Waterlily, closer to his mother and father, felt herself a stranger to her silent stepfather. But now his worried eyes said he was very much affected. "Daughter," he spoke to her, "I have tried in my humble way to provide for you because I do not want any child in my tipi to grow up in want. Yesterday you gave me a great fright, but if you will hurry and get well, then by and by you shall wear a gown and put red paint on your face."

It was not a very exciting promise to Waterlily. What was so extraordinary about wearing a gown, when one had always worn a gown? And red paint? She had worn that, too. But to the adults who understood the significance it was very important, for Rainbow was saying he would arrange and pay for a *hunka* ceremony for Waterlily. To become a *hunka* (child-beloved) was to be elevated to a high station in the tribe, and that was an honor that did not come to everyone.

Rainbow began at once to hunt for elk and to watch the hunting of other men so that he might buy from those who shot an elk the teeth that would be needed to decorate Waterlily's ceremonial gown. People were much impressed and spread the news about. "Have you heard? Rainbow is pledged to a great undertaking. He is making that little daughter of his wife a 'beloved.' Right now he is collecting elk teeth for her gown."

Everyone helped. But it was slow work because each animal yielded only two teeth that could be used. Moreover they must come only from the female elk. So widespread was the interest that even hunters from other camp circles saved elk teeth for Rainbow and sent or brought them to him from time to time. For these that were proffered he gave suitable presents in return. Only where he asked for teeth outright did he buy them.

When enough elk teeth were on hand, his sister Dream Woman made the gown; and it was something to behold. Many women, especially those who fancied themselves to be inspired artists, as Dream Woman was believed to be though she never said, came in to examine the finished gown and went away marveling at its beauty of material and workmanship. As usual, Dream Woman had dreamed an original design. It was worked into the wide border of embroidery that topped the heavy fringe around the bottom of the skirt and of the loose, open sleeves. The matched teeth, which had been painstakingly polished to a high luster by the grandfather, who was happy to help to that extent, were appliquéed in pleasing groups all over the upper half of the gown, above the belt and down over the sleeves. The gown was exactly alike both front and back.

Two whole years were spent in getting ready for the ceremony, and meantime Waterlily was preoccupied with a new baby sister, to the extent that she often forgot for long periods the great event awaiting her. The baby was named Mysterious Hand, and that was in compliment to her aunt Dream Woman, whose hands turned out unvarying beauty "too perfect to be human," as people said. But Mysterious Hand would be the ceremonial name, not to be spoken carelessly. Waterlily's descriptive term for the baby became her nickname, Smiling One.

But at last the great day arrived. At dawn Gloku began to prepare special foods for the *hunka* candidate and fed her as the sun appeared. Then Blue Bird bathed her at the stream and washed and oiled her long hair until it shone. She braided it in two long braids in the usual style and tied on the new hair ties that were part of the special outfit. They were fragrant, for

Dream Woman had made colorfully embroidered balls and stuffed them with perfume leaf, and these were attached to the ties.

The new gown and the necklace and belt and bracelet were put on Waterlily, and some long, wide pendants of tiny shells were hung from her ears. Though they were so heavy that they pulled the small lobes down, elongating them, Waterlily knew they must be endured for beauty's sake. Last of all, the new moccasins of solid red quillwork with matching leggings went on. A detail of the dreamed design on the gown was here skill-fully repeated, making of the entire costume a charming har-mony. And not only the tops but also the soles of the moccasins were covered with quillwork. This seemed extravagant and unnecessary, and Waterlily ventured to say so. "When I walk, I shall quickly break the quills and ruin the soles." Her aunt Dream Woman replied, "But you will not walk." Then she told the girl that child-be-loved moccasins for the *hunka* were always decorated so, and that one did not walk to the ceremonial tipi; one was carried.

And now Waterlily was sitting stiffly attired in the rare outfit, so heavy with elegance that she hardly dared move, nor even so much as look sideways because of the ear ornaments that hung well below her collarbone on either side. She was all ready, there in the honor-place of the tipi, but as yet she was not wearing the face paint Rainbow had promised her.

Leaping Fawn and Prairie Flower, her cousins, brought other girls in to admire her. Leaping Fawn thought it needful to explain, "You see, my cousin nearly died, but lived. That is why she is being honored. My uncle promised her this cere-mony." That was a perfectly acceptable explanation, for every-one knew that there was always a valid reason for parents to go to such expense—either because of a vow, as in Waterlily's case, or because a child was sickly and there was fear of its death, or something of the sort.

Now and then a child asked, but not often, "Mother, why is my brother a *hunka* and not I?" And then he was told, "Because we prayed for his recovery and promised to feast the people in his name if he should be spared to us, and he was." A feast always accompanied the ceremony, and through it everyone in the community was related to the child being honored. The singling out of a child for the honor was accepted by the other children when they understood. They had always been taught it was shameful to be jealous of a brother or sister. "You are all one," they were told. "Be happy for each other." Children with normal endowments and sound health did not need any such compensating honor, and the majority lived and died content without its coming to them personally.

Little Chief stayed around home today, as did everyone, for this was an occasion. He watched the ceremonial lodge being erected in the center of the circle and then ran home to wait for the ritual custom called the "pretended search" that was soon to start. Presently he shouted, "Here they come!" and ran telling everyone. But he knew what the searchers would do. He had seen them act out their role on similar occasions, for, like all boys, he often roamed throughout the circle and had watched many family ceremonies of several kinds, of which the *hunka* was one. He knew about the dramatics connected with bringing in the candidates, of the way the four men who were sent out as escorts for the candidate must pretend to lose their way.

That was what they were doing now. They came out of the ceremonial tipi and walked rapidly away, only to stop short, argue, and change their direction. Three times they did this, and only the fourth time did they head straight for Black Eagle's camp. And each time they stopped to confer and decide on another direction, they sang the traditional song that said,

> "Just where do they live?
> "Just where do they live?"

though they knew all the time.

The men arrived, entered the tipi, and lifted Waterlily gently onto the back of the one who was to carry her. Then the four men left the tipi, with Waterlily riding high and looking a little bewildered. The spectators who jammed the entrance made comments in praise of her costume, but she did not hear them.

Three other children whose parents were also honoring them were borne in the same way by their particular escorts to the ceremonial tipi. There they were seated in the honor-place and an immense curtain was held in front of them while the officials gave them the *hunka* painting: tiny pencil lines of red vermilion down their cheeks to signify their new status. They were now children-beloved. All their lives they would have the right to mark their faces in this manner for important occasions, and people would say of them, "There goes a *hunka!*" and that would be an honor. It would mean "There goes one whose family loved him so much that they gave a great feast and many presents to the people in his name." To have something given away in one's name was the greatest compliment one could have. It was better than to receive.

When the painting was finished and the curtain removed, the spectators saw the four children sitting in a row, each one holding a beautiful ear of blue corn mounted on a stick. This was to symbolize the hospitality to which they were in effect pledging themselves by accepting *hunka* status. They were now of the elect.

It was required of the officiant of every ceremony that he first declare his qualifications. Accordingly, the man who had been engaged to administer the *hunka* rite began by saying, "I have myself known this rite. And have ever striven to live up to its demands; all who hear me know that this is so. I have gladly accepted the obligation of hospitality. No one in need has opened my tipi entrance curtain in vain," and so he "presented his credentials."

Then he sang a very holy song while he waved the *hunka* wand over the heads of the candidates to invoke on them a blessing. The wand was wrapped solid with ornamental quill-work, and long strands of horsetail dyed in bright colors hung from it. At the end of the wand was a pipe.

After the song, the man offered a drink of water to each child and then withdrew it as they were about to take it, saying, "As you go on from here, there may be those about you who are faint and weary. Of such you shall be mindful. And though you would hastily bring water to your lips to quench your own thirst, yet you shall first stop to look about you," and only then he allowed them to drink.

Next he held a piece of food over incense and then cut it in two. He threw one piece in the fire and laid the other on the candidate's tongue, saying, "Whenever you sit down to eat, there may perhaps be someone waiting near, hungering for a swallow of your food. At such a time you shall remember what you have become here. And though you might be lifting meat to your mouth, yet you shall stop midway. You shall forbear to eat your food alone. Only half the morsel shall you eat, and with the other shall you show mercy."

This was all of the ritual; the feasts followed at the homes of the candidates. Rainbow gave some horses away in Waterlily's name and provided much of the food, allowing the other relatives to share in giving it, for that was the way of the people— that all those families who belonged together help each other.

Waterlily did not immediately understand what she had been committed to, but she would learn as time went on. She had been set apart as one of those who must make hospitality their first concern. Until she was a mature woman she would not be expected to carry on independently; till then, her mother and other relatives would carry on in her name. But the *hunka* obligation had been laid on her and it was a compelling thing. Its reward was high in prestige. The hairline stripes of red which she was thereafter privileged to wear were a sign of that.

Immediately after the feast the elaborate costume was laid away and once more Waterlily wore ordinary dress, so there was nothing in her daily appearance to make her different from other children. Nothing further was said about her recent honor. In time she would realize fully that she was of the elect, but the honor was something she must appear to wear casually. Let others speak of it—self-boasting was out.

Waterlily was beginning to take homely things and family doings with more appreciation. These she had always taken for granted, until this grand gesture of her stepfather brought them into focus. And so it was very much to her liking when one of her cousins, the youngest son of Black Eagle, came in one evening with the following report: "I came upon a stray buffalo with a broken leg today, so I shot him and left him in the hollow he rolled into and died."

News of meat was always a cause for rejoicing. For Black Eagle, this particular news was cause for pride and elation, for it was the boy's first real killing. Immediately he invited any of the family members who wished to go, to move out to the scene with him and camp there for the butchering. In short, it was to be a family outing.

At dawn, Rainbow and his sisters, First Woman and Dream Woman, and two or three cousins, all with their families, and of course the grandparents, Gloku and her old man, moved out there, leaving their homes standing in the camp circle and setting up temporary tipis near the ravine where the buffalo was. All the men were experienced butchers. They always cut up the animals they shot and brought the meat home in pieces. It was the Teton custom to skin the animal carefully, since hides were as important as the meat, and then to dissect the flesh according to the muscle structure. Each muscle was removed intact and called by name. The anatomical names of parts of animals were many. As each piece was removed and handed to the waiting women, they set at once to preparing it for drying. The old people took care of the bones, pounding them and then boiling them to derive their rich oils that took the place of butter, which they did not have.

But it was not all work. There was feasting on the side. Nothing seemed so desirable as meat broiled while still fresh. It was the men who took charge here, broiling the whole sides, on a grand scale called "warpath style." Over a huge fire of elm and oak they made a dome of green willows, and when the fire died down to a pile of hot coals, they flung the meat like an immense tent over the dome. It quite well covered the fire and caught all the rising heat. To a people subsisting principally on buffalo meat, the sound of sizzling juices dripping into the fire was delicious to hear; the occasional flare-up from the melting grease whetted all appetites. When the meat was cooked, it was lifted off by means of stout sticks sharpened to a point and was laid level on elm boughs spread on the ground. Then it was cut into juicy strips and passed around. And everyone had a wonderful time, the children making the most of it.

Inveterate givers of food as the Tetons were, it was not enough that Black Eagle's group of relatives were feasting after this windfall in their midst. No, they must share it. So they scanned the surrounding country for people passing in the distance and summoned them by waving a blanket or by calling to them, or some youth on a swift pony was dispatched to bring them in, to partake of the feast.

It was wonderfully pleasant to be out there. When all the meat had been cared for properly, nobody wanted to return to the camp circle just yet, though it was in sight and there was constant going in and coming out by different ones, especially the boys on horseback, who were sent back with meat for those who did not come out.

The fact that the *tinpsila,* wild prairie turnips, were at their best and grew plentifully on the hillsides offered a good excuse to stay; the women wanted to dig them for winter use. Meantime the men hunted desultorily. If one brought in a deer it was all to the good—more broiling of fresh meat. But they were too near the large circle to be hopeful of finding many.

To Waterlily these were memorable days, for this was the time she began to like her mother best and enjoy being with her more than with the other family members. Before, she had turned as readily to her grandmother, aunts, and other relatives as to her mother—it was the way of related families—but now she was learning to appreciate her mother for the rare and sympathetic person she was. The two were beginning to have little heart-to-heart talks on serious matters that were on Waterlily's mind, which her mother seemed to anticipate.

There was that lovely afternoon when they went from the camp for a walk, just Blue Bird and her three children, Waterlily, Ohiya, and Smiling One, who was now past two winters. Beyond the knoll they sat down to rest, and there was nobody and nothing in sight, only country. Blue Bird looked on her children fondly and said, "Now I am truly happy— surrounded by my children." And this she said because here was one of her rare opportunities to love them without limit, and to show them that she did. For in the larger family, where all adults acted parental toward all the children, they tried to be careful not to seem partial to any.

Waterlily said eagerly, "We are happy, too, Mother, having you to ourselves. Mother, let's play that game 'hard times' that we used to play with elder brother."

"Do you remember that, Waterlily?" Blue Bird was sur-

68

prised. "You were very little, you know, when your brother Little Chief invented it for the three of us. It was fun, wasn't it?" Then she added, looking far off, "Your brother is too big to play with us any more. He is out there somewhere, riding with the other boys. And that is right. These are the times when he must learn to ride. It is needful that all men ride well. Come now!"

She pulled her wrap over her head and brought her three children under it. They snuggled up to her as she began a running commentary about their "awful plight," and listened to the imagined misery with playful shudders.

"Now . . . here we are . . . all alone . . . just us four. On a wide, deserted, strange prairie. And worst of all, we have so little food, and it is not likely we shall find any more . . . Oh dear, isn't it terrible?"

"Terrible! Terrible!" The two older children repeated in a chorus, being well into the spirit of it.

"All we have is this tiny shelter . . . only a makeshift and not at all secure . . . Well, at least it protects us . . . if only the wind would not blow so hard!"

"The wind! The wind!" They shuddered again.

"Come, Ohiya," the mother said, "a little closer in. Waterlily, pull the tent downward and hold it firm, there, back of you . . . Oh, for some anchoring pins! But there is no tree to cut from, alas. The wind grows worse, and colder. It could rip our shelter right off . . . Hold tight! Oh, whatever shall become of us!" The children loved it—it was such fun to be so wretched when it was only play.

Ohiya added his bit of make-believe by crying, "Mother! Look at Smiling One, crawling out from under the tipi!"

"No, no, Smiling One, come back here or you will freeze! All of you, keep close so we can warm one another." They huddled still closer, in a tight knot. And then Ohiya began to moan in great misery. "What is it, my son?" "Mother, I am starving . . . soon I shall be dead. I have eaten nothing for three days and three nights . . ."

His mother was appropriately distressed, as she hastened to offer him food. "Here, son, I have a very little pemmican . . .

a mere handful. But at least hold a bit of it in your mouth . . . don't swallow it . . . swallow the juice only . . . That will sustain you. It is what warriors sometimes have to do."

"Give, give! Quick!" And Ohiya gasped and rolled his eyes in agony, according to his notion of correct dying from starvation. His mother passed out a pinch of the food to each one and took some herself and they sat holding it in the mouth, swallowing the juice only.

"I wonder, Ohiya, whether the storm has spent itself . . . it seems suddenly very quiet. Just peek out and see." She said this to find out if the children were tired of the game. Far from it. At least Ohiya wanted to prolong it, for he stuck his head out and then jerked it back in with teeth chattering noisily. "Ouch! My ears are nearly frozen off, it is so cold . . . I think we must stay here some more."

Waterlily said, "Mother, in that case, tell us a story." And so Blue Bird told them not one story but two and then a third. They were the same little stories long familiar but always welcome—about the stupid bear; the deceitful fox; the wily Iktomi, master of trickery; and about Meadowlark and her babies.

In due time the children, who had wriggled about into more comfortable position against their mother, were sound asleep, their heads on her lap. She gazed on them tenderly as she wiped their flushed faces damp along the hairline, for it was actually a very warm day. "A lapful of babies—what more should a woman want?"

She sat very still, her back against a rock, so they might have their rest, until someone called from beyond the hill telling them their evening meal was waiting.

On the way back she carried the baby while the two older ones walked ahead. Suddenly Waterlily turned back to her and said, "Mother, this was such fun! Can we go walking with you again—often?"

Waterlily went everywhere with her grandmother, Gloku, and her aunts and others, and always it was very pleasant, for they were all most agreeable. But now at last she had found her preference, her own mother, who could play games and talk about many things that were perplexing, clearing them away.

She would stay close to her from now on. It was well she decided this, for very soon she would be needing more guidance through the extraordinary days of adolescence that were not too far off. And then it would be her own mother who would be most understanding and helpful.

from LIFE AMONG THE PIUTES
Sara Winnemucca Hopkins

Born near Humbolt Lake, Nevada, in 1844, Sara Winnemucca *(Paiute) grew up to be a staunch advocate for her people and their rights. She traveled throughout the United States, lecturing about the cruel abuses faced by her tribe at the hands of unscrupulous Indian agents who stole and made personal profit from the government food and supplies meant for the tribe. In her autobiographical and historical work,* Life Among the Piutes: Their Wrongs and Claims, *Hopkins narrates the story of her family and the unjust treatment her people received after contact with and conquest by the United States government. Please note that the spelling "Piutes" in the title exemplifies the convention of the time. Today, the accepted form is "Paiute."*

In the excerpt that follows, she tells of a grandfather who kept his word even in the face of betrayal. And she writes of the terror of being buried alive by her mother in her attempt to hide Sara from invading white men whom the tribe believed were cannibals. This belief had its basis in the fate of the Donner party who, while trapped by a snowstorm in a mountain pass, had indeed survived by eating their dead. The party's Indian guides, Lewis and Salvadore, refused to do so. These heroic men, who had steadfastly remained with the doomed immigrants, fled for their lives, only after being told of plans to murder them for food. Nevertheless, they were eventually tracked down by members of the party. When they were found, exhausted and too weak to move, they were both shot in the head and consumed.

It is believed that Sarah Winnemucca Hopkins died in October 1891 and that she is buried at Henry's Lake, Montana.

OH, WHAT A FRIGHT WE ALL GOT ONE MORNING TO HEAR SOME
white people were coming. Every one ran as best they could.
My poor mother was left with my little sister and me. Oh, I
never can forget it. My poor mother was carrying my little
sister on her back, and trying to make me run; but I was so
frightened I could not move my feet, and while my poor mother
was trying to get me along my aunt overtook us, and she said
to my mother: "Let us bury our girls, or we shall all be killed
and eaten up." So they went to work and buried us, and told
us if we heard any noise not to cry out, for if we did they would
surely kill us and eat us. So our mothers buried me and my
cousin, planted sage bushes over our faces to keep the sun from
burning them, and there we were left all day.

Oh, can any one imagine my feelings *buried alive*, thinking
every minute that I was to be unburied and eaten up by the
people that my grandfather loved so much? With my heart
throbbing, and not daring to breathe, we lay there all day. It
seemed that the night would never come. Thanks be to God!
the night came at last. Oh, how I cried and said: "Oh, father,
have you forgotten me? Are you never coming for me?" I cried
so I thought my very heartstrings would break.

At last we heard some whispering. We did not dare to whisper
to each other, so we lay still. I could hear their footsteps coming
nearer and nearer. I thought my heart was coming right out of
my mouth. Then I heard my mother say, " 'T is right here!"
Oh, can any one in this world ever imagine what were my
feelings when I was dug up by my poor mother and father? My
cousin and I were once more happy in our mothers' and fathers'
care, and we were taken to where all the rest were.

I was once buried alive; but my second burial shall be for
ever, where no father or mother will come and dig me up. It
shall not be with throbbing heart that I shall listen for coming
footsteps. I shall be in the sweet rest of peace,—I, the chieftain's
weary daughter.

Well, while we were in the mountains hiding, the people that
my grandfather called our white brothers came along to where
our winter supplies were. They set everything we had left on
fire. It was a fearful sight. It was all we had for the winter, and
it was all burnt during that night. My father took some of his

74

men during the night to try and save some of it, but they could not; it had burnt down before they got there.

These were the last white men that came along that fall. My people talked fearfully that winter about those they called our white brothers. My people said they had something like awful thunder and lightning, and with that they killed everything that came in their way.

This whole band of white people perished in the mountains, for it was too late to cross them. We could have saved them, only my people were afraid of them. We never knew who they were, or where they came from. So, poor things, they must have suffered fearfully, for they all starved there. The snow was too deep.

Early in the following spring, my father told all his people to go to the mountains, for there would be a great emigration that summer. He told them he had had a wonderful dream, and wanted to tell them all about it.

He said, "Within ten days come together at the sink of Carson, and I will tell you my dream."

The sub-chiefs went everywhere to tell their people what my father had told them to say; and when the time came we all went to the sink of Carson.

Just about noon, while we were on the way, a great many of our men came to meet us, all on their horses. Oh, what a beautiful song they sang for my father as they came near us! We passed them, and they followed us, and as we came near to the encampment, every man, woman, and child were out looking for us. They had a place all ready for us. Oh, how happy everybody was! One could hear laughter everywhere, and songs were sung by happy women and children.

My father stood up and told his people to be merry and happy for five days. It is a rule among our people always to have five days to settle anything. My father told them to dance at night, and that the men should hunt rabbits and fish, and some were to have games of football, or any kind of sport or playthings they wished, and the women could do the same, as they had nothing else to do. My people were so happy during the five days,—the women ran races, and the men ran races on foot and on horses.

My father got up very early one morning, and told his people the time had come,—that we could no longer be happy as of old, as the white people we called our brothers had brought a great trouble and sorrow among us already. He went on and said,—

"These white people must be a great nation, as they have houses that move. It is wonderful to see them move along. I fear we will suffer greatly by their coming to our country; they come for no good to us, although my father said they were our brothers, but they do not seem to think we are like them. What do you all think about it? Maybe I am wrong. My dear children, there is something telling me that I am not wrong, because I am sure they have minds like us, and think as we do; and I know that they were doing wrong when they set fire to our winter supplies. They surely knew it was our food."

And this was the first wrong done to us by our white brothers.

Now comes the end of our merrymaking.

Then my father told his people his fearful dream, as he called it. He said,—

"I dreamt this same thing three nights,—the very same. I saw the greatest emigration that has yet been through our country. I looked North and South and East and West, and saw nothing but dust, and I heard a great weeping. I saw women crying, and I also saw my men shot down by the white people. They were killing my people with something that made a great noise like thunder and lightning, and I saw the blood streaming from the mouths of my men that lay all around me. I saw it as if it was real. Oh, my dear children! You may all think it is only a dream,—nevertheless, I feel that it will come to pass. And to avoid bloodshed, we must all go to the mountains during the summer, or till my father comes back from California. He will then tell us what to do. Let us keep away from the emigrant roads and stay in the mountains all summer. There are to be a great many pine-nuts this summer, and we can lay up great supplies for the coming winter, and if the emigrants don't come too early, we can take a run down and fish for a month, and lay up dried fish. I know we can dry a great many in a month, and young men can go into the valleys on hunting excursions, and kill as many rabbits as they can. In that way we can live in the mountains all summer and all winter too."

So ended my father's dream. During that day one could see old women getting together talking over what they had heard my father say. They said,—

"It is true what our great chief has said, for it was shown to him by a higher power. It is not a dream. Oh, it surely will come to pass. We shall no longer be a happy people, as we now are; we shall no longer go here and there as of old; we shall no longer build our big fires as a signal to our friends, for we shall always be afraid of being seen by those bad people."

"Surely they don't eat people?"

"Yes, they do eat people, because they ate each other up in the mountains last winter."

This was the talk among the old women during the day.

"Oh, how grieved we are! Oh, where will it end?"

That evening one of our doctors called for a council, and all the men gathered together in the council-tent to hear what their medicine man had to say, for we all believe our doctor is greater than any human being living. We do not call him a medicine man because he gives medicine to the sick, as your doctors do. Our medicine man cures the sick by the laying on of hands, and we have doctresses as well as doctors. We believe that our doctors can communicate with holy spirits from heaven. We call heaven the Spirit Land.

Well, when all the men get together, of course there must be smoking the first thing. After the pipe has passed round five times to the right, it stops, and then he tells them to sing five songs. He is the leader in the song-singing. He sings heavenly songs, and he says he is singing with the angels. It is hard to describe these songs. They are all different, and he says the angels sing them to him.

Our doctors never sing war-songs, except at a war-dance, as they never go themselves on the war-path. While they were singing the last song, he said,—

"Now I am going into a trance. While I am in the trance you must smoke just as you did before; not a word must be spoken while I am in the trance."

77

About fifteen minutes after the smoking was over, he began to make a noise as if he was crying a great way off. The noise came nearer and nearer, until he breathed, and after he came to, he kept on crying. And then he prophesied, and told the people that my father's dream was true in one sense of the word,— that is, "Our people will not all die at the hands of our white brothers. They will kill a great many with their guns, but they will bring among us a fearful disease that will cause us to die by hundreds."

We all wept, for we believed this word came from heaven.

So ended our feast, and every family went to its own home in the pine-nut mountains, and remained there till the pine-nuts were ripe. They ripen about the last of June.

Late in that fall, there came news that my grandfather was on his way home. Then my father took a great many of his men and went to meet his father, and there came back a runner, saying, that all our people must come together. It was said that my grandfather was bringing bad news. All our people came to receive their chieftain; all the old and young men and their wives went to meet him. One evening there came a man, saying that all the women who had little children should go to a high mountain. They wanted them to go because they brought white men's guns, and they made such a fearful noise, it might even kill some of the little children. My grandfather had lost one of his men while he was away.

So all the women that had little children went. My mother was among the rest; and every time the guns were heard by us, the children would scream. I thought, for one that my heart would surely break. So some of the women went down from the mountain and told them not to shoot any more, or their children would die with fright. When our mothers brought us down to our homes the nearer we came to the camp, the more I cried,—

"Oh, mother, mother, don't take us there!" I fought my mother,—I bit her. Then my father came, and took me in his arms and carried me to the camp. I put my head in his bosom, and would not look up for a long time. I heard my grandfather say,—

"So the young lady is ashamed because her sweetheart has come to see her. Come, dearest, that won't do after I have had such a hard time to come to see my sweetheart, that she should be ashamed to look at me."

Then he called my two brothers to him, and said to them, "Are you glad to see me?" And my brothers both told him that they were glad to see him. Then my grandfather said to them,—

"See that young lady; she does not love her sweetheart any more, does she? Well, I shall not live if she does not come and tell me she loves me. I shall take that gun, and I shall kill myself."

That made me worse than ever, and I screamed and cried so hard that my mother had to take me away. So they kept weeping for the little one three or four days. I did not make up with my grandfather for a long time. He sat day after day, and night after night, telling his people about his white brothers. He told them that the whites were really their brothers, that they were very kind to everybody, especially to children; that they were always ready to give something to children. He told them what beautiful things their white brothers had,—what beautiful clothes they wore, and about the big houses that go on the mighty ocean, and travel faster than any horse in the world. His people asked him how big they were. "Well, as big as that hill you see there, and as high as the mountain over us."

"Oh, that is not possible,—it would sink, surely."

"It is every word truth, and that is nothing to what I am going to tell you. Our white brothers are a mighty nation, and have more wonderful things than that. They have a gun that can shoot a ball bigger than my head, that can go as far off as that mountain you see over there."

The mountain he spoke of at that time was about twenty miles across from where we were. People opened their eyes when my grandfather told of the many battles they had with the Mexicans, and about their killing so many of the Mexicans, and taking their big city away from them, and how mighty they were. These wonderful things were talked about all winter long. The funniest thing was that he would sing some of the soldier's roll-calls, and the air to the Star-spangled Banner, which everybody learned during the winter.

He then showed us a more wonderful thing than all the others that he had brought. It was a paper, which he said could talk to him. He took it out and he would talk to it, and talk with it. He said, "This can talk to all our white brothers, and our white sisters, and their children. Our white brothers are beautiful, and our white sisters are beautiful, and their children are beautiful! He also said the paper can travel like the wind, and it can go and talk with their fathers and brothers and sisters, and come back to tell what they are doing, and whether they are well or sick."

After my grandfather told us this, our doctors and doctresses said, —

"If they can do this wonderful thing, they are not truly human, but pure spirits. None but heavenly spirits can do such wonderful things. We can communicate with the spirits, yet we cannot do wonderful things like them. Oh, our great chieftain, we are afraid your white brothers will yet make your people's hearts bleed. You see if they don't; for we can see it. Their blood is all around us, and the dead are lying all about us, and we cannot escape it. It will come. Then you will say our doctors and doctresses did know. Dance, sing, play, it will do no good; we cannot drive it away. They have already done the mischief, while you were away."

But this did not go far with my grandfather. He kept talking to his people about the good white people, and told them all to get ready to go with him to California the following spring.

Very late that fall, my grandfather and my father and a great many more went down to the Humboldt River to fish. They brought back a great many fish, which we were very glad to get; for none of our people had been down to fish the whole summer.

When they came back, they brought us more news. They said there were some white people living at the Humboldt sink. They were the first ones my father had seen face to face. He said they were not like "humans." They were more like owls than any thing else. They had hair on their faces, and had white eyes, and looked beautiful.*

I tell you we children had to be very good, indeed, during the winter; for we were told that if we were not good they would come and eat us up. We remained there all winter; the next spring the emigrants came as usual, and my father and grandfather and uncles, and many more went down on the Humboldt River on fishing excursions. While they were thus fishing, their white brothers came upon them and fired on them, and killed one of my uncles, and wounded another. Nine more were wounded, and five died afterwards. My other uncle got well again, and is living yet. Oh, that was a fearful thing, indeed!

After all these things had happened, my grandfather still stood up for his white brothers.

Our people had council after council, to get my grandfather to give his consent that they should go and kill those white men who were at the sink of Humboldt. No; they could do nothing of the kind while he lived. He told his people that his word was more to him than his son's life, or any one else's life either.

"Dear children," he said, "think of your own words to me;—you promised. You want me to say to you, Go and kill those that are at the sink of Humboldt. After your promise, how dare you to ask me to let your hearts be stained with the blood of those who are innocent of the deed that has been done to us by others? Is not my dear beloved son laid alongside of your dead, and you say I stand up for their lives. Yes, it is very hard, indeed; but, nevertheless, I know and you know that those men who live at the sink are not the ones that killed our men."

While my grandfather was talking, he wept, and men, women, and children, were all weeping. One could hardly hear him talking.

After he was through talking, came the saddest part. The widow of my uncle who was killed, and my mother and father

---

*When asked to explain this, she said, "Oh, their eyes were blue, and they had long beards."

81

all had long hair. They cut off their hair, and also cut long gashes in their arms and legs, and they were all bleeding as if they would die with the loss of blood. This continued for several days, for this is the way we mourn for our dead. When the woman's husband dies, she is first to cut off her hair, and then she braids it and puts it across his breast; then his mother and sisters, his father and brothers and all his kinsfolk cut their hair. The widow is to remain unmarried until her hair is the same length as before, and her face is not to be washed all that time, and she is to use no kind of paint, nor to make any merriment with other women until the day is set for her to do so by her father-in-law, or if she has no father-in-law, by her mother-in-law, and then she is at liberty to go where she pleases. The widower is at liberty when his wife dies; but he mourns for her in the same way, by cutting his hair off.

It was late that fall when my grandfather prevailed with his people to go with him to California. It was this time that my mother accompanied him. Everything had been got ready to start on our journey. My dear father was to be left behind. How my poor mother begged to stay with her husband! But my grandfather told her that she could come back in the spring to see her husband; so we started for California, leaving my poor papa behind. All my kinsfolk went with us but one aunt and her children.

The first night found us camped at the sink of Carson, and the second night we camped on Carson River. The third day, as we were travelling along the river, some of our men who were ahead, came back and said there were some of our white brothers' houses ahead of us. So my grandfather told us all to stop where we were while he went to see them. He was not gone long, and when he came back he brought some hard bread which they gave him. He told us that was their food, and he gave us all some to taste. That was the first I ever tasted.

Then my grandfather once more told his people that his paper talked for him, and he said, —

"Just as long as I live and have that paper which my white brothers' great chieftain has given me, I shall stand by them, come what will." He held the paper up towards heaven and kissed it, as if it was really a person. "Oh, if I should lose this," he said, "we shall all be lost. So, children, get your horses ready, and we will go on, and we will camp with them to-night, or by them, for I have a sweetheart along who is dying for fear of my white brothers." He meant me; for I was always crying and hiding under somebody's robes, for we had no blankets then.

Well, we went on; but we did not camp with them, because my poor mother and brothers and sisters told my grandfather that I was sick with crying for fright, and for him not to camp too close to them. The women were speaking two words for themselves and one for me, for they were just as afraid as I was. I had seen my brother Natchez crying when the men came back, and said there were white men ahead of us. So my grandfather did as my mother wished him to do, and we went on by them; but I did not know it, as I had my head covered while we were passing their camp. I was riding behind my older brother, and we went on and camped quite a long way from them that night.

So we travelled on to California, but did not see any more of our white brothers till we got to the head of Carson River, about fifteen miles above where great Carson City now stands.

"Now give me the baby." It was my baby-sister that grandpa took from my mother, and I peeped from under my mother's fur, and I saw some one take my little sister. Then I cried out,—

"Oh, my sister! Don't let them take her away."

And once more my poor grandfather told his people that his white brothers and sisters were very kind to children. I stopped crying, and looked at them again. Then I saw them give my brother and sister something white. My mother asked her father what it was, and he said it was *Pe-har-be*, which means sugar. Just then one of the women came to my mother with some in her hand, and grandpa said:—

"Take it, my child."

Then I held out my hand without looking. That was the first gift I ever got from a white person, which made my heart very glad.

When they went away, my grandfather called me to him, and said I must not be afraid of the white people, for they are very good. I told him that they looked so very bad I could not help it.

We travelled with them at that time two days, and the third day we all camped together where some white people were living in large white houses. My grandpa went to one of the houses, and when he came back he said his white brothers wanted him to come and get some beef and hard bread. So he took four men with him to get it, and they gave him four boxes of hard bread and a whole side of beef, and the next morning we got our horses ready to go on again. There was some kind of a fight,—that is, the captain of the train was whipping ne-groes who were driving his team. That made my poor grand-father feel very badly. He went to the captain, and told him he would not travel with him. He came back and said to his people that he would not travel with his white brothers any farther. We travelled two days without seeing any more of my grandfather's white brothers. At last we came to a very large encampment of white people, and they ran out of their wagons, or wood-houses, as we called them, and gathered round us. I was riding behind my brother. I was so afraid, I told him to put his robe over me, but he did not do so. I scratched him and bit him on his back, and then my poor grandfather rode up to the tents where they were, and he was asked to stay there all night with them. After grandpa had talked awhile, he said to his people that he would camp with his brothers. So he did. Oh, what nice things we all got from my grandpa's white brothers! Our men got red shirts, and our women got calico for dresses. Oh, what a pretty dress my sister got! I did not get anything, because I hid all the time. I was hiding under some robes. No one knew where I was. After all the white people were gone, I heard my poor mother cry out:—

"Oh, where is my little girl? Oh, father, can it be that the white people have carried her away? Oh, father, go and find her,—go, go, and find her!" And I also heard my brothers and sister cry. Yet I said nothing, because they had not called me to get some of the pretty things. When they began to cry, I began crawling out, and then my grandfather scolded me, and told me that his brothers loved good children, but not bad ones like me. How I did cry, and wished that I had staid at home with my father! I went to sleep crying.

I did not forget what had happened. There was a house near

where we camped. My grandfather went down to the house with some of his men, and pretty soon we saw them coming back. They were carrying large boxes, and we were all looking at them. My mother said there were two white men coming with them.

"Oh, mother, what shall I do? Hide me!"

I just danced round like a wild one, which I was. I was behind my mother. When they were coming nearer, I heard my grandpa say,—

"Make a place for them to sit down."

Just then, I peeped round my mother to see them. I gave one scream, and said,—

"Oh, mother, the owls!"

I only saw their big white eyes, and I thought their faces were all hair. My mother said,—

"I wish you would send your brothers away, for my child will die."

I imagined I could see their big white eyes all night long. They were the first ones I had ever seen in my life.

NI-BO-WI-SE-GWE

Ignatia Broker

I n Night Flying Woman, *Ignatia Broker (Ojibway) lovingly recounts the life of her great-great-grandmother, Ni-bo-wi-se-gwe. This is a story rich in Ojibway traditions and lifeways that moves from a life of precontact peace and contentment to the disruption and displacement caused by white settlers. In Broker's own words, it was a time of "great chaos and change."*

The following passage tells the story of a family's refusal to capitulate to government demands that they be placed on a reservation, their subsequent flight from white encroachment, and the sorrow and desolation of leaving playmates and loved ones behind, perhaps never to be seen again.

Ignatia Broker was an Ojibway elder and storyteller. Over the course of her life she worked to educate the public about Native American people. She was involved with the Upper Midwest American Indian Center in Minneapolis, Minnesota, and founded the Minnesota Indian Historical Society. She died in 1987.

NI-BO-WI-SE-GWE IS A GREAT-GREAT-GRANDMOTHER TO MANY people of the Wolf and Fish clans, and in our family we speak of her with pride. She was a great and unusual woman, and there are many stories told of her life and ways.

As it is told, many of the events and circumstances pertaining to Ni-bo-wi-se-gwe were unusual, even from the time before her birth. Her father, Me-ow-ga-bo (Outstanding), and mother, Wa-wi-e-cu-mig-go-gwe (Round Earth), were young, healthy, and strong. Usually such Ojibway couples have children early in marriage, and often they have at least five. But it was not so with this young couple. They had been three years together, a long time, and they had not had a child. The people of their village began to wonder and feel a sadness for the young couple. After the third year, Ni-bo-wi-se-gwe was born, and she was the only child.

The time of her birth was after the blueberry gathering and before the wild-rice harvesting. The day began bright and sunny, and it was so when Wa-wi-e-cu-mig-go-gwe felt the first pangs of birth. Just before the sun was high in the sky, at the exact time of birth, the sun and moon crossed paths and there was a pitch darkness. In this darkness the first wail of the child was heard, and because of this her parents knew that the tiny girl would be different. But they felt it was good because she was born of love and joy.

So out of the darkness, called the eclipse, was born a person who became strong and gave strength, who became wise and lent this wisdom to her people, who became part of the generation of chaos and change.

Me-ow-ga-bo and Wa-wi-e-cu-mig-go-gwe were happy, for it was a time of plenty. The velvet of the forest shone as soft and bright as the love they had for Tiny Girl. They had waited a long time for their child. Now that they were fulfilled, they would fill the life of their child with all that was necessary to honor her and thus the people and the Gitchi Manito, the Great Spirit.

Three weeks after birth, according to the custom of the people, came the time when the naming must be planned. The spirit of every person must be honored with a name, a song, and an animal. Tiny Girl must be given a name, and she must be given in honor to her grandparents.

Me-ow-ga-bo and Wa-wi-e-cu-mig-go-gwe consulted with Grandfather and Grandmother and decided that A-wa-sa-si (Bullhead) should be the namer, for A-wa-sa-si was old and wise and good. A-wa-sa-si was the storyteller, and when she placed her hands on the heads of the children, their crying and fears were stilled. The family lit a pipe and offered it to the Gitchi Manito. Then they sent Tiny Girl's cap with a bag of kin-nik-a-nik inside to old A-wa-sa-si. If A-wa-sa-si accepted the cap and smoked the kin-nik-a-nik it meant that she would, indeed, be the namer.

A-wa-sa-si took the cap and smiled, for it pleased her to be the namer. First she went into the forest to choose the medicine for the animal bag that she would make and give to the baby. Then she visited the child and returned to the forest to meditate and to choose an animal and a song. She visited Tiny Girl again. A day was set for the naming feast, and the family sent kin-nik-a-nik to all the people in the village to let them know that they were to come.

The family began to prepare the feast for the naming ceremony. There would be much food, for it was after the ricing time when food was stored and buried. Acorns were roasted. Hazel nuts were ground and mixed with dried berries to make small cakes. Ma-no-min, the precious wild rice, was popped and mixed with si-s-sa-ba-gwa-d, the maple sugar. There would be fish, deer, and rabbit for all, but the heads of the bear and buffalo were reserved for the Old Ones of the Mi-de-wi-wi-n.

The ceremony and feast were held in the beautiful autumn season. Although the days were cooling, they were yet sunny. The green of the forest was turning to orange, gold, and brown; this orange, gold, and brown fell and cushioned the earth and reflected the glory of the trees.

All the people of the village arrived bringing gifts. They came to hear the honor of the name given to the child of Me-ow-ga-bo and Wa-wi-e-cu-mig-go-gwe, for by honoring a child the people also honored the Gitchi Manito. A-wa-sa-si had chosen the name Ni-bo-wi-se-gwe, which means Night Flying Woman, because Tiny Girl had been born during the darkness of the day. A-wa-sa-si said that the shadows when the sun left the earth and the shadows when the day began would be the best time for her. But because Ni-bo-wi-se-gwe was such a long name for tiny tongues, the child was soon called Oona, for her first laughing sound.

Oona's first months were like those of all Ojibway children. The Ojibway know that a learning process begins at birth and that a baby's first learning experience is watching. So, as soon as possible, Oona was laced into a cradleboard and placed where she could see her family at work and at play. She watched Grandmother lacing muk-kuk-ko-ons-sug, the strong birch-bark containers, or winding wi-go-b, the tough string made from the bark of trees. People talked to her about things they saw and did. Oona was happy. She would look into the shadows in the lodge and smile, and the people would remember the time she came.

Being strapped in the cradleboard was also the beginning of her experience in restraint. She began to learn this in the custom-ary way. At certain times when she cried, a brushy stick was scraped across her face and her lips were pinched. These actions would be repeated if the family needed to make a silent journey; then Oona would know she must not cry. It was a matter of survival, especially if there were enemies in the forest.

During the first year of Oona's life the winter white piled high around the lodges, but she did not know this for inside the lodge all was warm and snug. The fire in the middle of the lodge leaped and shone and made patterns that made Oona laugh and coo. Many times old A-wa-sa-si would be in the lodge with Grandmother, for these two watched over Oona. Mother would go about her work, and often she would stop and whisper softly to Oona. Sometimes she made tiny clothes when she sat watching the meat roast over the fire. Father would come in blowing cold air and smiling, his strength and presence making everyone feel that all was well.

When the winter white turned to water, Oona, still in the cradle, went to the maple-sugar bush with the family. In the summer Oona tasted berries fresh from the bush. She walked her first steps in the fall at ricing time. For five years Oona's cycle of life was the same. Summer camp to ricing camp to winter village to sugar bush to planting time to summer camp. These years were filled with love and laughter and this cycle was the cycle of life of our people, the Ojibway.

It was the beautiful spring season. The days now were warm and clear and the sun shone through the new green of the trees. The stately birch, which had looked ghostly all through the winter, was sprinkled with the green. Once again it offered its yearly gift of bark to the forest people. Pale flowers, the violet and the crocus, lifted their faces and lent their fragile scent to the forest air, blending with the village smell of the wood fires and burning cedar leaves. The waters in the brooks whispered back and forth with the trees. Squirrels came out from their winter homes and they too chattered back and forth, holding their tails up high. This was a sign foretelling warmth for the coming days. Other Forest Brothers were standing, lean but shining, ready for another cycle of birth and life. Everything was so new, fresh, and good.

There was much excitement in the Ojibway village and the children felt it. It made them fearful. A do-daim, or clansman, from the east was visiting and the people held a feast in his honor. After the feast, in the evening, the people met in council to hear the news of the do-daim. He told of a strange people whose skins were as pale as the winter white and whose eyes were blue or green or gray.

"Yes," said A-bo-wi-ghi-shi-g (Warm Sky), the village leader, "I have seen these strangers."

"I also," said others.

"These strangers," said the do-daim, "are again asking the Ojibway to mark a paper. All the leaders of the A-sa-bi-ig-go-na-ya, the Nettle Fiber People, are to do this. The Ojibway to the east have made the mark, and now they are on the big water where they must stay forever. The strangers promised never to enter their forests but they came anyway to trade for the coats of the Animal Brothers. I have a muk-kuk they gave me, and I will leave it to you. It sits right on the fire and does not crack. It is called iron kettle, and the strangers have promised many of these when the papers are marked."

"Have you studied these strangers well? Are they good people, or are they those who will be enemies?" asked A-bo-wi-ghi-shi-g.

"Some are kind. Others speak good. Others smile when they think they are deceiving," replied the do-daim. "Many of the Ojibway have stayed with these people, but soon our people had great coughs and there were bumps on their skins, and they were given water that made them forget."

"I have seen these strangers before. They have come into the forests many times," said Grandfather. "I know that they desire the furs of our animal friends and wish to give us the strange things."

"Yes," said the do-daim, "these strangers are asking the Ojibway to trap the Animal Brothers. They give a stick that roars and that can kill faster than an arrow."

"Also," said Grandfather, "I have seen the men with the long dress. They speak many words about Gitchi Manito, the Great Spirit. And I have seen the men with the fire sticks. They have followed the Chi-si-bi (Mississippi) to its source."

"But now," said the do-daim, "these strangers are many. They intend to stay, for they are building lodges and planting food. Far to the east, the forests of the Eastern Keepers have been ripped from the face of the earth and the doors of the longhouses have been sealed.

"These strangers fight among themselves. They fought and killed each other for the land of the Mo-wi-ga-n (Mohegan) and now again they are fighting in the land of the Che-ro-ki (Cherokee).

"Our kinsmen, the O-ma-no-ma-ni-g (Menominee), the Wild Rice People, are crowded at the edge of the big water, and the O-da-wa (Ottawa) have crossed the big water. The O-bo-da-wa-da-mi-g (Potawatomi) have gone south, many of them. The Mi-s-gwa-ghi (Fox) are shivering with cold and hunger now. They are but a handful in number.

"Down by the Chi-si-bi at the place where the small gulls fly, the forests have become smaller. Strangers are there in great number. All day long they cut the trees and send them down the river. Although these strangers have said they will stay to the rising sun, already they are looking this way, for soon there will be no forest where they are now.

"Yes, my brothers," said the do-daim, "these strangers are looking this way."

When the do-daim left, the council fires burned. The people discussed what he had said.

A-bo-wi-ghi-shi-g, the leader, said, "We cannot escape for long the meeting with these strange people. Our kinsmen on the Chi-o-ni-ga-mig (Lake Superior) have marked the paper and now they must forever stay at O-bi-mi-wi-i-to-n (Grand

Portage), the carrying place. Also, I have been to where the Chi-si-bi and the A-bwa-na-g (Minnesota) waters meet. I have seen the strangers' lodges there. The lodges are many and the men called soldiers are many. They will forever be there, for they plant the corn."

Oona's grandfather said, "I also have been to the land where the small gulls live, where the strangers push the forest poles into the big river. I have seen their lodges and their planting. Soon all will be planted. But I have also been to the rainy country. The men who desire the furs are few there now. They use the waters only to pass on to the big north country, and this is seldom. The forests are thick there, and beneath the trees the earth is soft and boggy so the planting would not be good, although there are many dry places deep within the bogs. I am thinking that I shall take my family there and maybe escape these strangers for a while."

"Yes," said A-bo-wi-ghi-shi-g, "we shall do that. Those who wish to go with you will lay a stick in a pile. I shall take the others to the strangers at the Lake of Nettles if this must be so. But we all must move soon in order to plant the seed in our new places and find the ricing beds and the sugar bush."

The people met and talked for three days on the hill outside the village. They spoke of the many good things that had always been. Of grandfathers and grandmothers who were the dust of the forests. Of those who would be left in the journeying places. The women listened and there was a wailing sound to their voices when they talked together.

On the eve of the third day, the men smoked the pipe of peace in council and passed around the sacred kin-nik-a-nik. The voices of the people became stilled and a quiet purpose was reflected in their faces. The whole forest became silent.

Little Oona awoke one bright new day to the busy stirrings of the village. She had felt the excitement of the past few days, and she was fearful. "Bis-in-d-an, listen," Oona whispered to herself, heeding one of her first lessons. "Listen, and you will hear the patterns of life. Are they the same, or is there a change in the sounds?" So Oona listened. "Something different is happening today," Oona whispered again to herself. Quickly she rolled out from under the rabbitskin robe, dressed, and went out of the lodge. She saw Grandfather and Grandmother making bundles of food and clothing.

Oona was only five years old but she was already trained in many of the ways of a good Ojibway. She knew almost all that she could not do and all that she must learn to do. She went to her grandparents and stood before them with eyes cast down, knowing she could not speak the many questions she wished to ask, for they who are wise must speak first. Always, the first words spoken should be from the older people.

Oona wanted to look up at her grandfather's face, a face that was lined with many years. She had always sought comfort from her grandfather, who had a special look just for her. He would smile with his eyes and she felt well and cared for.

"Oona, my child," said Grandfather, "I hope you have slept well. I know by the roundness of your eyes that you are wondering what is doing today." Grandfather paused, sat down, and stretched out his hand to Oona. "Take my hand, and I will tell you what your eyes ask.

"Remember this day, my child," Grandfather continued. "For all of your small life, this village, this place, has been your home, but now we must move toward the setting sun. We have been happy here and we have lived here a long, long time. A very long time even before you were born. At the council it was decided that we shall seek a new place. We move because there is another people who are fast coming into the forest lands. Their ways are different and we wish to be free of them for as long as we can.

"Take the things you wish to take—your corn doll and rubbing rock toy. Put them in a bundle. There is room." Grandfather smiled and Oona felt comforted. She accepted the thoughts of change. With a feeling of excitement and anticipation, she went and stood before her mother.

"Mother," said Oona, "who will be leaving with us?"

"There will be eight families," replied Mother. "Four of your uncles and their families and three families of the do-daim of the Muk-kwa, and of course old A-wa-sa-si. Grandfather, since he is the oldest, will be the leader."

"When shall we be leaving, Mother?"

"We shall leave in a while, for we are all packed and the men have gone to get the canoes from the place of hiding. We must leave before the others go to the Lake of Nettles to be counted. That way the strange people will not know that we are not doing what they demand."

Mother looked down at her fragile daughter, she who was much smaller than the other children of her age. She brushed Oona's black shining hair and lifted up the small oval face with the huge dark eyes.

"It is sad to be leaving, my Oona," said Mother, "but in one's life there are many times when one must leave a place of happiness for the unknown. I have done this many times, but the beauty of a life remains forever in the heart. You must remember the beauty that was here. Go, my daughter, and say the words of friendship to those who were your playmates."

Oona made up her little bundle. Then she went to find her cousin, E-quay (Lady). They joined hands and circled the camp, smiling the smile of friendship to those they would not see again. They then went to the river to wait for the men and the canoes.

WASICHUS IN THE HILLS

Black Elk as told to John G. Neihardt

J ohn G. Neihardt *first met Black Elk, a holy man of the Oglala*
Lakota/Sioux, in August 1930 on the Pine Ridge Reservation in
South Dakota. The book that came out of that meeting describes
Black Elk's calling and life as a holy man. It is also the story of
the struggles of the Lakota people against the threat of white
encroachment and annihilation at the hands of the United States
cavalry—a struggle that culminated in the tragic massacre of the
peaceful people of Chief Big Foot's camp at Wounded Knee on
December 29, 1890.

When the Black Hills, sacred to the Lakota and guaranteed by
the Treaty of 1868 to remain in the possession of the tribe, were
invaded by General George Armstrong Custer and his men, Black
Elk was eleven years old. With the treaty broken, the influx of
white settlers and gold miners went unchecked. Racial tensions and
competition for land increased. This selection from Black Elk
Speaks *tells of some of the trials faced by Black Elk and his people*
during this turbulent time.

Today battles for land and tribal sovereignty take place in
courtrooms as the Lakota people continue their struggle for
autonomy and justice.

IT WAS THE NEXT SUMMER, WHEN I WAS 11 YEARS OLD (1874), THAT
the first sign of a new trouble came to us. Our band had been
camping on Split-Toe Creek in the Black Hills, and from there
we moved to Spring Creek, then to Rapid Creek where it comes

out into the prairie. That evening, just before sunset, a big thunder cloud came up from the west, and just before the wind struck, there were clouds of split-tail swallows flying all around above us. It was like a part of my vision, and it made me feel queer. The boys tried to hit the swallows with stones and it hurt me to see them doing this, but I could not tell them. I got a stone and acted as though I were going to throw, but I did not. The swallows seemed holy. Nobody hit one, and when I thought about this I knew that of course they could not.

The next day some of the people were building a sweat tepee for a medicine man by the name of Chips, who was going to perform a ceremony and had to be purified first. They say he was the first man who made a sacred ornament for our great chief, Crazy Horse. While they were heating the stones for the sweat tepee, some boys asked me to go with them to shoot squirrels. We went out, and when I was about to shoot at one, I felt very uneasy all at once. So I sat down, feeling queer, and wondered about it. While I sat there I heard a voice that said: "Go at once! Go home!" I told the boys we must go home at once, and we all hurried. When we got back, everybody was excited, breaking camp, catching the ponies and loading the drags; and I heard that while Chips was in the sweat tepee a voice had told him that the band must flee at once because something was going to happen there.

It was nearly sundown when we started, and we fled all that night on the back trail toward Spring Creek, then down that creek to the south fork of the Good River. I rode most of the night in a pony drag because I got too sleepy to stay on a horse. We camped at Good River in the morning, but we stayed only long enough to eat. Then we fled again, upstream, all day long until we reached the mouth of Horse Creek. We were going to stay there, but scouts came to us and said that many soldiers had come into the Black Hills; and that was what Chips saw while he was in the sweat tepee. So we hurried on in the night towards Smoky Earth River (the White), and when we got there, I woke up and it was day-break. We camped a while to eat, and then went up the Smoky Earth, two camps, to Robinson, for we were afraid of the soldiers up there.

Afterward I learned that it was Pahuska★ who had led his soldiers into the Black Hills that summer to see what he could find. He had no right to go in there, because all that country was ours. Also the Wasichus had made a treaty with Red Cloud (1868) that said it would be ours as long as grass should grow and water flow. Later I learned too that Pahuska had found there much of the yellow metal that makes the Wasichus crazy; and that is what made the bad trouble, just as it did before, when the hundred were rubbed out.

Our people knew there was yellow metal in little chunks up there; but they did not bother with it, because it was not good for anything.

We stayed all winter at the Soldiers' Town, and all the while the bad trouble was coming fast; for in the fall we heard that some Wasichus had come from the Missouri River to dig in the Black Hills for the yellow metal, because Pahuska had told about it with a voice that went everywhere. Later he got rubbed out for doing that.

The people talked about this all winter. Crazy Horse was in the Powder River country and Sitting Bull was somewhere north of the Hills. Our people at the Soldiers' Town thought we ought to get together and do something. Red Cloud's people said that the soldiers had gone in there to keep the diggers out, but we, who were only visiting, did not believe it. We called Red Cloud's people "Hangs-Around-The-Fort," and our people said they were standing up for the Wasichus, and if we did not do something we should lose the Black Hills.

In the spring when I was twelve years old (1875), more soldiers with many wagons came up from the Soldiers' Town at the mouth of the Laramie River§ and went into the Hills.

There was much talk all summer, and in the Moon of Making Fat (June) there was a sun dance there at the Soldiers' Town to give the people strength, but not many took part; maybe because everybody was so excited talking about the Black Hills. I re-

★Long Hair, General Custer.
§Colonel Dodge with 400 men and 75 wagons from Fort Laramie escorted a geological expedition into the Hills that spring and remained until October.

member two men who danced together. One had lost a leg in the Battle of the Hundred Slain and one had lost an eye in the Attacking of the Wagons, so they had only three eyes and three legs between them to dance with. We boys went down to the creek while they were sun dancing and got some elm leaves that we chewed up and threw on the dancers while they were all dressed up and trying to look their best. We even did this to some of the older people, and nobody got angry, because everybody was supposed to be in a good humor and to show their endurance in every kind of way; so they had to stand teasing too. I will tell about a big sun dance later when we come to it.

In the Moon When the Calves Grow Hair (September) there was a big council with the Wasichus on the Smoky Earth River at the mouth of White Clay Creek. I can remember the council, but I did not understand much of it then. Many of the Lakotas were there, also Shyelas and Blue Clouds*; but Crazy Horse and Sitting Bull stayed away. In the middle of the circle there was a shade made of canvas. Under this the councilors sat and talked, and all around them there was a crowd of people on foot and horseback. They talked and talked for days, but it was just like wind blowing in the end. I asked my father what they were talking about in there, and he told me that the Grandfather at Washington wanted to lease the Black Hills so that the Wasichus could dig yellow metal, and that the chief of the soldiers had said if we did not do this, the Black Hills would be just like melting snow held in our hands, because the Wasichus would take that country anyway.

It made me sad to hear this. It was such a good place to play and the people were always happy in that country. Also I thought of my vision, and of how the spirits took me there to the center of the world.

After the council we heard that creeks of Wasichus were flowing into the Hills and becoming rivers, and that they were already making towns up there. It looked like bad trouble coming, so our band broke camp and started out to join Crazy Horse on Powder River. We camped on Horsehead Creek, then on

*Cheyennes and Arapahoes.

the War Bonnet after we crossed the old Wasichu's road★ that made the trouble that time when the hundred were rubbed out. Grass was growing on it. Then we camped at Sage Creek, then on the Beaver, then on Driftwood Creek, and came again to the Plain of Pine Trees at the edge of the Hills.

The nights were sharp now, but the days were clear and still; and while we were camping there I went up into the Hills alone and sat a long while under a tree. I thought maybe my vision would come back and tell me how I could save that country for my people, but I could not see anything clear.

This made me sad, but something happened a few days later that made me feel good. We had gone over to Taking-The-Crow-Horses Creek, where we found many bison and made plenty of meat and tanned many hides for winter. In our band there was a man by the name of Fat, who was always talking about how fast his horse could run. One day while we were camping there I told Fat my pony could run faster than his could, and he laughed at me and said that only crows and coyotes would think my pony was any good. I asked him what he would give me if my pony could beat his, and he said he would give me some black medicine (coffee). So we ran, and I got the black medicine. All the while we were running I thought about the white wing of the wind that the Second Grandfather of my vision gave me; and maybe that power went into my pony's legs.

On Kills-Himself Creek we made more meat and hides and were ready to join Crazy Horse's camp on the Powder. There were some Hang-Around-The-Fort people with us, and when they saw that we were going to join Crazy Horse, they left us and started back to the Soldiers' Town. They were afraid there might be trouble, and they knew Crazy Horse would fight, so they wanted to be safe with the Wasichus. We did not like them very much.

We had no advisers, because we were just a little band, and when we were moving, the boys could ride anywhere. One day while we were heading for Powder River I was riding ahead

★The Bozeman Trail.

with Steals Horses, another boy my age, and we saw some footprints of somebody going somewhere. We followed the footprints and there was a knoll beside a creek where a Lakota was lying. We got off and looked at him, and he was dead. His name was Root-of-the-Tail, and he was going over to Tongue River to see his relatives when he died. He was very old and ready to die, so he just lay down and died right there before he saw his relatives again.

Afterwhile we came to the village on Powder River and went into camp at the downstream end. I was anxious to see my cousin, Crazy Horse, again, for now that it began to look like bad trouble coming, everybody talked about him more than ever and he seemed greater than before. Also I was getting older.

Of course I had seen him now and then ever since I could remember, and had heard stories of the brave things he did. I remember the story of how he and his brother were out alone on horseback, and a big band of Crows attacked them, so that they had to run. And while they were riding hard, with all those Crows after them, Crazy Horse heard his brother call out; and when he looked back, his brother's horse was down and the Crows were almost on him. And they told how Crazy Horse charged back right into the Crows and fought them back with only a bow and arrows, then took his brother up behind him and got away. It was his sacred power that made the Crows afraid of him when he charged. And the people told stories of when he was a boy and used to be around with the older Hump all the time. Hump was not young any more at the time, and he was a very great warrior, maybe the greatest we ever had until then. They say people used to wonder at the boy and the old man always being together; but I think Hump knew Crazy Horse would be a great man and wanted to teach him everything.

Crazy Horse's father was my father's cousin, and there were no chiefs in our family before Crazy Horse; but there were holy men; and he became a chief because of the power he got in a vision when he was a boy. When I was a man, my father told me something about that vision. Of course he did not know all of it; but he said that Crazy Horse dreamed and went into the world where there is nothing but the spirits of all things. That is the real world that is behind this one, and everything we see here is something like a shadow from that world. He was on his horse in that world, and the horse and himself on it and the trees and the grass and the stones and everything were made of spirit, and nothing was hard, and everything seemed to float. His horse was standing still there, and yet it danced around like a horse made only of shadow, and that is how he got his name, which does not mean that his horse was crazy or wild, but that in his vision it danced around in that queer way.

It was this vision that gave him his great power, for when he went into a fight, he had only to think of that world to be in it again, so that he could go through anything and not be hurt. Until he was murdered by the Wasichus at the Soldiers' Town on White River, he was wounded only twice, once by accident and both times by some one of his own people when he was not expecting trouble and was not thinking; never by an enemy. He was fifteen years old when he was wounded by accident; and the other time was when he was a young man and another man was jealous of him because the man's wife liked Crazy Horse.

They used to say too that he carried a sacred stone with him, like one he had seen in some vision, and that when he was in danger, the stone always got very heavy and protected him somehow. That, they used to say, was the reason no horse he ever rode lasted very long. I do not know about this; maybe people only thought it; but it is a fact that he never kept one horse long. They wore out. I think it was only the power of his great vision that made him great.

Now and then he would notice me and speak to me before this; and sometimes he would have the crier call me into his tepee to eat with him. Then he would say things to tease me, but I would not say anything back, because I think I was a little afraid of him. I was not afraid that he would hurt me; I was just afraid. Everybody felt that way about him, for he was a queer man and would go about the village without noticing people or saying anything. In his own tepee he would joke, and when he was on the warpath with a small party, he would joke to make his warriors feel good. But around the village he hardly ever noticed anybody, except little children. All the Lakotas like to dance and sing; but he never joined a dance, and they say nobody ever heard him sing. But everybody liked him, and they would do anything he wanted or go anywhere he said. He was a small man among the Lakotas and he was slender and had a thin face and his eyes looked through things and he always seemed to be thinking hard about something. He never wanted to have many things for himself, and did not have many ponies like a chief. They say that when game was scarce and the people were hungry, he would not eat at all. He was a queer man. Maybe he was always part way into that world of his vision. He was a very great man, and I think if the Wasichus had not murdered him down there, maybe we should still have the Black Hills and be happy. They could not have killed him in battle. They had to lie to him and murder him. And he was only about thirty years old when he died.

One day after we had camped there on Powder River, I went upstream to see him again, but his tepee was empty and he was gone somewhere, maybe with a war-party against the Crows, for we were close to them now and had to look out for them all the time. Later I did see him. He put his arm across my shoulder and took me into his tepee and we sat down together. I do not remember what he said, but I know he did not say much, and he did not tease me. Maybe he was thinking about the trouble coming.

We did not stay together there very long, but scattered out and camped in different places so that the people and the ponies would all have plenty. Crazy Horse kept his village on Powder River with about a hundred tepees, and our band made camp on the Tongue. We built a corral of poles for the horses at night and herded them all day, because the Crows were great horse-thieves and we had to be careful. The women chopped and stripped cottonwood trees during the day and gave the bark to the horses at night. The horses liked it and it made them sleek and fat.

Beside the mouth of the corral there was a tepee for the horse guard, and one night Crow Nose was staying there and his wife was with him. He had a hole in the tepee so that he could look through. Afterwhile he got very sleepy, so he woke his wife and told her to get up and watch while he had a little rest. By and by she saw something dark moving slowly on the snow out there, so she woke her husband and whispered, "Old man, you'd better get up, for I think I see something." So Crow Nose got up and peeped out and saw a man moving around the corral in the starlight looking for the best horse. Crow Nose told his wife to keep her eye at the hole and let him know when the man was coming out with a horse, and he lay down at the opening of the tepee with the muzzle of his gun sticking out of the flap. By and by they could hear the bar lifted at the mouth of the corral. When his wife touched him, Crow Nose thrust his head outside and saw the man just getting on a horse to ride away. He was black against the sky, so Crow Nose shot him, and the shot woke the whole camp so that many came running with guns and coup sticks. Yellow Shirt was the first to count coup★ on the dead Crow, but many followed. A man who has killed an enemy must not touch him, for he has already had the honor of killing. He must let another count coup. When I got there to see, a pile of coup sticks was lying beside the Crow and the women had cut him up with axes and scattered him around. It was horrible. Then the people built a fire right there beside the Crow and we had a kill dance. Men, women, and children danced right in the middle of the night, and they sang songs about Crow Nose who had killed and Yellow Shirt who had counted the first coup.

Then it was daylight, and the crier told us we would move camp to the place where Root-of-the-Tail died. Crow Nose dressed up for war, painted his face black and rode the horse the enemy had tried to steal. When the men paint their faces black, the women all rejoice and make the tremolo, because it means their men are going to kill enemies.

When we camped again, one of Red Cloud's loafers who had started back for the Soldiers' Town because they were afraid there might be trouble, came in and said the Crows had killed all his party but himself, while they were sleeping, and he had escaped because he was out scouting.

★ The act of striking an enemy, dead or alive, with a stick conferred distinction, the first coup naturally counting most.

During the winter, runners came from the Wasichus and told us we must come into the Soldiers' Town right away or there would be bad trouble. But it was foolish to say that, because it was very cold and many of our people and ponies would have died in the snow. Also, we were in our own country and were doing no harm.

Late in the Moon of the Dark Red Calves (February) there was a big thaw, and our little band started for the Soldiers' Town, but it was very cold again before we got there. Crazy Horse stayed with about a hundred tepees on Powder, and in the middle of the Moon of the Snowblind (March) something bad happened there. It was just daybreak. There was a blizzard and it was very cold. The people were sleeping. Suddenly there were many shots and horses galloping through the village. It was the cavalry of the Wasichus, and they were yelling and shooting and riding their horses against the tepees. All the people rushed out and ran, because they were not awake yet and they were frightened. The soldiers killed as many women and children and men as they could while the people were running toward a bluff. Then they set fire to some of the tepees and knocked the others down. But when the people were on the side of the bluff, Crazy Horse said something, and all the warriors began singing the death song and charged back upon the soldiers; and the soldiers ran, driving many of the people's ponies ahead of them. Crazy Horse followed them all that day with a band of warriors, and that night he took all the stolen ponies away from them, and some of their own horses, and brought them all back to the village.*

These people were in their own country and were doing no harm. They only wanted to be let alone. We did not hear of this until quite awhile afterward; but at the Soldiers' Town we heard enough to make us paint our faces black.

*Colonel Reynolds with six companies of cavalry attacked Crazy Horse's village as stated in the early morning of March 16, 1876.

AT LAST I KILL A BUFFALO

Luther Standing Bear

Luther Standing Bear, whose Lakota/Sioux name was Ota K'te, Plenty Kill, was born in the 1860s. In his informal memoir, My Indian Boyhood, *he affectionately recounts his family life and upbringing within traditional Lakota society.*

Luther Standing Bear was only eight years of age when his father allowed him to participate in his first buffalo hunt. For him, as for all Lakota boys, the first buffalo hunt served as a kind of test that would demonstrate his courage and ability. For the young Ota K'te, this event would do far more than challenge his bravery and skill, it would try his character as well.

Other books by Luther Standing Bear are My People the Sioux, Land of the Spotted Eagle, *and* Stories of the Sioux.

AT LAST THE DAY CAME WHEN MY FATHER ALLOWED ME TO GO ON a buffalo hunt with him. And what a proud boy I was!

Ever since I could remember my father had been teaching me the things that I should know and preparing me to be a good hunter. I had learned to make bows and to string them; and to make arrows and tip them with feathers. I knew how to ride my pony no matter how fast he would go, and I felt that I was brave and did not fear danger. All these things I had learned for just this day when father would allow me to go with him on a buffalo hunt. It was the event for which every Sioux boy eagerly waited. To ride side by side with the best hunters of the tribe, to hear the terrible noise of the great herds as they ran, and then to help to bring home the kill was the most thrilling day of any Indian boy's life. The only other event which could equal it would be the day I went for the first time on the warpath to meet the enemy and protect my tribe.

On the following early morning we were to start, so the evening was spent in preparation. Although the tipis were full of activity, there was no noise nor confusion outside. Always the evening before a buffalo hunt and when every one was usually in his tipi, an old man went around the circle of tipis calling, "I-ni-la," "I-ni-la," not loudly, but so every one could hear. The old man was saying, "Keep quiet," "Keep quiet." We all knew that the scouts had come in and reported buffalo near and that we must all keep the camp in stillness. It was not necessary for the old man to go into each tipi and explain to the men that tomorrow there would be a big hunt, as the buffalo were coming. He did not order the men to prepare their weapons and neither did he order the mothers to keep children from crying. The one word, "I-ni-la," was sufficient to bring quiet to the whole camp. That night there would be no calling or shouting from tipi to tipi and no child would cry aloud. Even the horses and dogs obeyed the command for quiet, and all night not a horse neighed and not a dog barked. The very presence of quiet was everywhere. Such is the orderliness of a Sioux camp that men, women, children, and animals seem to have a common understanding and sympathy. It is no mystery but natural that the Indian and his animals understand each other very well both with words and without words. There are words, however, that the Indian uses that are understood by both his horses and dogs. When on a hunt, if one of the warriors speaks the word "A-a-ah" rather quickly and sharply, every man, horse, and dog will stop instantly and listen. Not a move will be made by an animal until the men move or speak further. As long as the hunters listen, the animals will listen also.

The night preceding a buffalo hunt was always an exciting night, even though it was quiet in camp. There would be much talk in the tipis around the fires. There would be sharpening of arrows and of knives. New bow-strings would be made and quivers would be filled with arrows.

It was in the fall of the year and the evenings were cool as

father and I sat by the fire and talked over the hunt. I was only
eight years of age, and I know that father did not expect me
to get a buffalo at all, but only to try perhaps for a small calf
should I be able to get close enough to one. Nevertheless, I was
greatly excited as I sat and watched father working in his easy,
firm way.

I was wearing my buffalo-skin robe, the hair next to my
body. Mother had made me a rawhide belt and this, wrapped
around my waist, held my blanket on when I threw it off my
shoulders. In the early morning I would wear it, for it would
be cold. When it came time to shoot, I should not want my
blanket but the belt would hold it in place.

You can picture me, I think, as I sat in the glow of the camp-
fire, my little brown body bare to the waist watching, and
listening intently to my father. My hair hung down my back
and I wore moccasins and breech-cloth of buckskin. To my belt
was fastened a rawhide holster for my knife, for when I was
eight years of age we had plenty of knives. I was proud to own
a knife, and this night I remember I kept it on all night. Neither
did I lay aside my bow, but went to sleep with it in my hand,
thinking, I suppose, to be all the nearer ready in the morning
when the start was made.

Father sharpened my steel points for me and also sharpened
my knife. The whetstone was a long stone which was kept in a
buckskin bag, and sometimes this stone went all over the camp;
every tipi did not have one, so we shared this commodity with
one another. I had as I remember about ten arrows, so when
father was through sharpening them I put them in my rawhide
quiver. I had a rawhide quirt, too, which I would wear fastened
to my waist. As father worked, he knew I was watching him
closely and listening whenever he spoke. By the time all prepara-
tions had been made, he had told me just how I was to act when
I started out in the morning with the hunters.

We went to bed, my father hoping that tomorrow would be
successful for him so that he could bring home some nice meat
for the family and a hide for my mother to tan. I went to bed,
but could not go to sleep at once, so filled was I with the
wonderment and excitement of it all. The next day was to be a
test for me. I was to prove to my father whether he was or was

not justified in his pride in me. What would be the result of my training? Would I be brave if I faced danger and would father be proud of me? Though I did not know it that night I was to be tried for the strength of my manhood and my honesty in this hunt. Something happened that day which I remember above all things. It was a test of my real character and I am proud to say that I did not find myself weak, but made a decision that has been all these years a gratification to me.

The next morning the hunters were catching their horses about daybreak. I arose with my father and went out and caught my pony. I wanted to do whatever he did and show him that he did not have to tell me what to do. We brought our animals to the tipi and got our bows and arrows and mounted. From over the village came the hunters. Most of them were leading their running horses. These running horses were anxious for the hunt and came prancing, their ears straight up and their tails waving in the air. We were joined with perhaps a hundred or more riders, some of whom carried bows and arrows and some armed with guns.

The buffalo were reported to be about five or six miles away as we should count distance now. At that time we did not measure distance in miles. One camping distance was about ten miles, and these buffalo were said to be about one half camping distance away.

Some of the horses were to be left at a stopping-place just before the herd was reached. These horses were pack-animals which were taken along to carry extra blankets or weapons. They were trained to remain there until the hunters came for them. Though they were neither hobbled nor tied, they stood still during the shooting and noise of the chase.

My pony was a black one and a good runner. I felt very important as I rode along with the hunters and my father, the chief. I kept as close to him as I could.

Two men had been chosen to scout or to lead the party. These two men were in a sense policemen whose work it was to keep order. They carried large sticks of ash wood, something like a policeman's billy, though longer. They rode ahead of the party while the rest of us kept in a group close together. The leaders went ahead until they sighted the herd of grazing buffalo. Then they stopped and waited for the rest of us to ride up. We all rode slowly toward the herd, which on sight of us had come together, although they had been scattered here and there over the plain. When they saw us, they all ran close together as if at the command of a leader. We continued riding slowly toward the herd until one of the leaders shouted, "Ho-ka-he!" which means, "Ready, Go!" At that command every man started for the herd. I had been listening, too, and the minute the hunters started, I started also.

Away I went, my little pony putting all he had into the race. It was not long before I lost sight of father, but I kept going just the same. I threw my blanket back and the chill of the autumn morning struck my body, but I did not mind. On I went. It was wonderful to race over the ground with all these horsemen about me. There was no shouting, no noise of any kind except the pounding of the horses' feet. The herd was now running and had raised a cloud of dust. I felt no fear until we had entered this cloud of dust and I could see nothing about me—only hear the sound of feet. Where was father? Where was I going? On I rode through the cloud, for I knew I must keep going.

Then all at once I realized that I was in the midst of the buffalo, their dark bodies rushing all about me and their great heads moving up and down to the sound of their hoofs beating upon the earth. Then it was that fear overcame me and I leaned close down upon my little pony's body and clutched him tightly. I can never tell you how I felt toward my pony at that moment. All thought of shooting had left my mind. I was seized by blank fear. In a moment or so, however, my senses became clearer, and I could distinguish other sounds beside the clatter of feet. I could hear a shot now and then and I could see the buffalo beginning to break up into small bunches. I could not see father nor any of my companions yet, but my fear was vanishing and I was safe. I let my pony run. The buffalo looked too large for me to tackle, anyway, so I just kept going. The buffalo became more and more scattered. Pretty soon I saw a young calf that looked about my size. I remembered now what father had told me the night before as we sat about the fire. Those instructions were important for me now to follow.

I was still back of the calf, being unable to get alongside of him. I was anxious to get a shot, yet afraid to try, as I was still very nervous. While my pony was making all speed to come alongside, I chanced a shot and to my surprise my arrow landed. My second arrow glanced along the back of the animal and sped on between the horns, making only a slight wound. My third arrow hit a spot that made the running beast slow up in his gait. I shot a fourth arrow, and though it, too, landed it was not a fatal wound. It seemed to me that it was taking a lot of shots, and I was not proud of my marksmanship. I was glad, however, to see the animal going slower and I knew that one more shot would make me a hunter. My horse seemed to know his own importance. His two ears stood straight forward and it was not necessary for me to urge him to get closer to the buffalo. I was soon by the side of the buffalo and one more shot brought the chase to a close. I jumped from my pony, and as I stood by my fallen game, I looked all around wishing that the world could see. But I was alone. In my determination to stay by until I had won my buffalo, I had not noticed that I was far from every one else. No admiring friends were about, and as far as I could see I was on the plain alone. The herd of buffalo had completely disappeared. And as for father, much as I wished for him, he was out of sight and I had no idea where he was.

I stood and looked at the animal on the ground. I was happy. Every one must know that I, Ota K'te, had killed a buffalo. But it looked as if no one knew where I was, so no one was coming my way. I must then take something from this animal to show that I had killed it. I took all the arrows one by one from the body. As I took them out, it occurred to me that I had used five arrows. If I had been a skillful hunter, one arrow would have been sufficient, but I had used five. Here it was that temptation came to me. Why could I not take out two of the arrows and throw them away? No one would know, and then I should be more greatly admired and praised as a hunter. As it was, I knew that I should be praised by father and mother, but I wanted more. And so I was tempted to lie.

I was planning this as I took out my skinning knife that father had sharpened for me the night before. I skinned one side of the animal, but when it came to turning it over, I was too small. I was wondering what to do when I heard my father's voice calling, "To-ki-i-la-la-hu-wo," "Where are you?" I quickly jumped on my pony and rode to the top of a little hill near by. Father saw me and came to me at once. He was so pleased to see me and glad to know that I was safe. I knew that I could never lie to my father. He was too fond of me and I too proud of him. He had always told me to tell the truth. He wanted me to be an honest man, so I resolved then to tell the truth even if it took from me a little glory. He rode up to me with a glad expression on his face, expecting me to go back with him to his kill. As he came up, I said as calmly as I could, "Father, I have killed a buffalo." His smile changed to surprise and he asked me where my buffalo was. I pointed to it and we rode over to where it lay, partly skinned.

Father set to work to skin it for me. I had watched him do this many times and knew perfectly well how to do it myself, but I could not turn the animal over. There was a way to turn the head of the animal so that the body would be balanced on the back while being skinned. Father did this for me, while I helped all I could. When the hide was off, father put it on the pony's back with the hair side next to the pony. On this he arranged the meat so it would balance. Then he covered the meat carefully with the rest of the hide, so no dust would reach it while we traveled home. I rode home on top of the load.

I showed my father the arrows that I had used and just where the animal had been hit. He was very pleased and praised me over and over again. I felt more glad than ever that I had told the truth and I have never regretted it. I am more proud now that I told the truth than I am of killing the buffalo.

We then rode to where my father had killed a buffalo. There we stopped and prepared it for taking home. It was late afternoon when we got back to camp. No king ever rode in state who was more proud than I that day as I came into the village sitting high up on my load of buffalo meat. Mother had now two hunters in the family and I knew how she was going to make over me. It is not customary for Indian men to brag about their exploits and I had been taught that bragging was not nice. So I was very quiet, although I was bursting with pride. Always when arriving home I would run out to play, for I loved to be with the other boys, but this day I lingered about close to the tipi so I could hear the nice things that were said about me. It was soon all over camp that Ota K'te had killed a buffalo.

My father was so proud that he gave away a fine horse. He called an old man to our tipi to cry out the news to the rest of the people in camp. The old man stood at the door of our tipi and sang a song of praise to my father. The horse had been led up and I stood holding it by a rope. The old man who was doing the singing called the other old man who was to receive the horse as a present. He accepted the horse by coming up to me, holding out his hands to me, and saying, "Ha-ye," which means "Thank you." The old man went away very grateful for the horse.

That ended my first and last buffalo hunt. It lives only in my memory, for the days of the buffalo are over.

SCHOOLDAYS

Traditionally, Native American children were educated by their families and communities through a combination of hands-on instruction, gentle admonishment, and the passing on of tribal ethics and values through storytelling and ceremonial participation. Children were taught the responsibilities of kinship and respect for self and others so that one day they would become competent and contributing members of the tribal society. It was an educational experience marked by patience and consideration for each child's unique abilities.

Euroamerican educational policies regarding Native Americans began to take shape in the 1870s when Congress allocated monies for the instruction of tribal children. Assimilation and detribalization were the goals of this educational program and the task of overseeing instruction went to various religious institutions and organizations. Though these schools were initially established as day schools, officials soon decided that a boarding school environment away from family and tribal community would be a more effective means of achieving their desired goals. By the close of the nineteenth century, mandatory boarding school was firmly in place and became a grim fact of life for many Native American children. When these children were taken from their homes, often at the age of six, the military-style methods employed by missionary and government boarding schools had devastating effects on them. Separated from their families, punished for speaking their native languages, ill fed and brutally treated, these children often emerged emotionally and physically scarred.

Personal courage, memories of family and home, and love for one another allowed these young Native Americans to endure and resist the efforts of those who meant to destroy their tribal identities.

from THE MIDDLE FIVE: INDIAN SCHOOLBOYS OF THE OMAHA TRIBE

Francis La Flesche

*I*n his autobiographical recollection, The Middle Five: Indian Schoolboys of the Omaha Tribe, *Francis La Flesche offers a thorough and incisive account of student life in a Presbyterian mission school in northeastern Nebraska around the time of the Civil War. The students, whose ages ranged from four to seventeen, frequently banded together into groups that offered friendship, mutual comfort, and understanding as they tried to negotiate between the old world they had been torn from and the alien new world in which they found themselves. The Middle Five was the name of the group created by Francis La Flesche and four other schoolboys.*

In these selections, La Flesche tells several moving incidents illustrating the compassion, bravery, and friendship of a group of boys during one of the most difficult periods of their lives.

Francis La Flesche (Omaha) was born in 1857. He devoted his life to the study of his people's traditions and was awarded an honorary degree of Doctor of Letters by the University of Nebraska in 1926 for his outstanding scholarly achievements. He died in 1932.

JOE

IT WAS RECESS. THE LAUGHER AND SHOUTS OF THE BOYS, AS THEY chased each other and wrestled, mingled with the song of the wren and other birds that inhabited the woods surrounding the school. Not less merry or boisterous were the laughter and calls of the girls, although their territory for play was limited and fenced in, to keep them from too free a communication with the rougher sex. Study and work were forgotten, and every boy and girl romped in the sunshine, and the atmosphere around seemed to be alive with happiness.

Suddenly the boys began to gather curiously around two objects upon the ground. The girls, seeing this unusual stir, came running to their fence, climbed up as far as they dared, and asked the nearest boys what it was that attracted so large a crowd.

It was a pitiful scene,—there, sitting on the green grass, was a crippled old woman of about seventy or eighty years, speaking in the kindest and gentlest of tones, with inflections of the voice hard to describe, but which brought to one's mind the twittering of a mother bird to its young, and passing her crooked fingers and wrinkled hands over the brown back of a miserable, naked, little boy who was digging his chubby fists in his eyes to squeeze away the tears that flowed incessantly.

"Don't cry! my little grandson," she was saying; "don't cry! These White-chests are kind; they will clothe and feed you. I can no longer take care of you, so I must give you to them. See these boys, what nice caps and coats and pants they have! You will have these things, too, and you will have plenty to eat. The White-chests will be good to you; I will come and see you very often. Don't cry!"

But the boy cried all the harder, twisting his fists into his eyes, and the old woman continued her caressing twittering.

The bell rang, and there was a rush for the school-room. When the hard breathing, coughing, and shuffling into position at the desks had ceased, the door was gently pushed open, and the old woman entered, tenderly urging the unwilling little brown body forward into the room, still weeping. Addressing Gray-beard, who was watching the scene with a queer smile on his lips, the old woman said:

"I have brought my little boy to give him to the White-chests to raise and to educate. On account of my age and feebleness, I am no longer able to care for him. I give him to you, and I beg that he be kindly treated. That is all I ask."

Without waiting for an answer, the poor creature, with tears streaming down her furrowed cheeks, limped out of the room, making a cheerless clatter with her heavy stick as she moved away. The little boy, recovering from his bewilderment, turned to see if his grandmother was still near by, and, finding that she had gone, gave a piteous wail, and fell to the floor, sobbing violently.

Who was this wretched little boy? He was his mother's son, that's all. He had no father, that is, none to caress and fondle him as other boys had. A man had presented the name of the boy to the Agent to be entered on the annuity rolls, only to that selfish extent recognizing the lad as his son.

The mother died while the child still needed her tender care, and the little one was left all alone in this great world that plays with the fortunes of men and nations. The place of death was in a dreary little tent, the rags of which flapped and fluttered in the force of the merciless winds, as though in sympathy with the melancholy situation. No loving husband or father was there to prepare the body for its last resting-place, and to give the helpless babe the nourishment for which it cried. Not even a relative was there; the dead woman had none among the people; she belonged to another tribe.

As the mother lay an unburied corpse, and her child wailing, a figure bent with age was plodding by. It was an old woman; slowly she put her heavy stick forward, then took a step, as though measuring every movement. When she came near the tent, she stopped, for the distressing wail had pierced her ears. She raised her trembling hand to her brow, looked up to the tent, then to the surroundings. The wailing went on, and the decrepit old woman hastened toward the tent as fast as she was able to go, and entered. For a moment she stood still, contemplating the scene before her, then from the fountains of her tender heart arose tears, impelled not by the sympathy that naturally springs from the love of friend or kindred, but by that nobler and higher feeling which lifts one toward God,—the sympathy for human kind.

Thus it was that this kind-hearted old woman took the homeless little child to her tent and cared for him. The two were inseparable until the grandmother, as she was called by the boy, felt that she was fast approaching the time when she would be summoned to join her fathers in the spirit-land; so, to provide for the child's future, she had brought him to the school.

The naming of a new pupil was usually an occasion for much merriment, but this time there was no enthusiasm. The school seemed to be in sympathy with the grandmother who went away weeping. Instead of raising their hands, as was their wont, to suggest names, they sought to hide their feeling by poring over their books.

"Come," said Gray-beard, "we must have a name for this youngster. Be quick and suggest one."

There was no response. Finally a big boy, who was busy over his lessons, said without lifting his head, "Call him Joseph."

So Gray-beard entered that name on the school Register.

Joe, as he was called by the boys, grew rapidly, but the helplessness of infancy clung to him. Because he could not fight, he became the butt of every trick a school-boy could devise, and there was no one who would do battle for him. If a big boy looked hard at him he would howl, and if one of his size rushed at him threateningly, he would shrink with fear. He was incapable of creating any mischief, yet he was continually stumbling into scrapes.

One sultry afternoon as I was sitting in the shade of the walnut-tree in front of the school, busy making a sling for Bob out of an old shoe, Joe came up to us, and dropped on his hands and knees. With the greatest interest he watched me cut the leather into a diamond shape; after a while he ventured to ask, "What yer makin'?"

"Wait and see," I answered, and went on working. When I had finished the sling-strap or pocket, I cut from the lappets of my buckskin moccasin two strings, making a noose at the end of one, and then fastened both strings to the sling-strap. Although I did not say anything about it, I had determined to make one for Joe as soon as I had shown Bob how to use the sling. He tried to find out from Bob what I was making; but that little chap would not speak to him.

When the sling was finished, I told Bob to gather some rusty nails and pebbles. He was off with a jump, and returned with a good supply in an amazingly short time. Joe still sat watching, with eyes and mouth wide open. I put a nail in the sling-strap, and, to show Bob how to use the sling, swung it around three or four times, then threw out my arm with force, letting one end of the string slip, and the nail sped on its way through the air, singing. Bob clapped his hands with delight.

A crow was flying lazily over head, croaking as he went. I sent a stone whizzing up to him; it barely missed his head, and he turned a complete somersault in the air, to our great amusement.

"I'm goin' to make one too!" said Joe, suddenly rising and hunting around for materials.

I paid no attention to him, but went on teaching Bob how to throw stones with the sling, little thinking that we were drifting toward an incident which gave Joe much pain temporarily and left an impression on my immature mind unfavorable to the White-chests which lasted many, many years.

"Mine's done!" exclaimed Joe, holding up a sling he had made out of rotten rags.

"Don't use it," I made haste to say, "and I'll make you a good one."

He paid no heed to my words, but went on trying to balance stones in the old piece of rag. The stones dropped before he could swing the sling and throw them. Bob kept me busy throwing stones for him, for he was afraid of hitting the boys who were on the hillside near by playing tag, or of sending a pebble over the fence, where the girls were singing and chatting over some of their games.

"Look now, look!" cried Joe. I turned to see what he was doing. He had succeeded in balancing a clod of earth nearly as large as his head in the rag sling, and was about to swing it.

Just at this moment Gray-beard came out of the carpenter's shop and, shading his eyes with a newspaper, he called loudly to one of the boys who was playing tag, "Ulysses! Ulysses!" He inflated his lungs to call for the third time, and with greater volume of voice. Joe had swung the clod of earth around for the second time, and it was half way up for the third round when the string broke; released from its holdings, the clod flew into the air, revolving, and dropping loose particles as it went. I held my breath as I watched it, for I saw just where it was going to strike.

In throwing a stone at some object, I used to imagine that by keeping a steady eye on the stone and bending my body in the direction I desired it to go, I could make the missile reach the place aimed at. In this instance, although I did not throw the clod, I unconsciously bent my body sidewise, keeping my eyes steadily on the lump of earth to draw it away from the spot for which it was making. The two other boys watched with frightened faces.

Gray-beard with head thrown back, lips parted, and chest expanded, called, "Uly—!" when the diminutive planet, which I was trying to guide by my force of will, struck him in the chest, and burst in a thousand bits. For a moment there was coughing and sputtering; then Gray-beard drew out his hand-kerchief, dusted his beard, and his white shirt front. He looked around to see where the missile that struck him came from. I wished that we three could sink into the earth, or else turn into nothing, as Gray-beard's eyes rested upon us.

"Come here!" he demanded with a vigorous gesture. Like so many guilty curs we walked up to him.

"Which one of you did it?" he cried, grasping me by the collar and shaking me until my teeth chattered.

Joe cringed and cried; it was a confession. I was about to say, "he didn't mean to do it;" when the infuriated man turned, went into the shop, and in a moment came back with a piece of board.

"Hold out your hand!" he said, addressing the shrinking boy.

Joe timidly held out his left hand, keeping his eyes all the while on the uplifted board, which came down with force, but not on the little hand that had been withdrawn to escape the blow. Gray-beard sprang at the boy, caught his hand, and at-tempted to strike it; but the boy pulled away and the board fell with a vicious thud on the wrist of the man, who now turned white with rage. Catching a firm grip on the hand of the boy, Gray-beard dealt blow after blow on the visibly swelling hand. The man seemed to lose all self-control, gritting his teeth and breathing heavily, while the child writhed with pain, turned blue, and lost his breath.

It was a horrible sight. The scene in the school-room when the naked little boy was first brought there by the old woman rose before me; I heard the words of the grandmother as she gave the boy to Gray-beard, "I beg that he be kindly treated; that is all I ask!" And she had told the child that the White-chests would be kind to him.

Poor Joe, I did what I never would have done if a boy of his own size had thrashed him, I took him by the hand and tried to comfort him, and cared for his bruises.

As for Gray-beard I did not care in the least about the violent shaking he had given me; but the vengeful way in which he fell upon that innocent boy created in my heart a hatred that was hard to conquer.

The day was spoiled for me; I partly blamed myself for it, though my plans had been to make the two little boys happy, but misery came instead. After supper I slipped away from my companions, and all alone I lay on the grass looking up at the stars, thinking of what had happened that afternoon. I tried to reconcile the act of Gray-beard with the teachings of the Missionaries, but I could not do so from any point of view.

All the boys had come together in the yard, and some one called out, "Let's play pull." So they divided into two groups, grading each according to the size of the boys. Two of the strongest were selected, one from each side; they held a stout stick between them, then on each side the boys grasped each other around the waist. When all were ready, they began to pull, every boy crying, "Hue! Hue!" as he tugged and strained. In the dusk the contending lines looked like two great dark beasts tearing at each other and lashing their tails from side to side. Bob and Joe were at the very end of one side; Bob had tied a bit of rope around his waist, and Joe had hold of that with his only serviceable hand. The pulling lasted for quite a while; finally one side drew the other over the mark; the game ended, and the boys noisily disbanded.

"Frank! Frank!" I heard; it was Edwin and the rest of the "gang."

"Here I am," I called out, and they gathered around me.

"Joe's hand is awful swelled up," said Bob, as he threw himself down on the grass.

"What's the matter with him?" asked Warren.

"Gray-beard beat Joe's hand like everything; he was so mad I thought he'd kill the boy." Then I recounted the scene, adding, "I can't think of anything else; it was awful!"

"Did he do anything to you?" asked Edwin.

"He shook me right hard when he asked me who did it; but when he saw Joe crying he knew who it was; then he let go of me and whipped him."

Brush had been listening to my story without a word; now he arose and said, "Boys, stay here till I come back."

He went into the house and knocked at the superintendent's door.

"I'm glad to see you Brush," said the superintendent kindly. "Have you finished the book, and do you want another?"

"No, sir; I wish to speak to you about something that happened to-day, which I don't think is quite right, and I thought you ought to know about it." Then he told in a simple straightforward manner the story of Joe's punishment.

When Brush had finished, the superintendent sent for Gray-beard. For a long time the two men talked earnestly together. At length Brush returned, and said, as he took his seat among us:

"Boys, that will not happen again. Gray-beard says he's sorry he did it, and I believe him."

THE BREAK

"BRUSH! BRUSH! BRUSH!" I RAN CALLING ONE MORNING SOON AFTER breakfast, down to the barn, to the spring, and back to the house, but I could not find the boy; then I thrust my fingers into my mouth and blew a loud robin call, and the answer came from under a tree up on the hillside. I ran hurriedly to the place; there lay Brush in the shade on the green grass reading.

The occasion of this excited search and call was the announcement by the superintendent that the school would be closed that day, and the children dismissed, so that they might go and see their parents, it being reported by an Indian who had come for his little girl that the people had just returned from the hunt.

"I been everywhere trying to find you," I said to Brush. "My folks have come home. Put that old book away and come go with me to see them. There isn't going to be any school to-day."

"Frank, it's right good of you to ask me, but I don't feel very well; I think I better not go," he replied, in a tone of disappointment. "All my bones ache, and I don't know what's the matter with me; but you go 'long, boy, and have a good time; you can tell me all about your visit when you come back."

"I'm sorry you can't go, Brush; but I'll come back soon and bring you some buffalo meat," I said, starting to go; "you better think about it again and come."

"I think I better stay home and be quiet," he answered, opening his book.

I spent all the forenoon with my parents, and in the afternoon I went in search of some of my village playmates. I found a number of them on the hillside shooting with their bows and arrows. They gave me a noisy welcome in mock English, which made me laugh heartily; then I had to wrestle with one or two of them, and when our peculiar greetings were over, the boys resumed their play, in which they let me join, one of them lending me his bow and arrows.

Our shooting from mark to mark, from one prominent object to another, brought us to a high hill overlooking the ripe fields of corn on the wide bottom below, along the gray Missouri. Here and there among the patches of maize arose little curls of blue smoke, while men and women moved about in their gayly-colored costumes among the broad green leaves of the corn; some, bending under great loads on their backs, were plodding their way laboriously to the fires whence arose the pretty wreaths of smoke.

"They're making sweet corn," exclaimed one of the youngsters whose little naked brown back glinted against the afternoon sun, and he pointed to the workers in the field.

As we stood watching the busy, picturesque scene below us, one little fellow held his bow close to his ear and began strumming on the string, then all the rest played on their bows in the same manner, until one of them suddenly broke into a victory song, in which the others joined.

At the close of the song they gave me a graphic description of the attack on the camp when it was pitched on the Republican River. Although the enemy was repulsed, and the hunting ground secured to our people, the battle cost many lives, several of the enemy's warriors were left on the field, and the Omahas lost some of their bravest men.

While yet the boys were telling of the thrilling incidents of the battle, we arose with a sudden impulse and rushed down the hill with loud war-cries, as though attacking the foe, the tall grass snapping against our moccasined feet as we sped along. We were rapidly approaching a house which stood alone, when one of the older boys who was running ahead suddenly stopped and raised his hand as though to command silence. Immediately our shouts ceased, and, seeing the serious look on the lad's face, "What is it?" we asked in frightened tones as we gathered about him.

Without a word he pointed to a woman who was cutting the tall sunflower stalks that had almost hidden her little dwelling with their golden blossoms. Her long black hair flowed over her shoulders unbraided, a sign of mourning. Now and again she would pause in her work to look up at the humble home and utter sighs and sobs that told a tale of sorrow. Mingled with these outpourings of grief came often the words, "My husband! my little child!" with terms of endearment and tenderness for which I can find no equivalent in English. On a blanket spread over the ground near by sat a tot of a child babbling to itself and making the beheaded sunflowers kiss each other, innocently oblivious of its mother's grief. It was a sad home-coming for the woman; the spirit of her husband had fled to the dark clouds of the west to join the host of warriors who had died on the field of battle, and his bones lay bleaching in the sands of a far-off country.

"It is Gre-don-ste-win weeping for her husband who was killed in the battle last summer," whispered the big boy; "let us go away quietly."

When we had withdrawn to a distance where we were sure our noise would not disturb the mourner, one of the boys called out, "Let's play Oo-hae´ba-shon-shon!" (Tortuous path.) Years after I learned that this game was played by the children of the white people, and that they called it, "Follow my leader."

We graded ourselves according to size, the biggest boy at the head as leader. Each one took hold of the belt of the boy in front of him, and then we started off at a rapid jog-trot, keeping time to this little song which we sang at the top of our voices.

CHILDREN'S SONG
FOLLOW MY LEADER

Yo hay   yo ao   ha ra o ha

Ya hay   yo ao   yo ha o ha.

Whatever the leader did, all were bound to do likewise. If he touched a post, we touched it too; if he kicked the side of a tent, all of us kicked it; so on we went, winding around the dwellings, in and out of vacant lodges, through mud puddles and queer, almost inaccessible places, and even entering the village, where we made the place ring with our song.

At last, tired out, the boys broke line and scattered to their homes. It was then that I suddenly realized the lateness of the hour, and remembered my promise to Brush. I ran to the house, took a hurried leave of my parents, picked up the package of buffalo meat my mother had prepared for my school-mate, and fairly flew over the hill between the village and the Mission.

As I came running down the hill to the school I saw Lester, Warren, and Edwin sitting in a row on the fence.

"Hello!" I shouted, "what you sitting on that fence for, like a lot of little crows?"

No answer came, nor did the boys move. I began to wonder if they were displeased with me, although I could not think of anything I had done to give them offence. As I drew near, I noticed that the expression on their faces indicated alarm rather than displeasure, and, becoming anxious in my turn, I hurriedly asked, "What's the matter; what's happened; where's Brush?"

The boys looked at one another, then at me; finally Lester replied, almost with a sob, "Brush is awful sick; he's been raising blood; they sent for the Doctor."

"Where is he? I must go see him," I said, springing over the fence, and starting toward the house.

"He's in that little room next the girls' play-room; but they won't let anybody see him," said Warren.

I went to the room in which Brush lay, and knocked very gently on the door. There was a rustling movement inside, then the door slowly opened and one of the lady teachers stood before me.

"What is it, Frank?" she asked in a low tone.

I tried to look over her shoulder to see the bed, but she was too tall. "I want to see Brush; can't I see him? They say he is sick. I want to see him a moment," I pleaded. "I'm just come back from the village, and brought some buffalo meat I promised him."

"No, Frank, you cannot see him," was the reply. "He is very sick. The superintendent is with him trying to relieve his suffering. Run away now," said the lady, stroking my bare head with her small hand. "Don't make any noise, and tell the rest of the boys to be very quiet."

I went away reproaching myself for not coming back from the village soon, as I told Brush I would. When I rejoined the boys, they looked anxiously into my face, and Edwin asked, "Did you see him?"

"No, they would not let me." After a pause, I asked, "When did he get sick; who was with him?"

"It was under the walnut-tree," said Lester; "he was reading to us about Joseph, out of his little black Bible he always carries. He began to cough hard and choke; he dropped the book all covered with blood, and took hold of my brother's arm. I ran to tell the superintendent. Just as they carried Brush into the house, Edwin came back and we told him about it."

In the evening, after the small boys had gone to bed, the doctor came, a tall gray-haired man. At the gate he was met by the superintendent, and the two walked slowly up the steps, talking earnestly. We four had been watching for the doctor on the porch; as he came along we caught now and then a word, but we did not understand its meaning. We judged by the shaking of the doctor's head that he thought Brush's case was serious.

Days passed; the doctor came and went; yet Brush's door was closed to us, nor had we any hopeful news of him. We missed him sadly; we missed his whittling, his harmless scolding; and our play was only half-hearted.

Indians who came to the school on business missed his ready offer to help. There was no one to take his place; no one who could interpret for them as well as he. Each one, as he went away, left a word of cheer for the lad, with expressions of hope for his recovery.

As school was dismissed one afternoon, the teacher gave special injunctions to the scholars not to make any noise as they passed out, or while moving about the house, so as not to disturb the sick boy. We four strolled toward the spring. Frost had come, and the leaves were beginning to turn red and yellow. Wild geese flew noisily overhead, fleeing from the coming winter to sunnier climes. While we were counting, as we often did, the gray birds, floating through the air like a great V, Warren suddenly exclaimed, "Say, boys, plums!"

We looked at him inquiringly. "Let's go get plums for Brush!" he continued excitedly. Then we remembered that we had pre-empted a small grove of choice plum bushes at the head of the ravine, as against all the boys of the school, and acquired a right in it which even the Big Seven respected.

Edwin ran to the kitchen and borrowed from one of the cooks a small tin pail. We hurried to our orchard, where we saw no signs of trespass; the bushes were laden with beautiful ripe fruit. We filled the little pail with the choicest, then each one picked for himself. It was nearly supper-time when we appeared at Brush's door. The three boys looked at me; so I tapped very gently, and the teacher who was nursing the sick boy opened the door.

"We've brought some plums for Brush," I said, offering the tin pail.

"That's very nice," said the lady, softly; "I will give them to him." She was about to close the door, when I whispered, "Can we take just a little look at him?"

"Yes," she answered, throwing the door open.

We four leaned forward and looked in. A smile lit up Brush's face as he saw us. "How are you now?" I asked, in a loud whisper.

"I'm all right," he whispered back, although his hollow eyes and cheeks told a tale that stole away all our hopes. We withdrew, and the door was slowly closed.

Next morning as I was coming down from the dormitory I paused at Brush's door to listen. I heard footsteps moving about softly, then the door opened and one of the big girls came out with a white pitcher in her hand. I started to go on downstairs, when she called to me in a whisper, "Frank, go down to the spring and get some fresh water for Brush, will you, that's a good boy?"

I took the pitcher and went quietly downstairs. As soon as I was outside the yard, I ran as hard as I could to the spring, glad at the prospect of a chance to see my friend again. Warren and Lester met me as I was coming up the hill.

"Did you see him?" one of them asked.

"No, but I'm going to," I answered.

"Ask him if we can do anything for him?" said Lester.

Just as I reached the head of the stairs the same big girl appeared. I handed her the pitcher; she took it and was about to enter the room, when I caught her arm. "Just let me take a look at Brush, will you?" I whispered.

"No, Frank, I can't. Superintendent says to let nobody in."

I heard a cough, then a feeble voice say pleadingly, "Maria, let him in, just a minute!"

The girl looked cautiously around, then said to me, "Come, but don't let anybody see you. Don't stay long, be quick!"

I stepped in, and a thin hand was stretched out to receive me. "I can't talk much, I'm so weak," said Brush. Overcome with emotion, I could not speak but stood holding his hot hand. The girl at the door moved uneasily.

"Tell the boys I'm all right," said Brush. "They mustn't worry. Come nearer." I bent over him and he whispered, "To-night, when everybody is asleep, come down and see me. I want to talk to you when I'm alone."

As night came on we four sat under the walnut-tree watching Brush's window. A candle was lit, then the curtain was drawn.

Below in the dining-room, the large girls moved quietly to and fro, busy with their evening work. When this was finished, they gathered at the door, and softly sang that beautiful hymn, "Nearer my God to Thee." We joined in the chorus, the wind wafting the words to the broad skies. The singing came to a close; the dining-room lights were put out, and we were called to bed.

As we knelt by the side of our beds to repeat the Lord's Prayer, I could not keep back the tears that came, thinking of the emaciated little form that I was to see once more that night.

One by one the boys fell asleep, and I alone, among the forty or fifty in that big room, remained awake. The clock down in Gray-beard's room struck eleven; the only sounds that came to my ears were those of the heavy breathing of the boys, the soughing of the wind through the trees, the rushing of the waters in the river, and now and then the calls of the wild geese, migrating in the night.

The clock struck the hour of twelve; I sat up listening. There was a stir and the sound of a voice that startled me. It was only Warren moving and talking in his sleep. I went stealthily to the head of the stairs, then listened again. I could only hear the throbbing of my heart, and the rasping pulsations in my ears. After a pause which seemed interminable, I put one foot down the first step, the board sprang under my weight, and creaked. Again I paused to listen; there was no stir, and I went on. Every little sound in the stillness of the night seemed exaggerated, and I was often startled, but I went on and reached the door of Brush's room. I scratched the panel three times. There was a movement within, and a slight cough. Slowly I turned the knob and opened the door. I entered, closed the door, but left it unlatched.

A candle stood burning in the midst of a number of bottles on a little table near the head of the bed. I knelt by the bedside, and Brush put his arm around my neck. We were silent for a while, finally he whispered in the Omaha tongue:

"I'm glad you came; I've been wanting to talk to you. They tell me I am better; but I know I am dying."

Oppressed with ominous dread, I cried out, interrupting him, "Don't say that! Oh, don't say that!"

131

But he went on, "You mustn't be troubled; I'm all right; I'm not afraid; I know God will take care of me. I have wanted to stay with you boys, but I can't. You've all been good to me. My strength is going, I must hurry,—tell the boys I want them to learn; I know you will, but the other boys don't care. I want them to learn, and to think. You'll tell them, won't you?"

He slipped his hand under the pillow, brought out his broken-bladed jack-knife, and put it in my hand, then said, "I wish I had something to give to each one of the boys before I go. I have nothing in the world but this knife. I love all of you; but you understand me, so I give it to you. That's all. Let me rest a little, then you must go."

After a moment's stillness the door opened very gently, and the floor near it creaked as though there were footsteps. A breath of wind came and moved the flickering flame of the candle round and round. The boy stared fixedly through the vacant doorway. There was something strange and unnatural in his look as, with one arm still around me, he stretched the other toward the door, and, in a loud whisper, said, "My grandfather! He calls me. I'm coming, I'm coming!"

There was a sound as of a movement around the room; Brush's eyes followed it until they again rested upon the open door, which swung to with a soft click; then he closed his eyes.

I crept closer to the sick boy; I was quivering with fear. Brush opened his eyes again, he had felt me trembling. "Are you cold?" he asked.

Just then I heard footsteps in the girls' play-room; this time they were real; Brush heard them too.

"Superintendent," he said with an effort.

When I crept into my bed the clock below struck one. For a long while I lay awake. I could hear noises downstairs, Gray-beard's door open and close, and the door of Brush's room. I heard a window raised, then everything became still.

We did not know how fondly we were attached to Brush, how truly he had been our leader, until we four, left alone, lingered

132

around his grave in the shadowy darkness of night, each one reluctant to leave.

The Mission bell rang for evening service, and with slow steps we moved toward the school—no longer "The Middle Five."

from LAME DEER: SEEKER OF VISIONS

Lame Deer and Richard Erdoes

J ohn (Fire) Lame Deer (Lakota/Sioux) was born in 1903, after
the Sioux had been settled on reservations throughout North and
South Dakota. He pursued a number of interesting occupations,
including that of painter and rodeo clown, but his truest and most
important vocation was that of a Lakota holy man. Filled with good
humor and astute observations, his memorable life story was recorded
by Richard Erdoes in 1972. Lame Deer: Seeker of Visions offers
an adventure-filled life history and a rare glimpse into the world of
Lakota beliefs and spirituality.

This selection contrasts the traditional tribal education under the
wise and watchful eyes of grandparents with the forced, ineffectual
educational methods of the Bureau of Indian Affairs.

I WAS BORN A FULL-BLOOD INDIAN IN A TWELVE-BY-TWELVE LOG
cabin between Pine Ridge and Rosebud. *Maka tanhan wicasa
wan*—I am a man of the earth, as we say. Our people don't call
themselves Sioux or Dakota. That's white man talk. We call
ourselves Ikce Wicasa—the natural humans, the free, wild, common people. I am pleased to be called that.

As with most Indian children, much of my upbringing was
done by my grandparents—Good Fox and his wife, Pte-Sa-
Ota-Win, Plenty White Buffalo. Among our people the relationship to one's grandparents is as strong as to one's own father
and mother. We lived in that little hut way out on the prairie,
in the back country, and for the first few years of my life I had

no contact with the outside world. Of course we had a few white man's things—coffee, iron pots, a shotgun, an old buckboard. But I never thought much of where these things came from or who had made them.

When I was about five years old my grandma took me to visit some neighbors. As always, my little black pup came along. We were walking on the dirt road when I saw a rider come up. He looked so strange to me that I hid myself behind Grandma and my pup hid behind me. I already knew enough about riding to see that he didn't know how to handle a horse. His feet were hanging down to the ground. He had some tiny, windmill-like things coming out of his heels, making a tinkling sound. As he came closer I started to size him up. I had never seen so much hair on a man. It covered all of his face and grew way down to his chest, maybe lower, but he didn't have hair where it counted, on top of his head. The hair was of a light-brown color and it made him look like a mattress come to life. He had eyes like a dead owl, of a washed-out blue-green hue. He was chewing on something that looked like a smoking Baby Ruth candy bar. Later I found out that this was a cigar. This man sure went in for double enjoyment, because he was also chomping on a wad of chewing tobacco, and now and then he took the smoking candy bar from his mouth to spit out a long stream of brown juice. I wondered why he kept eating something which tasted so bad that he couldn't keep it down.

This strange human being also wore a funny headgear—a cross between a skillet and a stovepipe. He had a big chunk of leather piled on top of his poor horse, hanging down also on both sides. In front of his crotch the leather was shaped like a horn. I thought maybe he kept his man-thing inside to protect it. This was the first saddle I had seen. His pitiful horse also had strings of leather on its head and a piece of iron in its mouth. Every time the horse stuck out its tongue I could hear some kind of roller or gear grinding inside it. This funny human being wore leather pants and had two strange-looking hammers tied to his hips. I later found out these were .45 Colts.

The man started to make weird sounds. He was talking, but we couldn't understand him because it was English. He pointed at my grandmother's pretty beaded moccasins and he took some square green frog hides from his pocket and wanted to trade. I guess those were dollar bills. But Grandma refused to swap, because she had four big gold coins in her moccasins. That man must have smelled them. This was the first white man I met.

When I got home I had a new surprise waiting for me. My grandpa was butchering something that I had never seen before, an animal with hoofs like a horse and the body of a dog. Maybe somebody had mated a dog with a horse and this funny creature was the result. Looking at its pink, hairless body, I was reminded of scary old tales about humans coupling with animals and begetting terrifying monsters. Grandpa was chopping away, taking the white meat and throwing the insides out. My little puppy was sure enjoying this, his first pig. So was I, but the pig smelled terrible. My grandpa said to save the fat for axle grease.

Most of my childhood days weren't very exciting, and that was all right with me. We had a good, simple life. One day passed like another. Only in one way was I different from other Indian kids. I was never hungry, because my dad had so many horses and cattle. Grandma always got up early in the morning before everybody else, taking down the big tin container with the Government-issue coffee. First I would hear her roasting the beans in a frying pan, then I would hear her grind them. She always made a huge pot holding two gallons of water, put in two big handfuls of coffee and boiled it. She would add some sweetener—molasses or maple syrup; we didn't like sugar. We used no milk or cream in our *pejuta sapa*—our black medicine.

Before anything else Grandma poured out a big soup spoon of coffee as an offering to the spirits, and then she kept the pot going all day. If she saw people anywhere near the house she called out to them, regardless of who they were, "Come in, have some coffee!" When the black medicine gave out, she added water and a lot more coffee and boiled the whole again. That stuff got stronger and stronger, thicker and thicker. In the end you could almost stick the spoon in there and it would keep standing up-right. "Now the coffee is real good," Grandma would say.

To go with the coffee Grandma got her baking powder each morning and made soda bread and squaw bread. That squaw bread filled the stomach. It seemed to grow bigger and bigger inside. Every spring, as the weather got warmer, the men would fix up Grandma's "squaw-cooler." This was a brush shelter made of four upright tree trunks with horizontal lodge poles tied to the top. The whole was then covered with branches from pine trees. They rigged up an old wood burner for Grandma to cook on, a rough table and some logs to sit on. In the summer, much of our life was spent in the squaw-cooler, where you could always feel a breeze. These squaw-coolers are still very popular on the reservation.

Grandma liked to smoke a little pipe. She loved her *kinnickin-nick*—the red willow-bark tobacco. One time she accidentally dropped some glowing embers into an old visitor's lap. This guy still wore a breech cloth. Suddenly we smelled something burning. That breech cloth had caught fire and we had to yank it off and beat the flames out. He almost got his child-maker burned up. He was so old it wouldn't have made a lot of difference, but he still could jump.

One of my uncles used to keep a moon-counting stick, our own kind of calendar and a good one. He had a special staff and every night he cut a notch in it until the moon "died"—that is, disappeared. On the other side of his staff he made a notch for every month. He started a new stick every year in the spring. That way we always knew when it was the right day for one of our ceremonies.

Every so often my grandparents would take me to a little celebration down the creek. Grandpa always rode his old red horse, which was well known in all the tribes. We always brought plenty of food for everybody, squaw bread, beef, the kind of dried meat we called *papa,* and *wasna,* or pemmican, which was meat pounded together with berries and kidney fat. We also brought a kettle of coffee, wild mint tea, soup or stuff like that. Grandfather was always the leader of the *owanka osnato*—the rehearsal ground. He prepared the place carefully. Only the real warriors were allowed to dance there—men like Red Fish or Thin Elk, who had fought in the Custer battle. With the years the dancers grew older and older and fewer and fewer. Grandfather danced too. Everybody could see the scars all over his arm where he had been wounded by the white soldiers.

Some women had scars, too. Grandpa's brother, White Crane Walking, had three wives. They were not jealous of one another. They were like sisters. They loved one another and they loved their husband. This old man was really taking it easy; the women did all the work. He just lay around the whole day long, doing nothing. Once in a while some men called him lazy, but he just laughed and told them, "Why don't you get a second wife?" He knew their wives were jealous and didn't want them to get a second one. When this old man finally passed away, the two wives who survived him buried him in the side of a hill. They took their skinning knives and made many deep gashes in their arms and legs to show their grief. They might have cut off their little fingers too, but somebody told them that this was no longer allowed, that the Government would punish them for this. So they cut off their hair instead. They keened and cried for four days and nights; they loved their husband that much.

I was the *takoja*—the pampered grandson—and like all Indian children I was spoiled. I was never scolded, never heard a harsh word. "*Ajustan*—leave it alone"—that was the worst. I was never beaten; we don't treat children that way. Indian kids are so used to being handled gently, to get away with things, that they often don't pay much attention to what the grownups tell them. I'm a grandfather now myself and sometimes I feel like yelling at one of those brash kids, "Hey, you little son of a bitch, listen to me!" That would make him listen all right, but I can't do it.

When I didn't want to go to sleep my grandma would try to scare me with the *ciciye*—a kind of bogeyman. "*Takoja, istima ye*—Go to sleep, sonny," she would say, "or the *ciciye* will come after you." Nobody knew what the *ciciye* was like, but he must have been something terrible. When the *ciciye* wouldn't work anymore, I was threatened with the *siyoko*—another kind of monster. Nobody knew what the *siyoko* was like, either, but he was ten times more terrible than the *ciciye*. Grandma did not have much luck. Neither the *ciciye* nor the *siyoko* scared me for long. But when I was real bad, Grandma would say, *"Wasicun anigni kte"*—the white man will come and take you to his home," and that scared me all right. *Wasicun* were for real.

It was said that I didn't take after my grandpa Good Fox, whom I loved, but after my other grandfather, Crazy Heart, whom I never knew. They said I picked up where he left off, because I was so daring and full of the devil. I was told that Crazy Heart had been like that. He did not care what happened to other people, or to himself, once he was on his way. He was hot-tempered, always feuding and on the warpath. At the same time he saved lots of people, gave wise counsel, urged the people to do right. He was a good speech-maker. Everybody who listened to him said that he was a very encouraging man. He always advised patience, except when it came to himself. Then his temper got in the way.

I was like that. Things I was told not to do—I did them. I liked to play rough. We played shinny ball, a kind of hockey game. We made the ball and sticks ourselves. We played the hoop game, shot with a bow and arrow. We had foot races, horse races and water races. We liked to play *mato kiciyapi,* the bear game, throwing sharp, stiff grass stems at each other. These could really hurt you and draw blood if they hit the bare skin. And we were always at the *isto kicicastakapi,* the pit-slinging game. You chewed the fruit from the rosebush or wild cherries, spit a fistful of pits into your hand and flung them into the other fellow's face. And of course I liked the Grab-Them-by-the-Hair-and-Kick-Them game, which we played with two teams.

I liked to ride horseback behind my older sister, holding onto her. As I got a little bigger she would hold onto me. By the time I was nine years old I had my own horse to ride. It was a beautiful gray pony my father had given me together with a fine saddle and a very colorful Mexican saddle blanket. That gray was my favorite companion and I was proud to ride him. But he was not mine for long. I lost him through my own fault.

Nonge Pahloka—the Piercing of Her Ears—is a big event in a little girl's life. By this ceremony her parents, and especially her grandmother, want to show how much they love and honor her. They ask a man who is respected for his bravery or wisdom to pierce the ears of their daughter. The grandmother puts on a big feed. The little girl is placed on a blanket surrounded by the many gifts her family will give away in her name. The man who does the piercing is much admired and gets the most valuable gift. Afterward they get down to the really important part—the eating.

Well, one day I watched somebody pierce a girl's ears. I saw the fuss they made over it, the presents he got and all that. I thought I should do this to my little sister. She was about four years old at the time and I was nine. I don't know anymore what made me want to do this. Maybe I wanted to feel big and important like the man whom I had watched perform the ceremony. Maybe I wanted to get a big present. Maybe I wanted to make my sister cry. I don't remember what was in my little boy's mind then. I found some wire and made a pair of "ear rings" out of it. Then I asked my sister, "Would you like me to put these on you?" She smiled. "*Ohan*—yes." I didn't have the sharp bone one uses for the ear-piercing, and I didn't know the prayer that goes with it. I just had an old awl but thought would do fine. Oh, how my sister yelled. I had to hold her down, but I got that awl through her earlobes and managed to put the "ear rings" in. I was proud of the neat job I had done.

When my mother came home and saw those wire loops in my sister's ears she gasped. But she recovered soon enough to go and tell my father. That was one of the few occasions he talked to me. He said, "I should punish you and whip you, but I won't. That's not my way. You'll get your punishment later." Well, some time passed and I forgot all about it. One morning my father announced that we were going to a powwow. He had hitched up the wagon and it was heaped high with boxes and bundles. At that powwow my father let it be known that he was doing a big *otuhan*—a give-away. He put my sister on a rug, a pretty Navajo blanket, and laid out things to give away—quilts, food, blankets, a fine shotgun, his own new pair of cowboy boots, a sheepskin coat, enough to fit out a whole family. Dad was telling the people, "I want to honor my daughter for her ear-piercing. This should have been done openly, but my son did it at home. I guess he's too small. He didn't know any better." This was a long speech for Dad. He motioned me to come closer. I was sitting on my pretty gray horse. I thought

141

we were both cutting a very fine figure. Well, before I knew it, Dad had given my horse away, together with its beautiful saddle and blanket. I had to ride home in the wagon and I cried all the way. The old man said, "You have your punishment now, but you will feel better later on. All her life your sister will tell about how you pierced her ears. She'll brag about you. I bet you are the only small boy who ever did this big ceremony."

That was no consolation to me. My beautiful gray was gone. I was heart-broken for three days. On the fourth morning I looked out the door and there stood a little white stallion with a new saddle and a silver-plated bit. "It's yours," my father told me. "Get on it." I was happy again.

After I was six years old it was very hard to make me behave. The only way one could get me to sit still was to tell me a story. I loved to listen to my grandparents' old tales, and they were good at relating the ancient legends of my people. They told me of the great gods Wi and Hanwi, the sun and the moon, who were married to each other. They told me about the old man god Waziya, whom the priests have made into Santa Claus. Waziya had a wife who was a big witch. These two had a daughter called Ite—the face—the most beautiful woman in the universe. Ite was married to Tate, the wind.

The trouble with this pairing was that Ite got it into her mind that the sun, Wi, was more handsome than her own husband, the wind. Wi, on his part, thought that Ite was much more beautiful than his own wife, the moon. Wi was having a love affair with Ite, and whenever the moon saw them misbehaving she hid her face in shame. "That's why on some nights we don't see the moon," Grandma told me.

The Great Spirit did not like these goings-on, and he punished Ite. She still remained the most beautiful creature in the world, but only if one looked at her from one side. The other half of her face had become so hideous and ugly that there were no words to describe it. From that time on she was known as Anunk-Ite, or Double-Face. When it comes to love the women always have the worst of it.

Many of these legends were about animals. Grandma told me about the bat who hid himself on top of the eagle's back, screaming, "I can fly higher than any other bird." That was true enough; even the eagle couldn't fly higher than somebody who was sitting on top of him. As a punishment the other birds grounded the bat and put him in a mouse hole. There he fell in love with a lady mouse. That's why bats now are half mouse and half bird.

Grandpa Good Fox told me about the young hunters who killed a buffalo with a big rattle for a tail. After eating of its meat these young men were changed into giant rattle-snakes with human heads and human voices. They lived in a cave beneath the earth and ruled the underworld.

The stories I liked best had to do with Iktome, the evil spi-derman, a smart-ass who played tricks on everybody. One day this spider was walking by a lake where he saw many ducks swimming around. This sight gave him a sudden appetite for roast duck. He stuffed his rawhide bag full of grass and then he showed himself. When the ducks saw him they started to holler, "Where are you going, Iktome?"

"I am going to a big powwow."

"What have you got in your bag, Iktome?"

"It's full of songs which I am taking to the powwow, good songs to dance to."

"How about singing some songs for us?" begged the ducks.

The tricky spider made a big show of not wanting to do it. He told the ducks he had no time for them, but in the end he pretended to give in, because they were such nice birds. "I'll sing for you," he told the ducks, "but you must help me."

"We'll do what you want. Tell us the rules."

"Well, you must form three rows. In the front row, all you fat ones, get in there. In the second row go all those who are neither fat nor thin—the in-betweens. The poor scrawny ones go in the third row, way down there. And you have to act out the song, do what the words tell you. Now the words to my first song are 'Close your eyes and dance!' "

The ducks all lined up with their eyes shut, flapping their wings, the fat ones up front. Iktome took a big club from underneath his coat. "Sing along as loud as you can," he or-dered, "and keep your eyes shut. Whoever peeks will get blind." He told them to sing so that their voices would drown out the "thump, thump" of his club when he hit them over the head.

He knocked them down one by one and was already half done when one of those low-down, skinny ducks in the back row opened its eyes and saw what Iktome was up to.

"Hey, wake up!" it hollered. "That Iktome is killing us all!"

The ducks that were left opened their eyes and took off. Iktome didn't mind. He already had more fat ducks than he could eat.

Iktome is like some of those bull-shipping politicians who make us close our eyes and sing and dance for them while they knock us on the head. Democratic ducks, Republican ducks, it makes no difference. The fat, stupid ones are the first in the pot. It's always the skinny, no-account, low-class duck in the back that doesn't hold still. That's a good Indian who keeps his eyes open. Iktome is an evil schemer, Grandpa told me, but luckily he's so greedy that most of the time he outsmarts himself.

It's hard to make our grandchildren listen to these stories nowadays. Some don't understand our language anymore. At the same time there is the TV going full blast—and the radio and the phonograph. These are the things our children listen to. They don't care to hear an old-fashioned Indian story.

I was happy living with my grandparents in a world of our own, but it was a happiness that could not last. "Shh, *wasicun anigni kte*—be quiet or the white man will take you away." How often had I heard these words when I had been up to some mischief, but I never thought that this threat could become true, just as I never believed that the monsters *ciciye* and *siyoko* would come and get me.

But one day the monster came—a white man from the Bureau of Indian Affairs. I guess he had my name on a list. He told my family, "This kid has to go to school. If your kids don't come by themselves the Indian police will pick them up and give them a rough ride." I hid behind Grandma. My father was like a big god to me and Grandpa had been a warrior at the Custer fight, but they could not protect me now.

In those days the Indian schools were like jails and run along military lines, with roll calls four times a day. We had to stand at attention, or march in step. The B.I.A. thought that the best way to teach us was to stop us from being Indians. We were forbidden to talk our language or to sing our songs. If we disobeyed we had to stand in the corner or flat against the wall, our noses and knees touching the plaster. Some teachers hit us on the hands with a ruler. A few of these rulers were covered with brass studs. They didn't have much luck redoing me, though. They could make me dress up like a white man, but they couldn't change what was inside the shirt and pants.

My first teacher was a man and he was facing a lot of fearful kids. I noticed that all the children had the same expression on their faces—no expression at all. They looked frozen, deadpan, wooden. I knew that I, too, looked that way. I didn't know a word of the white man's language and very little about his ways. I thought that everybody had money free. The teacher didn't speak a word of Lakota. He motioned me to my seat. I was scared stiff.

The teacher said, "Stand," "Sit down!" He said it again and again until we caught on. "Sit, stand, sit, stand. Go and stop. Yes and no." All without spelling, just by sound.

We also had a lady teacher. She used the same method. She'd hold up one stick and say, "One." Then she'd hold up two sticks and say, "Two," over and over again. For many weeks she showed us pictures of animals and said "dog" or "cat." It took me three years to learn to say, "I want this."

My first day in school was also the first time I had beans, and with them came some white stuff, I guessed it was pork fat. That night, when I came home, my grandparents had to open the windows. They said my air was no good. Up to then I had eaten nothing but dry meat, *wasna, papa,* dry corn mixed with berries. I didn't know cheese and eggs, butter or cream. Only seldom had I tasted sugar or candy. So I had little appetite at school. For days on end they fed us cheese sandwiches, which made Grandma sniff at me, saying, "Grandson, have you been near some goats?"

After a while I lost some of my fear and recovered my daring. I called the white man teacher all the bad names in my language, smiling at him at the same time. He beamed and patted me on the head, because he thought I was complimenting him. Once I found a big picture of a monkey in the classroom, a strange animal with stiff, white side whiskers. I thought this must be the Great White Father, I really did.

I went to the day school on the Rosebud Reservation, twelve miles south of Norris, South Dakota. The Government teachers were all third-grade teachers. They taught up to this grade and that was the highest. I stayed in that goddam third grade for six years. There wasn't any other. The Indian people of my generation will tell you that it was the same at the other schools all over the reservations. Year after year the same grade over again. If we ran away the police would bring us back. It didn't matter anyway. In all those years at the day school they never taught me to speak English or to write and read. I learned these things only many years later, in saloons, in the Army or in jail.

When I was fourteen years old I was told that I had to go to boarding school. It is hard for a non-Indian to understand how some of our kids feel about boarding schools. In their own homes Indian children are surrounded with relatives as with a warm blanket. Parents, grandparents, uncles, aunts, older brothers and cousins are always fussing over them, playing with them or listening to what they have to say. Indian kids call their aunt "Mother," not just as a polite figure of speech but because that aunt acts like a mother. Indian children are never alone. If the grownups go someplace, the little ones are taken along. Children have their rights just as the adults. They are rarely forced to do something they don't like, even if it is good for them. The parents will say, "He hates it so much, we don't have the heart to make him do it."

To the Indian kid the white boarding school comes as a terrific shock. He is taken from his warm womb to a strange, cold place. It is like being pushed out of a cozy kitchen into a howling blizzard. The schools are better now than they were in my time. They look good from the outside—modern and expensive. The teachers understand the kids a little better, use more psychology and less stick. But in these fine new buildings Indian children still commit suicide, because they are lonely among all that noise and activity. I know of a ten-year-old who hanged herself. These schools are just boxes filled with homesick children. The schools leave a scar. We enter them confused and bewildered and we leave them the same way. When we enter the school we at least know that we are Indians. We come out half red and half white, not knowing what we are.

When I was a kid those schools were really bad. Ask the old-timers. I envied my father, who never had to go through this. I felt so lonesome I cried, but I wouldn't cooperate in the remaking of myself. I played the dumb Indian. They couldn't make me into an apple—red outside and white inside. From their point of view I was a complete failure. I took the rap for all the troubles in the school. If anything happened the first question always was "Did you see John do it?" They used the strap on us, but more on me than on anybody else.

My teacher was a mean old lady. I once threw a live chicken at her like a snowball. In return she hit my palms with a ruler. I fixed an inkpot in such a way that it went up in her face. The black ink was all over her. I was the first to smile and she knew who had done it right away. They used a harness thong on my back that time and locked me up in the basement. We full-bloods spent much time down there. I picked up some good fox songs in that basement.

I was a good athlete. I busted a kitchen window once playing stickball. After that I never hit so good again. They tried to make me play a slide trombone. I tore it apart and twisted it into a pretzel. That mean old teacher had a mouth like a pike and eyes to match. We counted many coups upon each other and I still don't know who won. Once, when they were after me again for something I didn't do, I ran off. I got home and on my horse. I knew the Indian police would come after me. I made it to Nebraska, where I sold my horse and saddle and bought a ticket to Rapid City. I still had twelve dollars in my pocket. I could live two days on one dollar, but the police caught me and brought me back. I think in the end I got the better of that school. I was more of an Indian when I left than when I went in. My back had been tougher than the many straps they had worn out on it.

Some doctors say that Indians must be healthier than white people because they have less heart disease. Others say that this comes from our being hungrier, having less to eat, which makes our bodies lean and healthy. But this is wrong. The reason Indians suffer less from heart disease is that we don't live long enough to have heart trouble. That's an old folks' sickness. The way we have to live now, we are lucky if we make it to age forty. The full-bloods are dying fast. One day I talk to one, the next day he is dead. In a way the Government is still "vanishing" the Indian, doing Custer's work. The strange-looking pills and capsules they give us to live on at the Public Health Service hospitals don't do us much good. At my school the dentist came once a year in his horse and buggy with a big pair of pliers to yank our teeth, while the strongest, biggest man they could find kept our arms pinned to our sides. That was the anesthesia.

There were twelve of us, but they are all dead now, except one sister. Most of them didn't even grow up. My big brother, Tom, and his wife were killed by the flu in 1917. I lost my own little boy thirty-five years ago. I was a hundred miles away, caught in a blizzard. A doctor couldn't be found for him soon enough. I was told it was the measles. Last year I lost another baby boy, a foster child. This time they told me it was due to some intestinal trouble. So in a lifetime we haven't made much progress. We medicine men try to doctor our sick, but we suffer from many new white man's diseases, which come from the white man's food and white man's living, and we have no herbs for that.

My big sister was the oldest of us all. When she died in 1914 my folks took it so hard that our life was changed. In honor of her memory they gave away most of their possessions, even beds and mattresses, even the things without which the family would find it hard to go on. My mother died of tuberculosis in 1920, when I was seventeen years old, and that was our family's "last stand." On her last day I felt that her body was already gone; only her soul was still there. I was holding her hand and she was looking at me. Her eyes were big and sad, as if she knew that I was in for a hard time. She said, "Onsika, onsika— pitiful, pitiful." These were her last words. She wasn't sorry for herself; she was sorry for me. I went up on a hill by myself and cried.

When grandfather Crazy Heart died they killed his two po- nies, heads toward the east and tails to the west. They had told each horse, "Grandson, your owner loved you. He has need of you where he's going now." Grandfather knew for sure where he was going, and so did the people who buried him according to our old custom, up on a scaffold where the wind and the air, the sun, the rain and the snow could take good care of him. I think that eventually they took the box with his body down from the scaffold and buried it in a cemetery, but that happened years later and by then he and his ponies had long gone to wherever they wanted to be.

But in 1920 they wouldn't even allow us to be dead in our own way. We had to be buried in the Christian fashion. It was as if they wanted to take my mother to a white boarding school way up there. For four days I felt my mother's *nagi*, her presence, her soul, near me. I felt that some of her goodness was staying with me. The priest talked about eternity. I told him we Indians did not believe in a forever and forever. We say that only the rocks and the mountains last, but even they will disappear. There's a new day coming, but no forever, I told him. "When my time comes, I want to go where my ancestors have gone." The priest said, "That may be hell." I told him that I'd rather be frying with a Sioux grandmother or uncle than sit on a cloud playing harp with a pale-faced stranger. I told him, "That Christian name, John, don't call me that when I'm gone. Call me Tahca Ushte—Lame Deer."

from LOVE MEDICINE
Louise Erdrich

Love Medicine *is the compelling and tumultuous tale of two Chippewa families, the Kashpaws and the Lamartines, whose lives are inextricably bound by blood and history. Filled with elements from the Chippewa oral tradition, it is an exhilarating legend of love, betrayal, and the search for identity.*

This chapter from the novel concerns a fourteen-year-old girl named Marie Lazarre who, determined to become a saint, ventures up the hill to enter the convent school, only to find herself locked in mortal combat with the formidable Sister Leopolda. Erdrich's unusual style, often described as "magical realism," adds a haunting, mythic quality to her work.

Novelist and poet, Louise Erdrich is a member of the Turtle Mountain band of Chippewas. She was born in Little Falls, Minnesota, in 1954 and grew up in Wahpeton, North Dakota. She has written numerous short stories, and two books of poetry, Jacklight *and* Baptism of Desire, *which have been widely acclaimed. Her best-selling novel,* Love Medicine, *won the National Book Critics Circle Award for Fiction in 1984, and the American Book Award from the Before Columbus Foundation.* Love Medicine *is the first novel in a tetralogy that includes* The Beet Queen *and* Tracks. *The fourth novel,* American Horse, *is yet to be published. Erdrich also wrote* The Crown of Columbus *with her husband, writer Michael Dorris. She currently lives in New Hampshire with him and their children.*

SO WHEN I WENT THERE, I KNEW THE DARK FISH MUST RISE. PLUMES of radiance had soldered on me. No reservation girl had ever prayed so hard. There was no use in trying to ignore me any longer. I was going up there on the hill with the black robe women. They were not any lighter than me, I was going up there to pray as good as they could. Because I don't have that much Indian blood. And they never thought they'd have a girl from this reservation as a saint they'd have to kneel to. But they'd have me. And I'd be carved in pure gold. With ruby lips. And my toenails would be little pink ocean shells, which they would have to stoop down off their high horse to kiss.

I was ignorant. I was near age 14. The length of sky is just about the size of my ignorance. Pure and wide. And it was just that—the pure and wideness of my ignorance—that got me up the hill to Sacred Heart Convent and brought me back down alive. For maybe Jesus did not take my bait, but them Sisters tried to cram me right down whole.

You ever see a walleye strike so bad the lure is practically out its back end before you reel it in? That is what they done with me. I don't like to make that low comparison, but I have seen a walleye do that once. And it's the same attempt as Sister Leopolda made to get me in her clutch.

I had the mail-order Catholic soul you get in a girl raised out in the bush, whose only thought is getting into town. For Sunday Mass is the only time my father brought his children in except for school, when we were harnessed. Our soul went cheap. We were so anxious to get there we would have walked in on our hands and knees. We just craved going to the store, slinging bottle caps in the dust, making fool eyes at each other. And of course we went to church.

Where they have the convent is on top of the highest hill, so that from its windows the Sisters can be looking into the marrow of the town. Recently a windbreak was planted before the bar "for the purposes of tornado insurance." Don't tell me that. That poplar stand was put up to hide the drinkers as they get the transformation. As they are served into the beast of their burden. While they're drinking, that body comes upon them, and then they stagger or crawl out the bar door, pulling a weight they can't move past the poplars. They don't want no holy witness to their fall.

Anyway, I climbed. That was a long-ago day. There was a

road then for wagons that wound in ruts to the top of the hill where they had their buildings of painted brick. Gleaming white. So white the sun glanced off in dazzling display to set forms whirling behind your eyelids. The face of God you could hardly look at. But that day it drizzled, so I could look all I wanted. I saw the homelier side. The cracked whitewash and swallows nesting in the busted ends of eaves. I saw the boards sawed the size of broken windowpanes and the fruit trees, stripped. Only the tough wild rhubarb flourished. Goldenrod rubbed up their walls. It was a poor convent. I didn't see that then but I know that now. Compared to others it was humble, ragtag, out in the middle of no place. It was the end of the world to some. Where the maps stopped. Where God had only half a hand in the creation. Where the Dark One had put in thick bush, liquor, wild dogs, and Indians.

I heard later that the Sacred Heart Convent was a catchall place for nuns that don't get along elsewhere. Nuns that complain too much or lose their mind. I'll always wonder now, after hearing that, where they picked up Sister Leopolda. Perhaps she had scarred someone else, the way she left a mark on me. Perhaps she was just sent around to test her Sisters' faith, here and there, like the spot-checker in a factory. For she was the definite most-hard trial to anyone's endurance, even when they started out with veils of wretched love upon their eyes.

I was that girl who thought the black hem of her garment would help me rise. Veils of love which was only hate petrified by longing—that was me. I was like those bush Indians who stole the holy black hat of a Jesuit and swallowed little scraps of it to cure their fevers. But the hat itself carried smallpox and was killing them with belief. Veils of faith! I had this confidence in Leopolda. She was different. The other Sisters had long ago gone blank and given up on Satan. He slept for them. They never noticed his comings and goings. But Leopolda kept track of him and knew his habits, minds he burrowed in, deep spaces where he hid. She knew as much about him as my grandma, who called him by other names and was not afraid.

In her class, Sister Leopolda carried a long oak pole for opening high windows. It had a hook made of iron on one end that could jerk a patch of your hair out or throttle you by the collar—

all from a distance. She used this deadly hook-pole for catching Satan by surprise. He could have entered without your knowing it—through your lips or your nose or any one of your seven openings—and gained your mind. But she would see him. That pole would brain you from behind. And he would gasp, dazzled, and take the first thing she offered, which was pain.

She had a stringer of children who could only breathe if she said the word. I was the worst of them. She always said the Dark One wanted me most of all, and I believed this. I stood out. Evil was a common thing I trusted. Before sleep sometimes he came and whispered conversation in the old language of the bush. I listened. He told me things he never told anyone but Indians. I was privy to both worlds of his knowledge. I listened to him, but I had confidence in Leopolda. She was the only one of the bunch he even noticed.

There came a day, though, when Leopolda turned the tide with her hook-pole.

It was a quiet day with everyone working at their desks, when I heard him. He had sneaked into the closets in the back of the room. He was scratching around, tasting crumbs in our pockets, stealing buttons, squirting his dark juice in the linings and the boots. I was the only one who heard him, and I got bold. I smiled. I glanced back and smiled and looked up at her sly to see if she had noticed. My heart jumped. For she was looking straight at me. And she sniffed. She had a big stark bony nose stuck to the front of her face for smelling out brimstone and evil thoughts. She had smelled him on me. She stood up. Tall, pale, a blackness leading into the deeper blackness of the slate wall behind her. Her oak pole had flown into her grip. She had seen me glance at the closet. Oh, she knew. She knew just where he was. I watched her watch him in her mind's eye. The whole class was watching now. She was staring, sizing, following his scuffle. And all of a sudden she tensed down, posed on her bent kneesprings, cocked her arm back. She threw the oak pole singing over my head, through my braincloud. It cracked through the thin wood door of the back closet, and the heavy pointed hook drove through his heart. I turned. She'd speared her own black rubber overboot where he'd taken refuge in the tip of her darkest toe.

Something howled in my mind. Loss and darkness. I understood. I was to suffer for my smile.

He rose up hard in my heart. I didn't blink when the pole cracked. My skull was tough. I didn't flinch when she shrieked in my ear. I only shrugged at the flowers of hell. He wanted me. More than anything he craved me. But then she did the worst. She did what broke my mind to her. She grabbed me by the collar and dragged me, feet flying, through the room and threw me in the closet with her dead black overboot. And I was there. The only light was a crack beneath the door. I asked the Dark One to enter into me and boost my mind. I asked him to restrain my tears, for they was pushing behind my eyes. But he was afraid to come back there. He was afraid of her sharp pole. And I was afraid of Leopolda's pole for the first time, too. I felt the cold hook in my heart. How it could crack through the door at any minute and drag me out, like a dead fish on a gaff, drop me on the floor like a gutshot squirrel.

I was nothing. I edged back to the wall as far as I could. I breathed the chalk dust. The hem of her full black cloak cut against my cheek. He had left me. Her spear could find me any time. Her keen ears would aim the hook into the beat of my heart.

What was that sound?

It filled the closet, filled it up until it spilled over, but I did not recognize the crying wailing voice as mine until the door cracked open, brightness, and she hoisted me to her camphor-smelling lips.

"He *wants* you," she said. "That's the difference. I give you love."

Love. The black hook. The spear singing through the mind. I saw that she had tracked the Dark One to my heart and flushed him out into the open. So now my heart was an empty nest where she could lurk.

Well, I was weak. I was weak when I let her in, but she got a foothold there. Hard to dislodge as the year passed. Sometimes I felt him—the brush of dim wings—but only rarely did his voice compel. It was between Marie and Leopolda now, and the struggle changed. I began to realize I had been on the wrong track with the fruits of hell. The real way to overcome Leopolda was this: I'd get to heaven first. And then, when I saw her coming, I'd shut the gate. She'd be out! That is why, besides the bowing and the scraping I'd be dealt, I wanted to sit on the altar as a saint.

To this end, I went up on the hill. Sister Leopolda was the consecrated nun who had sponsored me to come there.

"You're not vain," she said. "You're too honest, looking into the mirror, for that. You're not smart. You don't have the ambition to get clear. You have two choices. One, you can marry a no-good Indian, bear his brats, die like a dog. Or two, you can give yourself to God."

"I'll come up there," I said, "but not because of what you think."

I could have had any damn man on the reservation at the time. And I could have made him treat me like his own life. I looked good. And I looked white. But I wanted Sister Leopolda's heart. And here was the thing: sometimes I wanted her heart in love and admiration. Sometimes. And sometimes I wanted her heart to roast on a black stick.

She answered the back door where they had instructed me to call. I stood there with my bundle. She looked me up and down.

"All right," she said finally. "Come in."

She took my hand. Her fingers were like a bundle of broom straws, so thin and dry, but the strength of them was unnatural. I couldn't have tugged loose if she was leading me into rooms of white-hot coal. Her strength was a kind of perverse miracle, for she got it from fasting herself thin. Because of this hunger practice her lips were a wounded brown and her skin deadly pale. Her eye sockets were two deep lashless hollows in a taut skull. I told you about the nose already. It stuck out far and made the place her eyes moved even deeper, as if she stared out the wrong end of a gun barrel. She took the bundle from my hands and threw it in the corner.

"You'll be sleeping behind the stove, child."

It was immense, like a great furnace. There was a small cot close behind it.

"Looks like it could get warm there," I said.

"Hot. It does."

"Do I get a habit?"

I wanted something like the thing she wore. Flowing black cotton. Her face was strapped in white bandages, and a sharp crest of starched white cardboard hung over her forehead like a glaring beak. If possible, I wanted a bigger, longer, whiter beak than hers.

"No," she said, grinning her great skull grin. "You don't get one yet. Who knows, you might not like us. Or we might not like you."

But she had loved me, or offered me love. And she had tried to hunt the Dark One down. So I had this confidence.

"I'll inherit your keys from you," I said.

She looked at me sharply, and her grin turned strange. She hissed, taking in her breath. Then she turned to the door and took a key from her belt. It was a giant key, and it unlocked the larder where the food was stored.

Inside there was all kinds of good stuff. Things I'd tasted only once or twice in my life. I saw sticks of dried fruit, jars of orange peel, spice like cinnamon. I saw tins of crackers with ships painted on the side. I saw pickles. Jars of herring and the rind of pigs. There was cheese, a big brown block of it from the thick milk of goats. And besides that there was the everyday stuff, in great quantities, the flour and the coffee.

It was the cheese that got to me. When I saw it my stomach hollowed. My tongue dripped. I loved that goat-milk cheese better than anything I'd ever ate. I stared at it. The rich curve in the buttery cloth.

"When you inherit my keys," she said sourly, slamming the door in my face, "you can eat all you want of the priest's cheese."

Then she seemed to consider what she'd done. She looked at me. She took the key from her belt and went back, sliced a hunk off, and put it in my hand.

"If you're good you'll taste this cheese again. When I'm dead and gone," she said.

Then she dragged out the big sack of flour. When I finished

that heaven stuff she told me to roll my sleeves up and begin doing God's labor. For a while we worked in silence, mixing up the dough and pounding it out on stone slabs.

"God's work," I said after a while. "If this is God's work, then I've done it all my life."

"Well, you've done it with the Devil in your heart then," she said. "Not God."

"How do you know?" I asked. But I knew she did. And I wished I had not brought up the subject.

"I see right into you like a clear glass," she said. "I always did."

"You don't know it," she continued after a while, "but he's come around here sulking. He's come around here brooding. You brought him in. He knows the smell of me, and he's going to make a last ditch try to get you back. Don't let him." She glared over at me. Her eyes were cold and lighted. "Don't let him touch you. We'll be a long time getting rid of him."

So I was careful. I was careful not to give him an inch. I said a rosary, two rosaries, three, underneath my breath. I said the Creed. I said every scrap of Latin I knew while we punched the dough with our fists. And still, I dropped the cup. It rolled under that monstrous iron stove, which was getting fired up for baking.

And she was on me. She saw he'd entered my distraction.

"Our good cup," she said. "Get it out of there, Marie."

I reached for the poker to snag it out from beneath the stove. But I had a sinking feel in my stomach as I did this. Sure enough, her long arm darted past me like a whip. The poker lighted in her hand.

"Reach," she said. "Reach with your arm for that cup. And when your flesh is hot, remember that the flames you feel are only one fraction of the heat you will feel in his hellish embrace."

She always did things this way, to teach you lessons. So I wasn't surprised. It was playacting, anyway, because a stove isn't very hot underneath right along the floor. They aren't made that way. Otherwise a wood floor would burn. So I said yes and got down on my stomach and reached under. I meant to grab it quick and jump up again, before she could think up another lesson, but here it happened. Although I groped for the cup, my hand closed on nothing. That cup was nowhere to be found. I heard her step toward me, a slow step. I heard the creak of thick shoe leather, the little *plat* as the folds of her heavy skirts met, a trickle of fine sand sifting, somewhere, perhaps in the bowels of her, and I was afraid. I tried to scramble up, but her foot came down lightly behind my ear, and I was lowered. The foot came down more firmly at the base of my neck, and I was held.

"You're like I was," she said. "He wants you very much."

"He doesn't want me no more," I said. "He had his fill. I got the cup!"

I heard the valve opening, the hissed intake of breath, and knew that I should not have spoke.

"You lie," she said. "You're cold. There is a wicked ice forming in your blood. You don't have a shred of devotion for God. Only wild cold dark lust. I know it. I know how you feel. I see the beast . . . the beast watches me out of your eyes sometimes. Cold."

The urgent scrape of metal. It took a moment to know from where. Top of the stove. Kettle. Lessons. She was steadying herself with the iron poker. I could feel it like pure certainty, driving into the wood floor. I would not remind her of pokers. I heard the water as it came, tipped from the spout, cooling as it fell but still scalding as it struck. I must have twitched beneath her foot, because she steadied me, and then the poker nudged up beside my arm as if to guide. "To warm your cold ash heart," she said. I felt how patient she would be. The water came. My mind went dead blank. Again. I could only think the kettle would be cooling slowly in her hand. I could not stand it. I bit my lip so as not to satisfy her with a sound. She gave me more reason to keep still.

"I will boil him from your mind if you make a peep," she said, "by filling up your ear."

Any sensible fool would have run back down the hill the minute Leopolda let them up from under her heel. But I was snared in her black intelligence by then. I could not think straight. I had prayed so hard I think I broke a cog in my mind. I prayed while her foot squeezed my throat. While my skin burst. I prayed even when I heard the wind come through, shrieking in the busted bird nests. I didn't stop when pure light fell, turning slowly behind my eyelids. God's face. Even that did not disrupt my continued praise. Words came. Words came from nowhere and flooded my mind.

Now I could pray much better than any one of them. Than all of them full force. This was proved. I turned to her in a daze when she let me up. My thoughts were gone, and yet I remember how surprised I was. Tears glittered in her eyes, deep down, like the sinking reflection in a well.

"It was so hard, Marie," she gasped. Her hands were shaking. The kettle clattered against the stove. "But I have used all the water up now. I think he is gone."

"I prayed," I said foolishly. "I prayed very hard."

"Yes," she said. "My dear one, I know."

We sat together quietly because we had no more words. We let the dough rise and punched it down once. She gave me a bowl of mush, unlocked the sausage from a special cupboard, and took that in to the Sisters. They sat down the hall, chewing their sausage, and I could hear them. I could hear their teeth bite through their bread and meat. I couldn't move. My shirt was dry but the cloth stuck to my back, and I couldn't think straight. I was losing the sense to understand how her mind worked. She'd gotten past me with her poker and I would never be a saint. I despaired. I felt I had no inside voice, nothing to direct me, no darkness, no Marie. I was about to throw that cornmeal mush out to the birds and make a run for it, when the vision rose up blazing in my mind.

I was rippling gold. My breasts were bare and my nipples flashed and winked. Diamonds tipped them. I could walk through panes of glass. I could walk through windows. She was at my feet, swallowing the glass after each step I took. I broke through another and another. The glass she swallowed ground and cut until her starved insides were only a subtle dust. She coughed. She coughed a cloud of dust. And then she was only a black rag that flapped off, snagged in bob wire, hung there for an age, and finally rotted into the breeze.

I saw this, mouth hanging open, gazing off into the flagged boughs of trees.

"Get up!" she cried. "Stop dreaming. It is time to bake."

Two other Sisters had come in with her, wide women with hands like paddles. They were evening and smoothing out the firebox beneath the great jaws of the oven.

"Who is this one?" they asked Leopolda. "Is she yours?"

"She is mine," said Leopolda. "A very good girl."

"What is your name?" one asked me.

"Marie."

"Marie. Star of the Sea."

"She will shine," said Leopolda, "when we have burned off the dark corrosion."

The others laughed, but uncertainly. They were mild and sturdy French, who did not understand Leopolda's twisted jokes, although they muttered respectfully at things she said. I knew they wouldn't believe what she had done with the kettle. There was no question. So I kept quiet.

"*Elle est docile*," they said approvingly as they left to starch the linens.

"Does it pain?" Leopolda asked me as soon as they were out the door.

I did not answer. I felt sick with the hurt.

"Come along," she said.

The building was wholly quiet now. I followed her up the narrow staircase into a hall of little rooms, many doors. Her cell was the quietest, at the very end. Inside, the air smelled stale, as if the door had not been opened for years. There was a crude straw mattress, a tiny bookcase with a picture of Saint Francis hanging over it, a ragged palm, a stool for sitting on, a crucifix. She told me to remove my blouse and sit on the stool. I did so. She took a pot of salve from the bookcase and began to smooth it upon my burns. Her hands made slow, wide circles, stopping the pain. I closed my eyes. I expected to see blackness.

Peace. But instead the vision reared up again. My chest was still tipped with diamonds. I was walking through windows. She was chewing up the broken litter I left behind.

"I am going," I said. "Let me go."

But she held me down.

"Don't go," she said quickly. "Don't. We have just begun."

I was weakening. My thoughts were whirling pitifully. The pain had kept me strong, and as it left me I began to forget it; I couldn't hold on. I began to wonder if she'd really scalded me with the kettle. I could not remember. To remember this seemed the most important thing in the world. But I was losing the memory. The scalding. The pouring. It began to vanish. I felt like my mind was coming off its hinge, flapping in the breeze, hanging by the hair of my own pain. I wrenched out of her grip.

"He was always in you," I said. "Even more than in me. He wanted you even more. And now he's got you. Get thee behind me!"

I shouted that, grabbed my shirt, and ran through the door throwing it on my body. I got down the stairs and into the kitchen, even, but no matter what I told myself, I couldn't get out the door. It wasn't finished. And she knew I would not leave. Her quiet step was immediately behind me.

"We must take the bread from the oven now," she said.

She was pretending nothing happened. But for the first time I had gotten through some chink she'd left in her darkness. Touched some doubt. Her voice was so low and brittle it cracked off at the end of her sentence.

"Help me, Marie," she said slowly.

But I was not going to help her, even though she had calmly buttoned the back of my shirt up and put the big cloth mittens in my hands for taking out the loaves. I could have bolted for it then. But I didn't. I knew that something was nearing completion. Something was about to happen. My back was a wall of singing flame. I was turning. I watched her take the long fork in one hand, to tap the loaves. In the other hand she gripped the black poker to hook the pans.

"Help me," she said again, and I thought, Yes, this is part of it. I put the mittens on my hands and swung the door open on its hinges. The oven gaped. She stood back a moment, letting the first blast of heat rush by. I moved behind her. I could feel the heat at my front and at my back. Before, behind. My skin was turning to beaten gold. It was coming quicker than I thought. The oven was like the gate of a personal hell. Just big enough and hot enough for one person, and that was her. One kick and Leopolda would fly in headfirst. And that would be one-millionth of the heat she would feel when she finally collapsed in his hellish embrace.

Saints know these numbers.

She bent forward with her fork held out. I kicked her with all my might. She flew in. But the outstretched poker hit the back wall first, so she rebounded. The oven was not so deep as I had thought.

There was a moment when I felt a sort of thin, hot disappointment, as when a fish slips off the line. Only I was the one going to be lost. She was fearfully silent. She whirled. Her veil had cutting edges. She had the poker in one hand. In the other she held that long sharp fork she used to tap the delicate crusts of loaves. Her face turned upside down on her shoulders. Her face turned blue. But saints are used to miracles. I felt no trace of fear.

If I was going to be lost, let the diamonds cut! Let her eat ground glass!

"Bitch of Jesus Christ!" I shouted. "Kneel and beg! Lick the floor!"

That was when she stabbed me through the hand with the fork, then took the poker up alongside my head, and knocked me out.

It must have been a half an hour later when I came around. Things were so strange. So strange I can hardly tell it for delight at the remembrance. For when I came around this was actually taking place. I was being worshiped. I had somehow gained the altar of a saint.

I was laying back on the stiff couch in the Mother Superior's office. I looked around me. It was as though my deepest dream had come to life. The Sisters of the convent were kneeling to

163

me. Sister Bonaventure. Sister Dympna. Sister Cecilia Saint-Claire. The two French with hands like paddles. They were down on their knees. Black capes were slung over some of their heads. My name was buzzing up and down the room, like a fat autumn fly lighting on the tips of their tongues between Latin, humming up the heavy blood-dark curtains, circling their little cosseted heads. Marie! Marie! A girl thrown in a closet. Who was afraid of a rubber overboot. Who was half overcome. A girl who came in the back door where they threw their garbage. Marie! Who never found the cup. Who had to eat their cold mush. Marie! Leopolda had her face buried in her knuckles. Saint Marie of the Holy Slops! Saint Marie of the Bread Fork! Saint Marie of the Burnt Back and Scalded Butt!

I broke out and laughed.

They looked up. All holy hell burst loose when they saw I'd woke. I still did not understand what was happening. They were watching, talking, but not to me.

"The marks . . ."

"She has her hand closed."

"Je ne peux pas voir."

I was not stupid enough to ask what they were talking about. I couldn't tell why I was laying in white sheets. I couldn't tell why they were praying to me. But I'll tell you this: it seemed entirely natural. It was me. I lifted up my hand as in my dream. It was completely limp with sacredness.

"Peace be with you."

My arm was dried blood from the wrist down to the elbow. And it hurt. Their faces turned like flat flowers of adoration to follow that hand's movements. I let it swing through the air, imparting a saint's blessing. I had practiced. I knew exactly how to act.

They murmured. I heaved a sigh, and a golden beam of light suddenly broke through the clouded window and flooded down directly on my face. A stroke of perfect luck! They had to be convinced.

Leopolda still knelt in the back of the room. Her knuckles were crammed halfway down her throat. Let me tell you, a saint has senses honed keen as a wolf. I knew that she was over my barrel now. How it happened did not matter. The last thing

I remembered was how she flew from the oven and stabbed me. That one thing was most certainly true.

"Come forward, Sister Leopolda." I gestured with my heavenly wound. Oh, it hurt. It bled when I reopened the slight heal. "Kneel beside me," I said.

She kneeled, but her voice box evidently did not work, for her mouth opened, shut, opened, but no sound came out. My throat clenched in noble delight I had read of as befitting a saint. She could not speak. But she was beaten. It was in her eyes. She stared at me now with all the deep hate of the wheel of devilish dust that rolled wild within her emptiness.

"What is it you want to tell me?" I asked. And at last she spoke.

"I have told my Sisters of your passion," she managed to choke out. "How the stigmata . . . the marks of the nails . . . appeared in your palm and you swooned at the holy vision. . . ."

"Yes," I said curiously.

And then, after a moment, I understood.

Leopolda had saved herself with her quick brain. She had witnessed a miracle. She had hid the fork and told this to the others. And of course they believed her, because they never knew how Satan came and went or where he took refuge.

"I saw it from the first," said the large one who put the bread in the oven. "Humility of the spirit. So rare in these girls."

"I saw it too," said the other one with great satisfaction. She sighed quietly. "If only it was me."

Leopolda was kneeling bolt upright, face blazing and twitching, a barely held fountain of blasting poison.

"Christ has marked me," I agreed.

I smiled the saint's smirk into her face. And then I looked at her. That was my mistake.

For I saw her kneeling there. Leopolda with her soul like a rubber overboot. With her face of a starved rat. With the desperate eyes drowning in the deep wells of her wrongness. There would be no one else after me. And I would leave. I saw Leopolda kneeling within the shambles of her love.

My heart had been about to surge from my chest with the blackness of my joyous heat. Now it dropped. I pitied her. I pitied her. Pity twisted in my stomach like that hook–pole was driven through me. I was caught. It was a feeling more terrible than any amount of boiling water and worse than being forked. Still, still, I could not help what I did. I had already smiled in a saint's mealy forgiveness. I heard myself speaking gently.

"Receive the dispensation of my sacred blood," I whispered.

But there was no heart in it. No joy when she bent to touch the floor. No dark leaping. I fell back into the white pillows. Blank dust was whirling through the light shafts. My skin was dust. Dust my lips. Dust the dirty spoons on the ends of my feet.

Rise up! I thought. Rise up and walk! There is no limit to this dust!

A DAY IN THE LIFE OF SPANISH

Basil Johnston

Basil Johnston's Indian School Days *is the poignant autobiographical account of Native American students who were forced to attend St. Peter Claver's Indian Residential School, later called the Garnier Residential School, in Ontario, Canada. The school eventually came to be called "Spanish," after the village in which it was located. It was a name that, according to Johnston, was synonymous with "penitentiary, reformatory, exile, dungeon, whippings, kicks, slaps, all rolled into one." The young students, many of whom arrived already damaged from orphanhood or exile from family and friends, met with little understanding or compassion from their instructors, an ascetic group of Jesuits who had been trained to disavow the world of emotions and feelings.*

This excerpt, "A Day in the Life of Spanish," examines the monotony of life lived according to a rigid schedule, the never-ending struggle against hunger, and the dauntless courage of a group of Native American boys who practiced their own distinctive brand of resistance.

A member of the Ojibway nation, Basil Johnston is a writer and a linguist. Two of his books, Ojibway Heritage *and* Ojibway Ceremonies, *deal with Ojibway mythology and culture. He lectures in the Department of Ethnology at the Royal Ontario Museum in Toronto.*

6:15 A.M. CLANG! CLANG! CLANG! I WAS NEARLY CLANGED OUT of my wits and out of bed at the same time. Never had any-

167

thing—not wind, not thunder—awakened me with quite the same shock and fright.

Clang! Clang! Clang!

"Come on! Up! Up! Up! What's the hold-up? Not want to get up? Come on, Pius! What's wrong, Henry? You no like get up?"

Clang! Clang! Clang! Up and down the aisles between the beds Father Buck walked, swinging the bell as if he wanted to shake it from its handle.

"You deaf? You no can hear? Hmmm? You like sleep? No?" Father Buck asked as he stood beside Simon Martin's bed. He rang the bell even harder. There was no sign of movement from the still form. "Soooo! you won't get up, Simon!" And Father Buck seized one side of the mattress and lifted and overturned Simon, bedding and mattress together. Simon stirred.

"Ah! Come on, Father," Simon complained, articulating the expression in current usage at the school for "All right! Knock it off. Enough's enough."

Simon sat up, rubbing his eyes. He was taking far too much time to please the young scholastic.

"You! You want see Father Hawkins?" Father Buck asked.

Not wishing to see Father Hawkins, S.J., Simon got up—as slowly as he dared.

From the other end of the dormitory came a muffled and disrespectful challenge. "Whyn'tcha pick on someone your own size, Father?"

The reaction was instantaneous. "Who says this? Who says this?" demanded Father Buck, red in the face and redder still in the ears.

While Father's attention was elsewhere, Simon, now remarkably wide awake, stuck out his tongue and shook his fist at Father Buck, much to the delight and amusement of the boys in the immediate vicinity. Father Buck, guessing Simon's conduct behind his back, spun around, but Simon, knowing the tactics of adults in games of this kind and having considerable skill in outwitting the enemy, was instantly transformed into a groggy sleepy boy, all angelic innocence, struggling to replace his rebellious mattress, sheets and blankets back on his bed.

Meanwhile, during Simon's mutinous behaviour and irreverent charade, most of the boys, some fully awake others partly awake, and a few in a trance-like state, carried on as if nothing unusual were taking place, folding their pajamas, tucking them under the pillow and then rolling back the top sheet and blanket to air the bed. Not until they had performed these steps did anyone proceed to the washstand.

Clank! Clank! Clank! went the washbasins as they were flipped right side up on the bottom of a long shallow sink that resembled a cattle-feeding trough. To the clatter of basins was added a hiss as water gushed from many spigots into basins or streamed over toothbrushes that were then thrust into little round tins of tooth powder. Clank! Hiss! Gargle! Scrub-a-dub! Scrape! Choo-choo-choo! were the only sounds heard from the washing area.

Occasionally there was a complaint. "Come on, hurry up!" Lawrence Bisto or some other student would growl. "Ain't got all day." And, to lend force to the demand, he would prod the laggard.

"Hold your horses! Can't you see I ain't finished. What's a matter, you blind?" the laggard would retort, his tone of voice signalling that he was prepared to fight.

Clang! Clang! Clang!

"Line up!"

Two serpentine columns of listless boys formed.

"Okay! Quietly!"

But though tongues were quiet, boots beat down on the metal stairs, so that stairs, windows and railings rattled and reverberated from the bottom of the stairwell to the ceiling on the third floor.

In the recreation hall downstairs the boys either stood around in knots or sat slouched on the top board that served as a bench as well as a lid for the boxes that were built into the wall. But as I was to learn later, the boys were not really waiting in the commonly understood sense of the word "wait." Though they may have appeared to be waiting, the boys were in reality exercising a form of quiet disobedience directed against bells, priests, school and, in the abstract, all authority, civil and religious.

Since the boys could not openly defy authority either by

walking out of the school and marching north or south on Highway 17 or by flatly refusing to follow an order, they turned to the only means available to them: passive resistance, which took the form of dawdling.

Only once in my eight years of residence did I witness the phenomenon of boys racing to line up and then maintaining the strictest monastic silence when no bell had rung. As well as I can remember, the incident occurred in the following manner:

"Ice cream!" someone yelled.

"Ice cream! Ice cream! Ice cream!" was repeated a dozen times across the playground.

Well, the announcement "ice cream" uttered either by La Marr (Antoine Lafrance) or Neeyauss (Angus Pitwaniquot) had the same effect as the cry of "Fire!" except that in this instance it operated in reverse. As the magic words "ice cream" went echoing from mouth to mouth across the yard, bats, baseballs and scoreboards were abandoned and 130 boys rushed to line up in front of the veranda, where goodies such as ice cream and candies were often distributed to mark some special feast or event.

Prefects, too, clutching the hems of their soutanes, sprinted across the yard in pursuit of the boys.

Panting and flushed with impotent rage, Father Buck demanded to know: "Who says this?" Back and forth in front of the twelve rows of boys, every one of whom was anticipating the issue of ice cream, strode Father Buck, looking darkly into the faces of the boys as if he could discern the look of guilt. He paused directly in front of Donald Fox and Joe Coocoo, two of our fellow inmates, already well known for their habitual disregard for rules, regulations, laws and the Ten Commandments. He peered into their faces.

"You!" Father Buck snapped at Donald Fox. "Did you say this?"

Donald was deeply pained. In his most aggrieved tone he said, "Not me, Father. Honest to God. You always blaming me for nothing."

Father Buck continued to stare at Donald, dumbfounded that Donald should deny his guilt. Only Donald would sabotage a ball game and circulate false rumours. But before the young

scholastic could do anything rash, such as sending Donald to
Father Hawkins for a thrashing, Father Buck's fellow teachers,
Father Kehl and Father Mayhew, moved to his side. After a
brief whispered consultation and a quick glance at his watch,
Father Buck commanded, "You go back and play, until this
bell rings."

6:45 A.M. Clang! Clang! Clang!
   Boys shuffled into lines as slowly as they dared without having their names inscribed in the prefects' little black books. It
would have been easier to line up immediately without waiting
for the bell, but that would have been seen as surrender.
   Father Buck must have imagined himself a commander and
we his soldiers as he stood in front and stared us into silence.
Even when there was silence all around, he still felt constrained
to command it. *"Quiet!"* It was not until he had obtained a
sepulchral silence that he nodded to his colleague, Father Kehl,
to open the door. "Okay! And no talking."
   Our route from the recreation hall to the chapel was not
direct, through the first corridor, but round about outside, along
the south side of the building. We trod it in hail, sleet, blizzard
and deluge. Had there been fire and brimstone, we would have
walked in that as well.
   At the word "okay," the teams proceeded outside, where they
converged into two columns, with the youngest and smallest in
front and the oldest and biggest boys at the back. When the two
columns shuffled to a halt in the left aisle, they stood at reverent
attention.
   "Clap," snapped the clapper in Father Kehl's hand. Down on
one knee we dropped in united genuflection, remaining in that
position until the clapper clapped a second time in signal for us
to rise and to stand once more at attention. Only after one more
clap did we slide into our assigned places in the pews.
   Moments later, under the heavy escort of Miss Strain and
Miss Chabot and wearing pretty hats and dresses, the girls from
St. Joseph's entered the chapel in much the same way as we had
done except in one particular. Their movements, pace, halting,
genuflecting, rising and entering the pews from the right aisle
were regulated not by a wooden clapper but by the clapping of

the hands of female prefects who glowered and frowned just as severely as our own keepers, in an effort to make sure the girls did not cast lustful glances at the boys or receive similar glances.

When mass was over, we were ushered out with the same order and precision as we had entered . . . clack! clack! clack! We went directly back upstairs to make our beds according to a pattern more than likely of Jesuit invention. The dormitory, even though the beds had received a thorough airing, was rank with the smell of piss from the "pisskers' section." Once the beds were made we were led downstairs.

7:25 A.M. Clang! Clang! Clang!

For once the prefect did not have to yell to bring about peace and order. The older boys, anxious to eat, assumed the role of enforcement officers, delivering what were called "rabbit punches" to those who persisted in talking, as samples of what was to come if the talker did not at once desist.

Silently we filed into the refectory, which, from the state of the furnishings and settings, was a more appropriate term than "dining room." There were sixteen long tables of an uncertain green flanked by benches of the same green. On each table were eight place settings, consisting of a tin pie plate, a tablespoon and a chipped granite cup. In the middle were two platters of porridge, which, owing to its indifferent preparation, was referred to as "mush" by the boys; there were also a box containing sixteen slices of bread, a round dish bearing eight spoons of lard (Fluffo brand), and a huge jug of milk. It was mush, mush, mush, sometimes lumpy, sometimes watery, with monotonous regularity every Monday, Wednesday, Friday and Saturday. The boys would have vastly preferred the Boston baked beans that, along with a spoonful of butter, were served on Tuesdays, Thursdays and Sundays.

Not until we had said grace—"Bless this mush," some boys said in secret, "I hope it doesn't kill us"—could we begin. But no matter how indifferent the quality, no boy, to my recollection, ever refused his portion of mush. During the meal there was little conversation except for the occasional "Pass the mush" or "Pass the milk" and the clatter of spoons, which served as knives and forks as well.

★ ★ ★

7:55 A.M. Clang! Clang! Clang!

After grace of thanksgiving, it was outside to the recreation hall. Except for the lucky ones in Grades 1, 2 and 3, everyone went to his assigned place of work. The seniors, in Grades 6, 7 and 8, went to their permanent occupations: to the barn, to tend horses, cows, sheep, pigs and all their products; to the chicken coop, to look after chickens; to the tailor shop, shoe shop, electrical shop, carpentry shop, blacksmith shop, mill or plumber's shack. These were jobs of standing and responsibility in the adolescent community. The other boys, from grades that had no status, waited outside the storeroom for the issue of mops, pails, sponges, soap, rags, brooms, dustpans, dust-bane and other janitorial paraphernalia for performing the menial tasks of washing, sweeping, mopping, dusting, polishing toilets, corridors, refectory, chapels, kitchen, dormitory, scullery, every conceivable area.

"*Johnston!* Number *forty-three!*"

"Yes, Father."

"I have special job for you," Father said, handing me a mop, pail, soap and a peculiar, curved oval brush such as I had never before seen. Up to this time in my life the hardest and most detestable forms of work that I had performed were reluctantly carrying either wood or water for my mother. I really didn't want to work but, if work I must, it was better to begin with something special rather than with some plebeian labour.

"Come with me!"

Father Buck led me directly to the toilets, which were so vile with the reek of human waste that I nearly choked and disgorged my mush. Even Father Buck, who must have been aged about twenty-three or twenty-four, gasped as he issued his instructions: "Wash the bowls with this and the walls with this, and the urinals with this, and the floors with this, no? . . . And make clean and smell good . . . no? I come back." I thought that Father Buck staggered slightly as he went out and breathed deeply to cleanse his lungs.

I too had to go out to avoid being overcome. While I stood outside breathing in oxygen, I developed a stratagem for cleaning up the toilets without collapsing. For self-preservation the job had to be done in stages. Flush the toilets, run outside. Wash the bowls, run outside. Hold breath, wash urinals, run outside. Hold breath, wash partitions, run outside. Spread sawdust on the floor, run outside. Sweep up sawdust, run outside. The toilets may not have completely lost their miasma of dung as I swept up the last pile of sawdust, but they at least looked vastly cleaner. I staggered out, inhaling huge quantities of the "breath of life," and waited, proud of my labours . . . almost. "Achtung! You finish this, already?" Father asked as if he were astounded.

"Yes," I replied with a considerable burst of pride.

"Well! We shall see."

Father Buck didn't have to go into the lavatory to reach the conclusion that, "They not smell good." I was going to say that the smell was stuck in the walls, in the ceiling, on the floor, in the corners, everywhere, but I didn't get a chance. Father entered the lavatory and went directly into a compartment. Inside, he bent down in order to run his finger in the back of and under the bowl. He showed me a black fingertip.

"Sooooo! You like this fight but no like it work. Then you work extra week in these toilets until you learn it like work or until you learn it meaning of clean."

It was back to work.

8:50 A.M. Clang! Clang! Clang!

"Put it away tools."

From every part of the institution and the grounds boys scurried back to the recreation hall with their equipment.

8:55 A.M. Clang! Clang! Clang!

Line up again. According to the system then in operation half the senior boys went to class, while the other half went to work not only to practise a trade but also to provide the labour needed to run the institution. In the afternoon the seniors switched shifts. The younger boys went to classes the entire day.

"Number forty-*three!*"

There was no answer.

"Number forty-*three!*" A little louder.

Silence.

"You! Johnston!"

"Yes, Father!"

"You are number *forty-three*! Do you understand?"

I nodded.

"You answer, when I call *forty-three*!"

"Yes, Father."

"Now, you go with this Grade 5 to Father Mayhew's class."

"But Father, I'm supposed to be in Grade 6. I was in Grade 5 last year."

"Sooooo! You like it fight, you no like it work, and you like it argue! . . . sooooo!" And Father Buck fished out of his cassock pocket a black book in which he scribbled something while looking severely at me. "Soooo, you say you in Grade 6. That's what they all say. Now you be quiet. And no more trouble. You go with this Grade 5."

On the way upstairs, Ovilla Trudeau commented with a snicker, "You didn't think you'd get away with that, did you?"

"What's that teacher's name? I can't understand dat pries'."

"Father Mayhew."

After the Lord's Prayer I went directly to the teacher's desk.

"Father. Someone made a mistake. I'm supposed to be in Grade 6. I passed Grade 5 already. I tol' Father Buck, but he won't believe me."

Father Mayhew just looked at me. "I'm told you're in Grade 5. There's nothing that you can do about it."

But my appointment to Grade 5, as I learned years later, was not a product of misunderstanding but a coldly calculated decision made "for my own good." For if I had been allowed to proceed to Grade 6 as I should have been, it would have disrupted the entire promotion and graduation schedule that decreed that all boys committed to a residential school remain in the institution until age sixteen, or until their parents, if living together, arranged an early parole. If I had progressed at my normal rate through the elementary school I would have been ready for "entrance examinations" by age twelve. According to the administration it would not have been appropriate or in the best interests of society to release me or any one of my colleagues prior to age sixteen. The only solution was to have a boy repeat grades until Grade 8 and age sixteen were synchronized. I was not the only one to be so penalized.

Hence I was mired in Grade 5, forced to listen to dull and boring lessons rendered even duller and more boring by my sense of unjust treatment. What unspeakable fate I might have suffered had it not been for a collection of Tom Swift books and other volumes of doubtful merit, it is hard to say. That Father Mayhew turned a blind eye to my reading in class helped enormously; he didn't seem to mind as long as I didn't disturb the class and passed the tests. The only time I paid attention was during the reading of *The Song of Hiawatha*, whose Indian words Father Mayhew mangled and garbled. Inspired by the success of *Hiawatha*, Father Mayhew next tried to inflict *Winnie the Pooh* and *Anne of Green Gables* on us, but we denounced them as insipid so frequently that eventually Father Mayhew stopped reading them.

11:55 A.M. Clang! Clang! Clang!

Father Mayhew closed his book, looking relieved that the morning had finally come to an end. Wearily he made his way to the door, which he opened. Protocol decreed that he had to wait for Brother O'Keeffe to dismiss his class, the seniors, first. Only after Brother O'Keeffe and the seniors had gone out did Father Mayhew issue the order: "Okay!" As he did so, he stepped back to avoid being trampled by a rush of boys who leaped over desks and shoved one another in their anxiety to get out of the classroom. Moments later the "little shots" came down.

12:00 noon. Clang! Clang! Clang!

"*Line up! Shut up!*" The command need not have been shouted, but it was nevertheless bellowed, in the belief that a shout always obtained quicker compliance.

"Shshshshsh."

For dinner there was barley soup with other ingredients, including chunks of fat and gristle, floating about in it. Finding a chunk of fat in one's soup was like receiving a gift of manna, for it could be used to garnish the two slices of bread that came with the meal if one had lacked the foresight or the prudence to hide a chunk of lard from breakfast for one's dinner needs by sticking the lard under the table. Barley soup, pea soup (not the French or Quebec variety), green and yellow, vegetable soup, onion soup, for dinner and supper. Barley soup prepared in a hundred different combinations. "Barley soup! Don't that cook have no imagination?" Barley soup in the fall. "Hope they run outa that stuff pretty soon." Barley soup in the spring. "How much o' this stuff they plant, anyways? Hope a plague o' locusts eat all the barley this summer." Besides the soup there was a large jug of green tea diluted with milk. Clatter, clatter. "Pass the tea." Shuffle, scrape.

12:30 P.M. Clang! Clang! Clang!

After grace, except for the team scheduled to clean the refectory and wash dishes that week, everyone congregated near "the store" for the issue of baseball equipment before proceeding to one of the three baseball diamonds to play until 1:10, the seniors to the diamond hard by the chicken coop, the intermediates to the diamond near the horse barn and the juniors to the diamond near the windmill.

The only ones excluded from playing were the dishwashers, and the team not scheduled to play that day. The latter was required to provide umpiring, score-keeping and cheering services. Otherwise, there was no exemption for anyone. Cripples like Sam Paul were expected to, and did, derive as much fun and benefit from baseball, softball, touch football, basketball and hockey as Benjamin Buzwa and Eddie Coocoo; the stiff-jointed, like Reuben Bisto and David Jocko, were required to pursue fly balls or give chase to grounders with as much diligence if not grace as the more agile, like Steve Lazore and Tony Angus.

1:10 P.M. Clang! Clang! Clang!

This bell was harsher and therefore even more resented than the previous bells, for it put an end to forty minutes of relative freedom and distraction from sorrows. Hence bases, balls, bats, gloves and score-cards were collected—slowly—and returned to "the store" without haste. For the seniors, or the "big shots," as the intermediates sometimes referred to them, it was time to

change shifts; for the rest of us, it was back to the dreary classroom with its dreary lessons . . . or to look out over the Spanish
River, across the far portage at Little Detroit and beyond, into
the dim shapes and shadows of the past or the physically distant,
of mother and father and grandmother, of sisters and brothers
and friends, of aunts and uncles and their friends, of happiness
and freedom and affection . . . somewhere beyond Little Detroit
. . . as distant as the stars.

4:15 P.M. Clang! Clang! Clang!

By now our sole preoccupation, as hunger displaced the
shapes and shadows, was food. On our way downstairs one of
our colleagues expressed our collective fear: "If I starve to death,
it's going to be their fault; we never have enough but they have
lots for themselves."

In the recreation hall a line formed bearing in the direction of
the refectory, in front of whose doors was set one of the refectory tables. Behind this makeshift counter were two boys, one
of whom was lopping off the green tops of carrots with a large
butcher knife which he handled like a machete, while the other
distributed two raw carrots to each customer. "Collation" they
called this lunch. Today it was carrots; tomorrow it would be
a wedge of raw cabbage; the day after, a turnip, raw like everything else. As each boy received his ration he was directed to
take his collation outside. Despite its lofty name, collation was
regarded as little better than animal fodder. Nevertheless, every
boy ate the fodder to stave off starvation.

Collation was intended, I guess, not only to allay hunger
pains, but also to restore flagging energies. It was our first real
period of leisure in a day that had begun at 6:15 A.M., but if
anyone hoped for or expected an extended period of idleness,
as I then did, he was soon set straight by the sight of the accursed
bell in Father Buck's hand.

"Hey! Father!" an anonymous voice called out. "How come
you not eating carrots like us?" To which there was no answer.

4:30 P.M. Clang! Clang! Clang!

"Time for work, boys."

For me it was back to the lavatory. But with the five compartments or stalls in continuous occupation, as if most of the boys had suddenly been afflicted with a particularly virulent strain of diarrhea, I could not easily carry out Father Buck's instruction to "clean good." Even a lineup of boys outside commanding the occupants to "Hurry up! Ain't got all day!" could not make the incumbents accelerate the defecatory process. Sometimes threats worked. "Wait till you come out." Or, if threats and exhortations did not work, there was always "the drench," carried out by means of a wet rag squeezed over the top of the stall onto the incumbent. But this method of encouraging haste in the patrons only made my job worse.

4:55 P.M. Clang! Clang! Clang!
  "*Line up! . . . Quiet.*"
After quiet was established the prefects counted heads in each line by waggling a pencil and mouthing numbers.
  "Where's Shaggy [Joe Missabe]?"
  "Helping Brother Grubb."
  "Where's Cabootch?"
  "Working for Brother Van der Moor."
The young priest made a notation in his little black book, frowning in worry as he did so. Later, he would check the work schedule and consult the brothers to verify the information given him. Woe betide the student who gave false information; double woe betide the absentee.
  "All right! Upstairs, and no talking." Father Buck hated talking.

5:00 P.M. As we filed into the study hall, there was Brother Manseau from Asbestos, Quebec, standing to one side of the doorway, greeting the boys by name—or names. "Ah, Ti Phonse! Ti Bar Poot! Moustaffa! Monsieur le Snowball! Ti Blue!" Brother Manseau was of medium height, almost but not quite dark enough to be regarded as swarthy, with a light five o'clock shadow beclouding his face. His hair was grey and frizzy, swept back from his temples and from a point of recession at about the middle of his head, something like Harpo Marx's hair.
  To the boys, Brother J. B. Manseau was B. J. or "Beedj-

mauss" or "Beedj," from a reversal of his initials, which stood for "Jean-Baptiste." The "Beedj-mauss" also represented a play on words, which, if pronounced with the proper accent and inflection, would mean in our tribal language (Anishinaubae or Ojibway), "He comes reeking of the smell of smoke," a reference to Brother Manseau's pipe-smoking habit. He did not seem to mind "Hey Beedj!", just as he never seemed to mind too much a thumbtack on his seat. To my knowledge he never sent a boy to see Father Hawkins for punishment.

When he had settled down, Brother Manseau reminded us not to disturb him and, as an afterthought, gave us a verbal abstract of the book that he was then reading, *Twenty Thousand Leagues under the Sea*, by Jules Verne. After recommending that we read it, he warned us, "Now I don't want anybody to disturb me; I don't care what you do but don't bother me, otherwise, I kick his ass." And though Beedj had one short leg, he could deliver a mean kick, especially with the discarded Mountie's riding boots that he wore.

No one wanted his ass kicked, or to serve "jug" on Thursday; everyone settled down to do homework, draw, snooze or read, leaving Beedj-mauss to read his book undisturbed.

5:55 P.M. Father Buck slipped into the study hall almost as noiselessly as a ghost. He nodded for Brother Manseau to close his book, and Brother Manseau promptly disappeared. Believing that study was now over, many of us, in imitation of Brother Manseau, closed our books and put them away.

"STUDY IS NOT OVER! PUT THESE BOOKS BACK! AND NOT PUT AWAY TILL I TELL YOU!"

Father Buck looked at his watch. Not until the malefactors had reopened their books and resumed study, or appeared to do so, did the prefect dismiss us. Everything was by the clock, by the book, by regulations.

"Downstairs!"

6:00 P.M. Not one second before the minute or the hour would Father ring that bell, Clang! Clang! Clang! Clangity-clang! "Hurry up! Shshshsh!" There was silence, almost absolute except for the scuffle of boots and the odd sniffle and cough. This is the way it should have been, the way that it was intended to be, the way that would have gratified and edified the prefects and the way that would have pleased Father Buck.

Father Buck nodded, as he always did, to his colleague, Father Kehl, to open the door. In we filed and, for the next twenty minutes or a little longer, gave ourselves wholeheartedly to pea soup, bread, lard and green tea from Java. In quantity served there was just enough food to blunt the sharp edge of hunger for three or four hours, never enough to dispel hunger completely until the next meal. Every crumb was eaten, and the last morsel of bread was used to sponge up any residue of soup that might still be clinging to the sides or to the bottom of the plates, thereby leaving the plates clean and dry, the way puppies lick their dishes clean. There was the same quantity for every boy, regardless of size or need. Yet not even the "little shots," whose ingestive capacities were considerably less than those of their elders and who therefore should have required and received less, were ever heard to extol a meal with "I'm full." "I'm full" was an expression alien in our world and to our experience.

Never having the luxury of a second serving or an extra slice, the boys formed a healthy regard for food that bordered on reverence that shaped their eating habits. If they could not glut themselves, they could at least prolong the eating by carnally indulging in every morsel of food. To eat with such carnality may have constituted a sin, but we never considered it as such. Meals became rituals almost as solemn as religious services in their intensity, the only sounds the clatter of spoons on plates and mugs and the muted "Pass the mush" or "You owe me a slice"; "When you going to pay me that lard you owe me?" "I'm so hungry right now, can you wait till tomorrow?"

As deliberate as the boys were at table, few could match the solemnity or the sensuousness with which "That's the Kind" (Jim Wemigwans) presided over his meal. During the entire course of supper "That's the Kind" broke his bread, one pinch at a time, as one might nip petals off a bloom; each pinch was then deposited with delicacy on his tongue. Our colleague ate every morsel, be it barley, green beans, peas, onions, potatoes—

every spoonful of every meal—with as much deliberation and relish as if it were manna or ambrosia . . . or his last meal prior to execution.

6:30 to 7:30 P.M. If the prefects had not prearranged some event—swimming, a short walk, a choir practice, a game, a play practice—the hour was relatively free for the boys to do what they felt like doing. But it was during this free time that mischief and misdeeds were perpetrated and fights most often broke out. Hence, it was to forestall the commission of mischief and to reduce the number of fights that the administration planned each day—each hour—so that there was as little free time as possible.

Now such fights as did break out from time to time were in the main instigated merely to infuse some excitement into the monotony of institutional life, a monotony that may have suited the clergy, but was not to the liking of the boys.

Like many other pursuits and diversions in the school, fights were conducted according to certain customs and codes. They never broke out amid the shouts and accusations that usually precede fights, nor did one aggressor, as from ambush, spring upon his victim to deliver the coup de grace with one blow. Nor yet was a fight conducted to the finish. Not allowed during the course of a fight were kicking, biting, hitting an opponent from behind or striking an opponent while he was on the ground. No one was allowed to interfere on behalf of a friend or brother; every boy was expected to fight his own battles. Fights were to be fair and square.

By custom, the challenger, usually one of the intermediates anxious to prove his worth or to avenge some wrong, would deliberately seek out his foe with a wood chip or a flat stone on his shoulder, placed there either by his own hand or by that of someone else. In the school, "walking around with a chip on his shoulder" was not merely an expression but a literal reality. Some challengers, not satisfied with the obvious meaning of the act, issued a dare in addition: "Betcha too scairt to knock it off."

But no one was "too scairt" ever to refuse such a challenge, even if he knew from previous experience that he could never win in the proverbial "hundred years." For among the boys it had long been established that refusal was a sign of cowardice, and boys would sooner suffer a black eye, a bloodied nose or puffed lips than bear a reputation of being "yellow." Hence, it was a matter of honour for the challenged to rise to the dare and, with as much scorn and deliberation as he could muster, knock the chip off the challenger's shoulder. And there was no greater sign of contempt than, in knocking the chip off the shoulder, to brush the cheek of the challenger at the same time; to do so was comparable to a slap on the cheek with a pair of white gloves. In more formal fights, if there could be such things as more formal or less formal fights, a "second" would retrieve the chip and hand it to the challenged, who in his turn placed the object on his shoulder to make certain that the challenge was no bluff.

"Fight! Fight!" resounded throughout the recreation hall as the adversaries stood up to square off like boxers. The words were magnetic, at once drawing an audience, prefects included, who formed a ring around the contestants.

It was Eugene Keeshig and Michael Taylor, two senior students (Grade 6) who could never see eye to eye on anything. They circled each other like professional boxers.

All of a sudden there was a "pow, pow, pow," and the next moment Mike was on the ground, stricken by three blows delivered with lightning speed by Eugene, who had launched himself forward with the suddenness of a panther. Eugene now stepped back to allow his opponent to get back on his feet. Once Mike was upright the fight resumed, arms flailing and fists driving forward like pistons, with some grunts and growls. The skirmish was spirited but brief. Down went Michael who, in a kneeling position, held up one hand as a sign of submission; with the other he held his nose to stanch the flow of blood.

The fight was over in five minutes, but not the feud. Mike would never yield to anyone—or to anything, for that matter. In his ongoing feud with Eugene and Charlie Shoot, Mike took many lumps in living up to the basic principles of survival at the school: "taking it like a man" and "toughing it out."

Sometimes in the cold dreary evenings of October and November, when the weather was too inclement for playing outside, the call "mushpot" rang out. Instantly, all the boys, including those well settled on the pottie, suspended their operations to answer the summons. No fireman or soldier responded to a call more quickly. No one wanted to be "it," "mushpot." Hence, when the cry was uttered, everyone scrambled for a place in the circle—seniors, intermediates and juniors, all except the babies.

The last to arrive, the one who was "it," fashioned a mushpot from an old rag or a handful of toilet tissue soaked in water, the soggier the better. With the dripping mushpot, the boy who was "it" ran around the perimeter of the circle proposing to plant the soggy object behind somebody. This was difficult to accomplish, because the boys in the circle kept a watchful eye on "it." For if one of the players failed to notice the mushpot behind him by the time "it" came back around, "it" was entitled by tradition to bash the victim over the head with the mushpot and to kick him "in de hass" at the same time. The boy so walloped now became "it." However, if the intended victim noticed the "plant" behind him, he instantly took up the mushpot and gave chase and, if he overtook the planter, was allowed by the rules to wallop him over the head with the mushpot, causing "it" to continue to be "it." Some mushpots couldn't take it. As well as being mushpots, they were soreheads.

"Come on, Father! You ring that bell too soon . . . jis' when we were having fun. You don' want us to have fun."

Bells and whistles, gongs and clappers represent everything connected with sound management—order, authority, discipline, efficiency, system, organization, schedule, regimentation, conformity—and may in themselves be necessary and desirable. But they also symbolize conditions, harmony and states that must be established in order to have efficient management: obedience, conformity, dependence, subservience, uniformity, docility, surrender. In the end it is the individual who must be made to conform, who must be made to bend to the will of another.

And because prefects were our constant attendants and superintendents, regulating our time and motions, scheduling our comings and goings, supervising our work and play, keeping surveillance over deeds and words, enforcing the rules and maintaining discipline with the help of two instruments of control and oppression—bells and the black book—we came to dislike and to distrust these young men. Most were in their early twenties and had completed their novitiate of four years' study at Guelph, Ontario. Regardless of their dispositions or their attitudes toward us, they were the archenemies, simply because they held the upper hand both by virtue of their calling and by the exercise of threats. If one of our fellow inmates grew too contumacious even for the strap there was always the "reform school."

While most of these young novices (referred to as first, second or third prefects) superintended our lives by the book, a few possessed a degree of compassion. But even they were helpless to show their sympathy in a tangible way, for the prefects, too, were under the close and keen observation of the Father Superior and "the Minister," the administrator of the school. During their regency, the prefects, sometimes called "scholastics" by the priests, had to demonstrate that they had the stuff to be Jesuits.

Once one of the boys, after being warned to "*Shut up!*," continued to whisper, or perhaps just uttered one more word, which, if left unsaid, would have rendered his entire message meaningless. It must have been a very important word to risk its utterance in the presence of Father Buck. Anyway, the prefect flew into a rage and struck the offender on the head with the bell. At least, it appeared as if Father Buck had clouted the offender with the bell, for he struck our colleague with the same hand in which he held the bell—not hard enough to draw blood but forcefully enough to raise a contusion and to elicit an "Eeeeeyow!" and cause the victim to clutch his head in pain.

Even before the outcry had subsided, the senior boys at the back—Renee Cada, Tom White, Louis Mitchell, Jim Coocoo, John Latour and Louis Francis—protested: "Come on, Father! That's going too far." They wrenched the bell from Father Buck's hand and threatened to knock him on the head to "See how you'd like it. . . ."

The boy who had seized the bell raised his hand as if to strike . . . but, instead of bringing it down on Father Buck's head, returned the instrument to the disconcerted young prefect, whose face turned from ash to crimson and then back again. Had our colleague carried out his threat, he would most likely have been committed to the nearest reformatory, and also excommunicated from the church. There was a hushed silence throughout the recreation hall, both at the moment the bell was suspended over the prefect's head and afterward.

Father Buck opened the door in silence. What saved the senior boys then and other boys on other occasions from retribution was the prefect's own uneasiness about his superiors. Of course, we knew nothing of the prefects' fears.

9:00 P.M. At that hour we were dismissed from study (the babies having gone to bed at 7:30) to retire to the dormitory where everyone—or nearly everyone—loitered around the washing area, either brushing his teeth or washing . . . or just pretending to wash. Anything to waste time. While many boys dallied near and around the trough, others made their way to the infirmary, there to linger and to have their pains, bruises, aches and cuts attended to by Brother Laflamme.

9:25 P.M. The lights were switched on and off in a radical departure from bell clanging as a signal for all the boys to return to their bedsides.

"Kneel down and say your prayers."

We prayed, imploring God to allow us release from Spanish the very next day.

9:30 P.M. "All right! Get in bed . . . and no noise!"

The lights went out. The only illumination in the dormitory came from two night lights glowing red like coals at either end of the ceiling of the huge sleeping quarters. In the silence and the darkness it was a time for remembrance and reflection. But thoughts of family and home did not yield much comfort and strength; instead such memories as one had served to inflame the feelings of alienation and abandonment and to fan the flames of resentment. Soon the silence was broken by the sobs and whimpers of boys who gave way to misery and sadness, dejection and melancholy, heartache and gloom.

Besides the sobs and whimpers, which would come to an end

by the finish of a boy's first week at the school, there were the muted fall of footsteps and the faint motion of the phantom form of the prefect as he patrolled the dormitory.

"Shut up!"

But the dormitory was not always given to either golden or angelic silence or to the frigid winds that blew in through the open windows or to maudlin whimperings. More often there were muted whispers commingled with muffled giggles from the various regions of the dormitory. Sometimes one boy would cup his hand under his armpit and bring his arm down abruptly to produce a most obscene backfire, such as one would hear in a horse barn produced by an overwrought horse. Within moments there would be similar eruptions all over the dormitory.

For the prefects, who had a highly developed sense of law and regulation and of what was proper and improper, these night watches must have been harrowing. They were ever on the prowl to quell sobs, whispers or whatever disturbed the silence. They dashed from one side to the other in a vain attempt to catch the guilty party by asking for a confession. "Who makes thees noise?" For all the good their investigations did, they might as well have tried to quell spring peepers in a pond in May.

But there were times when Father Buck and Father Kehl brought the harassment on themselves.

Late at night they would sometimes confer in hushed but excited tones.

"Father! Did you hear the news today? The Fatherland sunk two hundred thousand tons of these enemy ships. Heil Hitler."

There was always someone awake, someone to hear, someone to whisper aloud, "Nazi"; and the word "Nazi" echoed and re-echoed throughout the dormitory.

"Who says thees?"

"Nazi," in the north corner.

"Who says thees?"

"Nazi," in the south end.

"Who says thees?"

"Nazi."

Eventually the two prefects would have to terminate the search and punish everyone by making us all stand stock still by our bedsides for half an hour.

Then to prevent being understood they spoke in German, with even worse results.

Eventually they stopped talking to one another in the dormitory; and finally they learned that it was better to grit their teeth and to bear whatever names the boys called them. And in due time, the boys too desisted in their practice of calling names.

For some, sleep, the friend of the weary and troubled, came soon; for others, later.

Though some days were eventful and were memorable for some reason, most passed by as the seconds, the minutes and the hours mark the passage of time, in work, study, prayer and proper play. Were it not for the spirit of the boys, every day would have passed according to plan and schedule, and there would have been no story.

6:15	Rise
6:45–7:25	Mass
7:30–8:00	Breakfast
8:05–8:55	Work
9:00–11:55	Class/work
12:00–12:25	Dinner
12:30–1:10	Sports/games/rehearsal
1:15–4:15	Class/work
4:15–4:30	Collation
4:30–4:55	Work/chores
5:00–5:55	Study
6:00–6:25	Supper
6:30–7:25	Sports/games/rehearsal
7:30–10:00	Study and prepare for bed

TWENTIETH
CENTURY

The policies that oppressed Native Americans continue almost unabated into the twentieth century. The issues that were at the heart of nineteenth-century tribal struggles (autonomy, self-determination, the retention of land, tribal lifeways, and religious freedom) remain central concerns.

The latter half of the twentieth century has brought forth an ever-increasing effort toward self-determination by indigenous peoples. The formation of the American Indian Movement (AIM) in 1968 created an enormous resurgence of tribal pride and a commitment to fight for the rights guaranteed under numerous treaties that have never been upheld. Over the years, protest actions carried out by members of AIM have played a significant part in capturing media attention and bringing the contemporary problems of Native Americans—both on the reservations and in urban areas—to the attention of the American public.

The battle against prejudice and racism has not ended for Native American people. The stories in this section illustrate the despair and alienation sometimes felt by many tribal people surrounded by a society that is often hostile to them. These stories also demonstrate that Native Americans are not curious cultural artifacts to be consigned to dusty museum shelves. The so-called vanishing American has not vanished. Native American peoples throughout the North American continent persevere. They are adapting to the conditions of the times and transforming themselves and their identities as they move forward.

from SUNDOWN
John Joseph Mathews

Challenge Windzer, the Osage protagonist of John Joseph Mathews's Sundown, was given his unusual name by his father in the hope that he would be a challenge to the enemies of his people. This penetrating and true-to-life novel traces Chal's increasing alienation as he tries to bridge the chasm between cultures during the social and economic upheaval in Oklahoma in the 1920s.

In this selection, young Chal invents his own private fantasy world, a world in which even religious images can take on flesh. When Chal invites the figure of the Christ Child to join his group of imaginary playmates, the real world intervenes with swift and sudden cruelty to shatter his childhood innocence.

John Joseph Mathews (Osage) was born in 1894 in Indian Territory, which is now the state of Oklahoma. He held a degree in geology from the University of Oklahoma, and a degree in natural sciences from Merton College at Oxford. Among his scholarly and literary achievements are Wah'Kon-Tah: The Osage and the White Man's Road and Talking to the Moon, a book of poetry. Sundown is his only work of fiction. Mathews died in 1979.

ONE MIGHT HAVE SAID THAT CHAL'S EARLY CHILDHOOD WAS CONtemplative rather than one of action. Yet this would not be true; it was both a life of contemplation and action. Contemplation, mostly in the form of dreams wherein he played the role of hero, whether in the form of man or animal.

Sometimes he was a panther lying lazily in his den and blink-

ing in physical contentment, or a redtail hawk circling high in
the blue of the sky. Often at night, when he heard the raindrops
on the tin roof of his bedroom, he would be an animal; an
indefinite animal in a snug den under the dripping boughs of a
tree. Sometimes real pain would be the result of these dream-
world metamorphoses; pain caused by the desire to fly over the
green world high in the air, like the turkey vulture and the
hawk. Unhappiness would descend on him as he lay on his back
in the prairie grass, watching the graceful spirals of the redtail.
He would get up with a feeling of helpless defiance and walk
slowly to where his pinto cropped the grass with reins dragging.
It was a hopeless feeling of inferiority in being earthbound, and
at such times he would find assuagement in racing the pony
over the prairie with the mane whipping his face; racing as fast
and as carelessly as the discreet little pinto would run; racing
until his attention was attracted to a coyote slinking off, or to
some movement on the horizon.

Eventually his thoughts would flow into other channels, and
later, as he rode into the barn lot erect and magnificent as a
bemedalled general at the head of a dusty, victorious army, he
would have forgotten his earlier unhappiness. The black surrey
mares coming up to the gate to greet the lathered pinto were an
escort, and the chickens the enthusiastic crowd. Of course there
was a sort of "time out" as he opened the gate and spoke sharply
to the black mares as they attempted to run past him; time out
until the general could climb back into the saddle. The gate just
wasn't there, and the opening and closing of it had no part in
the dream. The "general" would ride stiffly to the center of the
lot, whirl about, much to the amazement and annoyance of the
pinto, and stand like a statue for a few seconds. If he happened
to remember, he looked around to see that there was no one
within hearing of his voice, then he would make a high sounding
speech to his trusting, brave, and victorious troops, then dismiss
them with a flourish of his hand.

His final address to his soldiers was stilted and praiseful—the
kind of thing which he believed would float down the corridors
of time. No matter what high-sounding words came to his
mind, he always ended with a note of defiance and profound
warning: "Let England remember this day—let her remember

that the men of America will defend their mother country to the last man, shouting, 'Don't give up the ship!' You have covered yourselves with glory, and I am proud of you, and your memory will be green to the end of time."

Oddly enough, he was forever leading charges against England. Sometimes he led gaily painted warriors; Osages and Sioux against the mythical tyranny of an England who was taking Indian land, but most of the time he led an army of picture book soldiers, who were of course inevitably victorious. This was the influence of the stories which his father read to him from American history books, which gave to the American every virtue and to the Englishman every vice.

He was a boy of great action though he even dreamed during the playing of games. Often he would start out on the long dusty road over Cedarvale Hill toward the Kansas line, foxtrotting. Going on under the hot sun of August until his heart pumped like drum beats in his thin chest, and his throat became dry and he was in pain. But on he would run until he halted, staggering, then fall into the hot shade of a blackjack, where he would lie on his back and gaze up at the restless leaves.

He was not a little Indian boy even then, but a coyote, that had just outrun his uncle's greyhounds by tricking them. He had heard the pounding of their feet behind him, and could visualize the slavers flying back from their mouths, and the concentrated excitement in their eyes. When his breathing became regular, he would pull off his shirt which was already almost off, remove his denim pants, and with only his moccasins from which the beads had been worn, he would lie back and let the leaf shadows dance over his bronze body. If by this time he had not become something else or had not gone off on another line of dreaming, which would take him far away from the indolent summer voices, he would half rise and move the muscles of his nose in simulation of a coyote testing the air currents in quest of some trace of his enemies. In this simulation he often did no better than "make a face" with his nose wrinkled, but it answered the purpose; he was a coyote.

Often, his role was suddenly changed by a grasshopper climbing slowly up a grass stem, with the purposelessness of all grasshoppers. Or a cicada breaking into monotonous song just above him. Perhaps the hot breeze would stir the leaves more violently and there would be a subdued roar, like a moan; like a protest from Nature who had fallen into a soothing somnolence. A nuthatch moving like a shadow up a dark tree bole, fussing weakly, might send him into another dream world.

Sometimes he would not get home until after dark, walking or riding over the prairie and into the belt of blackjack where the density of the darkness, or half darkness of the twilight always produced other stimuli. If he were riding he would wheel his pony and dash off through the trees; the stiff, tough arms of the blackjacks catching at his clothing if he did not manage to dodge them by lying flat on the back of the pony or clinging to its side as he raced; enemies in pursuit of a fleeing brave. He would come to the edge of the sandstone hills and burst from the fringe of trees to look down upon the scattered red lights of the Agency; dim red lights like the eyes of prowling animals. At such times he would become a scout creeping into the camp of the enemy; leading the pony cautiously over the second growth oaks and slipping and sliding over the clay. But as he approached the barn and heard the restrained, inquisitive whinny of the mares, or the soft questioning of the Jersey cow, he would suddenly return to the world of reality with the thought of what his father might have to say about "mistreatin' stock."

Soon he would be back in the world of fantasy as he moved the heavy bales of hay from the loft to the mangers; as he thrust his head into the hot flank of the cow, as she lazily swished her tail against his back.

Whether he was alone on the prairie or swimming with little Running Elk, Little Wild Cat, Sun-on-His-Wings, and other boys of the camp, these days seemed always to be a part of the life he was destined to live; the quieter part of a stream near its source, lazy, murmuring and dappled.

But of this earlier life from babyhood, he remembered only a few outstanding things; like impressions made in fresh cement which would remain distinct throughout the years. Behind these impressions would be the silence, the tranquillity of his home. Always he remembered the silence, and though he grew more loquacious as he learned to say meaningless things, he had a reverence for it as long as he lived; even when he had assumed that veneer which he believed to be civilization.

His first lasting impression was when as a fat, bronzed baby sitting on the floor he was suddenly flooded with emotion; emotion that suffused him and left an impression which he never forgot, but he knew the source of that emotion only after years had passed and he had learned the details from his mother.

There were no servants in the Agency and those desiring them had to go into Kansas and induce the daughter of some starving settler to come to them, after getting permission from the agent and duly registering the girl, who was thereafter known as a "har'd gurl."

It was thus that a flaming red skirt worn by one of these har'd gurls produced in the baby the first intense emotion of his life. He learned from his mother later that upon seeing the swishing skirt as the girl passed him, his baby hands clutched the air convulsively, his mouth flew open and he began to drool lavishly. Then his two chubby fists were placed in his mouth and his whole body quivered, and unconsciously, red became his favorite color; long before he learned of the religion of his people, red was sacred to him; long before He-Who-Walks-With-Stick told him that red was the color of the Sun, who was Grandfather, and of Fire, who was Father, and of the Dawn, sacred to Wah 'Kon-Tah.

Again, an isolated impression, the circumstances of which he half guessed and vaguely learned from his mother, disturbed his whole life. It must have been a Fourth of July celebration under the shade of the elms along the creek. The tinny music, the horns, the popping firecrackers and the sweating people he remembered. He remembered having held someone's hand as he walked along, probably the hand of a har'd gurl; when suddenly his hand was dropped, and he seemed to be left alone. Then a towering, disheveled figure came toward him; a mad woman with her iron gray hair flying, cursing as she strode toward him. Her face was distorted and ugly and her eyes were gleaming. As she reached him she swung her great arm and knocked him sprawling. He did not remember being picked up, but the har'd gurl in charge of him must have come immediately to his rescue. But burnt forever in his memory was the intense emotion of that moment; so intense and so searing that it affected his whole nervous system, and the picture of that wild white woman with iron gray hair and eyes flaming with hate and madness, had ever the vividness of a white scar. Always thereafter, when the veneer dropped from a woman and she became excited and angered, he was suffused with that which seemed to be a strange chemical running through his veins, and he felt sick and his knees grew weak, and dejection sat on his spirit like black wings hovering.

He must have been older when the still, hot, summer evenings impressed themselves on his memory; evenings filled with the scent of honeysuckle and wistaria, when the insects chorused from the grass roots, led and almost drowned by the katydids. Evenings when there were no lights in the house and his parents sat for two or more hours in the silence. From his mother's lap with his head on her gently heaving breast, he could hear the singing on Wednesday evenings come from the lone frame church in the valley. The little church to which the few white people of the Agency came from all directions along the dark, dusty road, swinging lanterns which they left by the front entrance.

For an hour or more he would lie thus, without day-dreaming, lulled by the bread and milk in his stomach and the sleepy, murmuring night. He would sometimes concentrate on the bass chirruping of the cricket, out of harmony with the rest of the chorus and much nearer, perhaps under the porch. If an Indian dog did not bark to bring him back to sharp consciousness, or the coyotes yap from Cedarvale Hill, a veil would come over his thoughts, smothering them in sensuous torpor, and he would be conscious only of a very slight squeak in his mother's corsets as she breathed. Even this squeak was soporific, and soon, under the weight of the hot stars and the heated air that often in midsummer was like the breath of a panting dog; under the monotonous fiddling, buzzing and rasping from the grass and the singing that shrilled across the quiet valley, he would pass into sleep.

One day during the hot summer when he had been running through the house on his bare feet over the pine flooring that had begun to splinter, he ran a large splinter of wood into his foot. He remembered the smell of turpentine and the calm silence and the deftness of his mother. He remembered sitting on her lap in the kitchen. Pride in his independence must have been hurt, and to assuage it his mother was telling him that he should soon have a warm piece of the cake which the har'd gurl was baking as she hummed "Barbara Ellen." To make her argument stronger his mother had told him that screwflies would get into his foot and it would be very bad if he got down on the floor again—and soon he would have a nice piece of cake and the screwflies would go away and he would be well again in a few days.

For a long time he thought that hot cake, just out of the oven, was an antidote for screwflies, and he had thought at the time that perhaps the screwflies were already at his foot and that his mother, with her usual calmness, was pretending that they were not; that his mother knew that the cake would drive them away, and that warm cake was the only thing with which to cure a wound which already had flies in it. What a screwfly was he didn't know, but immediately pictured it with large red eyes and a proboscis shaped like a screw, with which it bored its way into fresh wounds.

It was at this time in his life that an intense dislike came to him. There was a cousin of his father, a thin woman with graying hair, who through his father had secured a position as teacher in the government school. For several weeks she stayed at the house and Chal was fascinated by her; one of the few white women he had ever seen. But he eyed her with suspicion when she attempted to get him to sit on her knees. He much preferred standing in a corner and listening with fascination to her almost continuous talk. Her room on the north side of the house was filled with a sickening, sweet odor, but it was also filled with the strangest things he had ever seen. There were pale little men and women made of china, like his mother's cups, and bottles of delicate pink and green shades, and one in particular with a little red rubber ball attached to a red rubber tube, which in turn was attached to the top of the bottle. This he wanted very much, but certainly would never ask her for it; she would probably have talked too much in giving it to him, and that would have embarrassed him painfully.

The most fascinating thing in the room was a large hat which, as far as he knew, never left the hanger on the back of the door. It had a bright ribbon around the crown, and delight of delights, the ribbon was red. And above this ribbon, sitting eternally asleep on the crown, was a gorgeous golden bird with red hackles and long tail feathers, and he, after spending many minutes just standing and looking at this incredible bird, desired it with all his heart. That bird flitted into his day-dreams and was many times present in the fantastic experiences one has when he is asleep. And always when he came into the house from play, he would go and with a little thrill running through him, stand looking at the golden bird with a desire so intense that it made him unhappy.

But it was from his father's cousin that he learned about Jesus and His birth; travail and death. He thought about the story so much that the carpenter's little Son became his playmate in fantasy. He showed this fanciful Boy the place under the grape arbor where one could hide when he dreamed that he was a wolf or a wildcat. He told his fanciful playmate about a wild turkey that came into the barn lot with her brood and had taken corn from his hand but had run when his father came. But the fanciful playmate and the fanciful turkey never met, although he promised the former that he might see her some day if he could be very quiet and peek through the cracks in the loft.

One day cousin Ellen came into the house simulating breath-lessness and sat down with her feet extended and her legs apart. She fanned herself with her large hat, saying that it was just as hot as it could be and that's all there was to it.

"I bet I've walked miles," she said. "But I tell yu though, it's cooler in this room, all right." For goodness sake, she just didn't know how a person could stand it if it got any hotter than this— she thought she reely would die. Chal's mother had stood with the wise, benign expression of fatalism and had said simply, "Well—it is hot," as though she would pat cousin Ellen on the shoulder and say, "Never mind," then left the room quietly.

Cousin Ellen stopped fanning herself and began to unwrap a small package, looking at Chal with a tight-lipped smile, "Guess what I got for a good little boy—something very nice—look." She drew some picture cards from the paper and began looking at them. "Come here," she said. "Here are all the pictures about the Christ child and the crucifixion. Here's the Christ child in the manger—isn't He sweet, and here's Joseph and Mary coming to Bethlehem—see Mary on the mule." She believed it indelicate to say "ass." "Now take them and take good care of them." Chal took the pictures in his brown hands and backed off, then turned and started to go. "Wait a minute," she said, and lifted a finger. "What do you say?" He muttered a "Thank you" over his shoulder as he went out into the yard. He went to the grape arbor and crawled under.

Certainly they were beautiful pictures: there were Mary and Joseph and the mule, the three wise men and a great, shining, abnormal star, about which he was rather doubtful. He had once asked his father if he had ever seen that star, and his father had said that he didn't guess he ever had and he reckoned no one else had neither.

There was a picture of Jesus in white robes, floating among the clouds with a great red heart on his breast toward which he was pointing. This was his favorite; Jesus was certainly not bound to the earth like other things without wings. He looked long at the card which showed the crucifixion. There was the stripped, emaciated and pale body of Jesus with red wounds, against a background of clouds. At the foot of the cross were Magdalen and Mary the mother, the latter in a robe which he thought the most beautiful blue he had ever seen—a soft blue that made you happy. In skirts like women wear, only not so long, were the Roman soldiers with metal breastplates and long spears. One of them in particular he noticed; the one who stood with upraised spear and shiny helmet; the one with the mocking look on his face.

The picture held him. It fascinated him so that he couldn't look away from it, although he wanted very much to do so. That soldier in those short skirts, with his beautifully muscled legs and arms. The beautiful blue of that robe which Mary wore, bowed at the foot of the cross. For many minutes he looked at the picture, then a slow anger rose within him. As he looked steadily, the sardonic face of the Roman, the beautiful blue robe, and the pale body of Christ all became blurred and he felt a tear on his hand. He put the other pictures aside, then dug a hole in the soft earth under the vines and buried that picture of the crucifixion face down, picked up the others, and walked back to the house. But all day he thought of that Roman's face.

After dinner, before the long summer twilight, he went back to the arbor and unearthed the picture. He was surprised to see the same expression on the Roman's face, and his anger was so great that he said aloud the bad white man's words which he had heard a freighter use when his mules got stuck in the mud in front of their house. He walked into the kitchen and from a little cigar box in which he kept his treasures he took a stub pencil and began furiously to mark out all the soldiers in the picture. He thought of the group just beyond the cross as young soldiers, because in perspective they were of course smaller. The pencil marks didn't seem to have the desired effect and he rubbed harder, but still no use. In his anger and his defeat the tears came again.

His parents and cousin Ellen were on the front porch—he could hear cousin Ellen talking. He took the big butcher's knife out of the drawer and began cutting the soldiers out of the picture—cutting until there was very little left. Just then cousin Ellen came into the kitchen to get a drink of water and saw him. "Why—I never," she exploded. "Is that the way you do the nice pictures I give you!" She picked up the cards and made a clucking sound: "Where are the others? I bet you cut 'em up, too." He reached in his blouse and took out the others and gave them to her, but remained silent. "I'm goin' straight and tell your mother," she warned, and her skirts flipped around the high tops of her buttoned shoes as she left the room, saying under her breath, "Little savage!"

His heart was broken. A queer world. Hadn't she told him with much show of anger and with sadness about the crucifixion, and the "mean old soldiers" of Rome? Hadn't she said that when He had called for water they had given Him vinegar to drink? And he was sure that the big soldier with the mean face was the one that had stuck a spear into the side of poor Jesus and had made Him die.

He went to the barn lot fence and climbed upon the top rail. He wanted to stop sobbing but he couldn't. One of the mares attempted to muzzle his foot, but he kicked her and she looked at him with surprise in her great soft eyes. He didn't care. He didn't care if he died.

There was no stern voice from the house—he didn't expect one. Cousin Ellen would be talking and talking, and his father and mother would remain silent, even when she would say what she had said to his mother in the bedroom one day—something about "respect," and coming to a "bad end." Suddenly he knew that he hated her, and anger relieved his leaden heart just a little, and though his sobs were less frequent they came, much to his humiliation.

Then he became conscious of the sunset. It was red; his beloved red, with the tops of the blackjacks cutting into it. They seemed strange and far away and he felt intensely that he should like to go there; go where the familiar blackjacks were like the strange scenes in his picture book. Above, there was a large dark cloud with its edges colored red by the sun. His uncle, Fire Cloud, chief of the Panther clan of the Big Hills, had been named for a cloud like that, his father had told him. He liked Fire Cloud, who came to eat at the house during payment time and sat talking with his father in Osage. He liked the tall Fire Cloud with wrinkles around his eyes, who patted him on the head and said he would bring a fawn next time he came to the Agency.

At the thought of the fawn trailing him, he forgot for the present the heaviness of his heart and was happy with plans for the dreamy future.

from MEAN SPIRIT

Linda Hogan

W hen oil was discovered on Osage lands in the 1920s,
unscrupulous white men, moved by greed, embarked on a vicious
crusade to defraud the newly wealthy from their property and profits
by every means possible, including murder. In her novel, Mean
Spirit, Linda Hogan gives voice to this little-known chapter in
American history as she tells the story of the Grayclouds and the
Blankets, two families who find themselves suddenly caught in a
whirlwind of death and destruction.

   This passage recounts the Graycloud family's journey into terror
and uncertainty. And it tells of the terrible evil that would always
be remembered as the hour of childhood's end for Nola Blanket.

   Linda Hogan (Chickasaw) was born in Denver, Colorado, in
1947. Her book of poetry, Seeing through the Sun, won a Before
Columbus Foundation American Book Award. Both a poet and
novelist, Hogan currently teaches creative writing in the English
department at the University of Colorado.

WHAT HAD HAPPENED THAT MORNING WAS THIS: AFTER DAWN,
before Grace and Nola Blanket walked up to Belle's white bedstead, they passed the oil field. An oilman named John Hale
nodded at them. Hale was a lanky white man who wore a
gray Stetson hat. He'd been a rancher in Indian Territory for a
number of years before he invested in the oil business. He was
known as a friend to the Indians. He'd always been generous

and helpful to his darker compatriots, but Grace didn't care for him.

Once, feeling Hale's eyes on her, Grace glanced back, quickly, over her shoulder. Hale watched her, but she was a beautiful woman and it wasn't unusual for men to stop and stare, so she thought little about it.

On their way to Woody Pond that Sunday morning, the girls walked a little behind Grace. They whispered to each other the secret things girls share. Nola bent and picked a sunflower. She handed it to Rena. Rena pulled the yellow petals from the flower, looked at its black center, and said, "He loves me."

"Who?" asked Nola.

"How should I know? But it's grand to be loved, isn't it?" Rena smiled.

Grace walked faster. "Hurry! We'll be late for church!" The sun moved up in the sky. They had another mile to go. But the girls didn't keep up with her and they lagged farther behind and there were more distances between Grace and the girls than just that stretch of road; there was a gap in time between one Indian way of life and another where girls were sassy and wore satin ribbons in their hair.

They turned and walked up the red dirt path to the pond. Grace gave each of the girls a small knife. "Cut those thin ones." She pointed to the willows she wanted for her baskets, and in their chalk-white dresses, the girls bent and pared them off, then handed the cuttings to Grace. She put them, one at a time, neatly in the sling she carried looped up over the padded shoulder of her dress.

It was hot and the white sun had risen further up the sky when Grace heard a car. It wasn't unusual for whiskey peddlers to drive past Woody Pond on Sunday mornings, nor was it odd for drivers on their way home from the city to stop there and rest.

The car kicked up a cloud of dust. When it cleared, Grace saw the black Buick. She smiled at first, thinking it belonged to Moses Graycloud, and that he was picking them up because they were late for church, but then her hand froze in the air.

The men in the car turned their faces toward her, as if something was wrong.

They talked while they watched her. She thought she saw a pistol, then thought she must have imagined it. The driver seemed to be saying "No" to the other man, and they drove in closer, still arguing. Hale was driving. Grace didn't know the passenger. He was a broad man with dark hair. She looked at them, then moved behind a tree. They turned the car around and drove slowly away down the road, but Grace remained nervous and watchful. "Hurry, it's getting late," she urged the girls. She glanced back toward the car. The girls worked faster. The sun was hot and the bees sounded dizzy, and then the car returned, and again the men's eyes were on Grace.

When the car braked, Grace panicked and held still, like a deer in danger, rooted to where she stood. Even the air became still, and not a hair on Grace's head moved as she stood still and fixed, a hand poised on the branches in the sling at her side. In desperate hope, she looked around for other Indians who might have been at the pond searching for turtles, or a Sunday morning rabbit hunter. But they were alone, and the girls felt Grace's fear, like electricity, rising up their skin, up the backs of their necks.

Nola looked around. "What is it?" she started to ask, but without turning toward her, Grace hissed at her, hoarse with a fear so thick that Nola dropped down to the ground. She hardly breathed. Grace scanned the oaks and hilly land. "Don't move!" she told the girls. "Whatever you do, don't follow me."

The car went by and turned around another time, with the men still looking, and in a split second before it returned, Grace whispered dryly, "Stay down. Stay there." Then she dropped her sling on the ground and ran, crashing through the bushes, away from the pond, toward town.

The girls fought their impulse to run. Even their own breathing sounded dangerous to them.

Grace was an easy target, and she knew it, but she wanted to, had to, lure the car away from the girls. She hoped and prayed she could turn and cut through rocky land a car couldn't cover, but the Buick followed her down the road, and when she ran faster, the car speeded up. Then she saw the rocky land and with relief, she veered off and cut through a field, and even from where they hid, the girls could hear the car turn and follow, grinding across the summer grass. The driver struggled with the dark steering wheel over stones and clumps of earth. In spite of her fear, Nola rose up to look, stood just enough to see her mother kick the shoes off her feet and race into the forest. As Nola watched, Grace disappeared in the dark green shadows of leaves and branches.

Rena was crying. She pulled Nola close to earth, tugging at her skirt. "Stay down."

The car braked, and Nola peered over the brush to see a man jump out. The driver remained inside, though, and the motor idled. Then in day's full light, a gunshot broke through air. Like a stone cracking apart, something falling away from the world.

The girls lay flat in the shallow water, hidden in the silty pond between the reeds. Nola covered her eyes with one of her muddy hands, but it was too late, she had already seen her mother run barefoot across the field, followed by the black car, and in her mind's eye she saw her mother wounded.

The car doors slammed shut. The girls heard the car begin to grind and jam once more across the field. They pressed themselves deeper into the marshy pond, still and afraid. Only their heads were out of the muddy red water. They barely breathed. Nola dropped her knife and searched the silt frantically, with shaking fingers, until she found it and held it tight and ready in her fist. Then the wind began to blow, hot and restless, drowning out the sound of the car. The men had propped Grace's body between them as if she were just a girlfriend out for a Sunday drive. They drove up to the pond where water willows were quaking in the wind, and when they lifted the woman out of the car, both of her dark braids came loose and fell toward earth. The wind blew harder. The men placed Grace's body behind a clump of wind-whipped black bushes, then they straightened their backs, turned around, and searched for Nola.

Nola could barely hear them speak over the sound of wind.

"I thought you said the girl was with her."

"She was."

Nola held her breath. She heard nothing else, for a sudden gust of wind whistled across the water and rattled the cattails. The girls were afraid to look. They heard the men search among the rushes, close to where they remained paralyzed with fright, but by then, the girls could not tell the difference between wind and the men's hands pilfering through the reeds.

The turn wind, a current from the south, blew grit up from the ground. The hillsides stirred with dust devils. Branches broke off the older trees.

As the hot wind quickened, tree branches began to creak. The storm drowned out the sound of the car and when the men drove away, the girls did not hear them. A mallard moved across the pond and took cover, hiding as the girls hid, in the blowing reeds.

A short while later, the car returned. Its motor sounded like the wind. The girls were sure the men were searching for children in Sunday dresses. One man got out and walked through the wind-swept grass toward Grace Blanket's body. From between the reeds, Nola could almost see his face. The wind blew his jacket open and away from his shirt. Behind him the trees bent. He placed a pistol in the dead woman's hand. Nola caught another glimpse of him. She couldn't tell who he was. She had never seen him before. He opened a bottle of whiskey and poured it on Grace Blanket's body, and the wind blew the smell of whiskey across the pond. The girls held their breaths while the man buttoned his dark jacket and laid down the empty bottle. He got back in the car and it rattled off toward town, erased by a storm cloud of dust.

The girls were drowning in the heat and wind of the storm. They didn't hear the sound of Michael Horse's gilt-colored car, nor did they hear Belle call out their names. They heard only the howling wind, and when it finally died down, they heard the horrible flies already at work on the body of Grace and then the afternoon sun turned red in the west sky, and then the long day was passing and the frogs began their night songs, and then it was night and the stars showed up on the surface of the dark pond. Nola crawled out of the water and up the bank of the pond on her elbows and knees. She half crawled toward her mother's body. Rena followed, shivering even in the heat. Her thin-skinned hands and feet were cracked open from the water. And in the midst of everything, the moon was shining on the water. Grace was surrounded by black leaves in the moonlight, and the whiskey smell was still thick and sickening. Grace was twisted and grotesque and her head turned to the side as if she'd said "No" to death. In her hand was the gun. The girl stood there for what seemed like a long time. She laid her head against her mother, crying, "Mama," and wept with her face buried in the whiskey-drenched clothing.

"Come on," Rena pulled Nola back into the world of the living.

Nola started to take the pistol. "Leave it," Rena told her, so Nola reached down and unclasped the strand of pearls from her mother's neck. With Rena's arm around her, she walked away, then looked back, hoping against all hope that her mother would move, that her voice would call out the way it had always done, "Come here, little one," but there were only the sounds of frogs and insects.

Rena took Nola's hand. They walked toward the Grayclouds' house, hiding themselves behind bushes or trees. The muddy weight of their dresses dragged heavily against their legs.

That night, the lights of fireflies and the songs of locusts were peaceful, as if nothing on earth had changed. How strange that life was as it had been on other summer nights, with a moon rising behind the crisscross lines of oil derricks and the white stars blinking in a clear black sky.

At the dark turnoff to the Graycloud's house, sweet white flowers bloomed on the lilac bush. The mailbox, with its flag up, was half hidden by the leafy branches. The house, too, looked as it always did, with an uneven porch and square windows of light. The chickens had gone to roost for the night, and they were softly clucking, and out in the distance, the white-faced cattle were still grazing, looking disembodied.

When they passed through the gate and neared the front door, the girls saw something white at the azalea bush. They were startled. They stopped and stared, thinking at first it was a ghost. But then the ghost in its white apron stepped toward them and said, "Where's your mother, child?" and the ghost became solid and became Belle Graycloud. Between sobs that night, Rena tried to tell the story of what had happened, and before the loss of Grace turned to grief in the old woman,

Belle raised her face to the starry sky and thanked the Great Something that the girls were alive.

Neither Belle nor Lettie Graycloud could sleep that night. They were still awake when Moses returned home from the livestock auction in Walnut Springs. He was wearing a new straw hat. Belle heard him whistling as he led a new palomino pony—they were the fashion that year—through the dark lot and into the barn.

She opened the door and called his name.

"I'm coming," he said from the darkness, then she saw him in the light from the house. He walked through the door and set his hat on the table. "What is it?"

She told him about Grace.

Moses was stunned with the news. He sat down heavily in a chair, and slumped over the table. He covered his face with his hands and was silent a long while, then he asked, "Did they see who did it?"

Belle shook her head. "All they know is that they drove a car like ours." She sat beside him. Her eyes were swollen.

He said, "Belle, I'm so sorry." He had doubted her. Then he said, "Black Buicks are everywhere." He took a deep breath, stood up, and put the new hat back on his head.

Belle was alarmed. "What are you doing?"

He answered slowly. "I'd better go talk to the sheriff."

She put up her hand to stop him. "I don't think you should."

He was puzzled. "Why not?"

She hesitated. She was weary and hoped she wasn't making a mistake. "Because, Moses, the killers didn't see the girls. I'm afraid that if they knew there were witnesses, they might come looking for them."

He turned it over in his mind, then took his hat off and, without an argument, he sat back down and rubbed the grit off his face.

Belle put her hand over his. She fingered one of the scars that crossed his knuckles. They sat that way, in silence for a while, Moses deep in thought, Belle too shaken to say more.

Then Moses pulled at one of his dark braids and said, "It was probably a lover's fight."

Belle studied his face. Moses was trying to push away his fear. It made her twice as cautious, as if to make up for him. "And if it wasn't?" she said, but before he could answer, she was on her feet. She took a pistol from a cabinet. It was a small handgun, one she used to frighten coyotes away from her nervous chickens. She loaded it. Moses said nothing.

Upstairs, the girls slept in Lettie's bed. It was hot. In the dim light of the lamp, they looked vulnerable in the large bed. Lettie watched over them. She also held a pistol. She straightened the sheet tenderly over them and smoothed the hair back from their damp faces. She wanted to hold them, to offer solace, but their breathing was deep and the waking world was dangerous, so she left them to the gift of sleep.

After a while, Belle relieved her of her watch, and the old woman set up her own silent vigil over the girls. But Lettie was overwhelmed with a feeling of loneliness, and around two in the morning, she returned to the bedside of the girls. She looked haggard. She wore a dark, worn robe. "Go on now, Mama," she said. "You need rest."

But Belle made no attempt to leave the room. "I can't sleep anyway," she said. Lettie was insistent, though, until Belle pulled herself up from the chair and went down the hall to her own room. She was restless, gripped in a hot fear, afraid for Rena and Nola.

She sat at the mirror. Out of habit, she brushed her long silver hair while she thought. In the dark, sparks flew and snapped through the air around her. She was sure something was afoot. She put the brush down.

Moses seemed to sleep. Through hell and high water, Belle thought, he always slept, and she was angry at him, but then she noticed that his breathing was uneven. He turned over.

Belle rocked herself in the rocker and gazed out the window. The floor creaked. She was watchful as she looked into the dark. She wanted to read the deep night and decipher the story of what had happened to Grace Blanket. She believed it was a plot since Grace's land was worth so much in oil. All along the smell of the blue-black oil that seeped out of the earth had smelled like death to her.

Belle climbed into bed beside Moses and tried to sleep. The old wood house settled and creaked. It was too hot. The sheets felt stiff against her skin. She climbed out of bed once more, and crept down the staircase. The furniture downstairs was dark and heavy, with ominous silence living in the shadows. Belle checked the latches on the doors.

Moses pulled on his pants and followed her downstairs. In the kitchen, he poured water into a glass and carried it over to Belle. "I'll stay up," he said. "You go rest."

She smiled at him. His wide chest looked soft beneath his undershirt. She laid her head against his chest briefly, long enough to hear his heart, and then she went back up the stairs.

Moses sat at the kitchen table in the darkness. He was waiting for his daughter, Louise, and her white husband, Floyd, to return home. By now, he thought, they were drunk and driving in from the city. The thought made him angry. He put his elbows on the oilcloth.

Once, before dawn, when the house made a noise, Belle climbed out of bed and in her big dressing gown, she looked out the window. In the gray light, she could have sworn a man was standing at the edge of the berry grove. "Moses!" she called down to him, but by the time Moses reached the window, the man was gone. She went down the stairs and peered out the window. He followed. She tried to convince him. "Someone was there. I saw him."

In the bedroom, Lettie Graycloud sat beside the sleeping girls. She held the pistol on her lap. She was uncomfortable with the weapon, but the murder, even if it had been a crime of passion like her father thought, had struck too close to home. A cool breeze from the window blew in across her face and hair.

In the first red light of morning, both girls breathed softly. Exhaustion had overcome even Nola's grief. But her face, almost overnight, had begun to look somehow hollow and older. Her skin was tight across her bones. Gazing at her, Lettie felt the first pain of her own loss, the first ache of missing her friend, Grace Blanket.

Lettie studied Nola's dark skin, the widow's peak, the distant quality that had once prompted Lettie to remark to Grace that if anyone's prayers were going to be heard in this life, she knew Grace's would.

Lettie's mind went back to the time when Grace had first traveled down from the bluffs above Watona and moved into the Graycloud house. Grace and Lettie became fast friends. They'd lived together in this same room, slept in this bed as their bones grew longer. They'd whispered together at night, and now here was this girl, the same bone, blood, and skin as Grace. Lettie felt overwhelmed with love for the girl, whose dark, slender hand hung peacefully over the side of the bed.

But then, as the room lightened more, what Lettie saw frightened her. At first, she thought Nola was awake and staring at her, like a person half dead, gazing into her own watching eyes. But Nola's eyes stared through Lettie and beyond, looking through the ceiling and roof to some far distant point in the sky. While some part of her was awake, was looking perhaps at the other world, the one where her mother had gone, the rest of her slept. She breathed deeply and evenly, and she did not so much as blink her open eyes.

Lettie looked away. She felt clammy. She went to the window. Another day of heat was blowing in. Already the ground was dry, and dust filtered into the room. Lettie leaned over, to feel the thin breeze of air. That was when she saw him. The man stood in front of the house. Without changing her position, Lettie raised the pistol to the window and aimed, but even as she did, she noticed that his legs looked rooted to earth, and he stood like one of the Hill Indians, as if he'd never lived among white people or their dry goods, or the cursed blessing of oil. His face was smooth and calm. Instantly, Lettie knew he was from the same band as Grace Blanket. She lowered the gun back down to her side and buried it in a fold of her robe as if she were afraid it would fire against her will. She knew, somehow, that he was there for Nola, to help her.

The man raised his eyes. Lettie wanted to step back, out of the light, but instead she remained in full view of the watcher, and for a brief moment their eyes met. He was one of the sacred runners from the hills. Lettie felt calm in his gaze, but as she looked out the window he seemed to vanish from her view.

Behind her, Rena began to stir. She opened her golden eyes and looked at her aunt's red and blue scarves that hung like flames on the wall above her. At first Rena thought they were burning, they were on fire, and she gasped awake, full of fear, and fought her way out of the tangle of hot sheets.

Outside, the rooster crowed and the little dog, Pippin, ran toward the road, barking at Louise and Floyd. The couple walked past the watcher without seeing him. Lettie heard their footsteps on the gravel, then the opening door and voices downstairs, and then the sound of high heels clapping up the stairs.

The door sprang open. Louise rushed into the bedroom. Rena smelled the whiskey on her mother's breath. She pulled away, remembering Grace's body and the odor of whiskey that had drifted across the pond, but Louise held tight to the girl, asking over and over, "What happened?" and saying "I can't believe it. I just can't believe it. My God." Her shrill voice woke Nola. The girl turned over in the bed, then sat up like a ghost. She was damp with the heat and with shock. Her eyes were black and haunted-looking, with dark circles beneath them. Looking at the ash-pale girl, Lettie felt a chill wash over her skin. Even Louise went silent. The air seemed to go out of the room.

After Louise took Rena back downstairs, Lettie could think of nothing to do, so she dressed Nola in one of her own dresses. "Raise your arms," she told her.

Nola did as she was told, and lifted both arms above her head. Lettie pulled the blue, too-large dress down over Nola's head. "Turn around now, honey," she said. Nola flatly obeyed. She stood vacantly as Lettie pinned the back of the dress to fit her limp and silent body.

Then, out of daily habit, while Nola stood in the poor-fitting woman's dress, Lettie took a dark blue hat off one of the hooks on the wall and settled it on top of her own thick black hair. She always wore a hat, it was her custom. She pushed the hat pin through her hair, and while she looked in the mirror she saw Nola's expression change. A look of surprise passed over Nola's face as she caught sight of the watcher outside. She ran over to the window and looked out, her face pitiful and broken. The watcher looked up. Lettie felt the whole room fill with sorrow, but she took the girl's cold hand and led her from the curtained square of light, and said to Nola, "Stay away from the windows. It's not safe." But something tugged at the girl and she pulled out from Lettie's grasp and went into the hall. Lettie followed behind her in through the door of Belle's room. Nola pulled aside the curtain and looked out. Down on the ground, near the berry grove, was another one of the watchers.

There were four altogether. They had come in the night.

from *THE NAMES: A MEMOIR*
N. Scott Momaday

*I*n The Names, *N. Scott Momaday combines family history, mythology, and personal reminiscences to weave a poetic tapestry spanning several generations.* The Names *chronicles Momaday's personal quest for identity, a search that culminates near a hollow log in the legendary emergence place of the Kiowa people.*

In this part of his autobiography, Momaday uses the power of his imagination to envision his grandfather, Mammedaty. He conjures his ancestor with words of remembrance and regeneration from inside a drawing. For Momaday, boyhood was a time in which to begin to form an idea of himself as a Kiowa.

Writer, poet, and artist, N. Scott Momaday (Kiowa) was born in Oklahoma in 1934. His novel House Made of Dawn *won the Pulitzer Prize for fiction in 1969. He has published a number of books including* The Way to Rainy Mountain, *a compilation of myth and personal memory. His most recent novel is* The Ancient Child. *Momaday holds a Ph.D. in English literature from Stanford University. He currently teaches at the University of Arizona in Tucson.*

CHILDREN TRUST IN LANGUAGE. THEY ARE OPEN TO THE POWER and beauty of language, and here they differ from their elders, most of whom have come to imagine that they have found words out, and so much of magic is lost upon them. Creation says to the child: Believe in this tree, for it has a name.

★ ★ ★

If you say to a child, "The day is almost gone," he will take you at your word and will find much wonder in it. But if you say this to a man whom the world has disappointed, he will be bound to doubt it. *Almost* will have no precision for him, and he will mistake your meaning. I can remember that someone held out his hand to me, and in it was a bird, its body broken. *It is almost dead.* I was overcome with the mystery of it, that the dying bird should exist entirely in its dying. J. V. Cunningham has a poem, "On the Calculus":

> *From almost nought to almost all I flee,*
> *And almost* has almost confounded
> > me;
> Zero my limit, and infinity.

I can almost see into the summer of a year in my childhood. I am again in my grandmother's house, where I have come to stay for a month or six weeks—or for a time that bears no common shape in my mind, neither linear nor round, but it is a deep dimension, and I am lonely in it. Earlier in the day—or in the day before, or in another day—my mother and father have driven off. Somewhere on a road, in Texas, perhaps, they are moving away from me, or they are settled in a room away, away, thinking of me or not, my father scratching his head, my mother smoking a cigarette and holding a little dog in her lap. There is a silence between them and between them and me. I am thoughtful. I see into the green, transparent base of a kerosene lamp; there is a still circle within it, the surface of a deeper transparency. Do I bring my hands to my face? Do I turn or nod my head? Something of me has just now moved upon the metal throat of the lamp, some distortion of myself, nonetheless recognizable, and I am distracted. I look for my image then in the globe, rising a little in my chair, but I see nothing but my ghost, another transparency, glass upon glass, the wall beyond, another distortion. I take up a pencil and set the point against a sheet of paper and define the head of a boy, bowed slightly, facing right. I fill in quickly only a few details, the line of the eye, the curve of the mouth, the ear, the hair—all in a few simple strokes. Yet there is life and expression in the face, a conjugation that I could not have imagined in these markings. The boy looks down at something that I cannot see, something that lies apart from the picture plane. It might be an animal, or a leaf, or the drawing of a boy. He is thoughtful and well-disposed. It seems to me that he will smile in a moment, but there is no laughter in him. He is contained in his expression— and fixed, as if the foundation upon which his flesh and bones are set cannot be shaken. I like him certainly, but I don't know who or where or what he is, except that he is the inscrutable reflection of my own vague certainty. And then I write, in my child's hand, beneath the drawing, "This is someone. Maybe this is Mammedaty. This is Mammedaty when he was a boy." And I wonder at the words. *What are they?* They stand, they lean and run upon the page of a manuscript—I have made a manuscript, rude and illustrious. The page bears the likeness of a boy—so simply crude the likeness to some pallid shadow on my blood—and his name consists in the letters there, the words, the other likeness, the little, jumbled drawings of a ritual, the nominal ceremony in which all homage is returned, the legend of the boy's having been, of his going on. I have said it, I have set it down. I trace the words; I touch myself to the words, and they stand for me. My mind lives among them, moving ever, ever going on. I lay the page aside, I imagine. I pass through the rooms of the house, slowly, pausing at familiar objects: a quiver of arrows on the wall, old photographs in oval frames, beaded emblems, a Bible, an iron bedstead, a calendar for the year 1942. Mammedaty lies ten years in the ground at Rainy Mountain Cemetery. What is there, *just there*, in the earth, in the bronze casket, under Keahdinekeah's shawl? I go out into the yard; the shadows are long to the east, and the sunlight has deepened and the red earth is darkened now to umber and the grasses are burnished. Across the road, where the plain is long and undulant and bears the soft sheen of rose gentian and rose mallow, there are figures like fossils in the prisms of the air. I see a boy standing still in the distance, only his head and shoulders visible above the long, luminous grass, and from the place where he stands there comes the clear call of a meadowlark. It is so clear, so definite in the great plain! I believe that it circles out and out, that it touches like ancient light upon the thistles at Saddle Mountain, upon the broken floor of Boke's store, upon the thin shadows that follow on the current of the Washita. And round on the eastern shelves I see the crooked ravines which succeed to the sky, a whirlwind tracing a red, slanting line across the middle distance, and there in the roiling dust a knoll, a gourd dance and give-away, and Mammedaty moves among the people, answers to his name; low thunder rolls upon the drum. A boy leads a horse into the circle, the horse whipping its haunches around, rattling its blue hooves on the hard earth, rolling its eyes and blowing. There are eagle feathers fixed with ribbons in the braided mane, a bright red blanket on the back of the black, beautiful hunting horse. The boy's arms are taut with the living weight, the wild will and resistance of the horse, swinging the horse round in a tight circle, to the center of the circle where Mammedaty stands waiting to take the reins and walk, with dignity, with the whole life of the hunting horse, away. It is good and honorable to be made such a gift—the gift of this horse, this hunting horse—and honorable to be the boy, the intermediary in whose hands the gift is passed. My fingers are crisped, my fingertips bear hard upon the life of this black horse. *Oh my grandfather, take hold of this horse. It is good that you should be given this horse to hold in your hands, that you should lead it away from this holy circle, that such a thing should happen in your name.* And the southern moon descends; light like phosphorus appears in the earth, blue and bone, clusters of blue-black bunch grass, pocks in pewter. Flames gutter momently in the arbor and settle to the saffron lamps; fireflies flicker on the lawn; frogs begin to tell of the night; and crickets tell of the night, but there is neither beginning nor end in their telling. The old people arrive, the thin-limbed, deep-eyed men in their hats and braids, the round-faced women in their wide half sleeves and fringed shawls, apron-bound, carrying pots and pans and baskets of food—fried bread, boiled cracked corn, melons, pies and cakes—and for hours my grandmother has been cooking meat, boiled beef, fried chicken, chicken-fried beefsteaks, white and brown gravies. *Cohn' Tsotohah, Tsoai-talee, come here; I want to tell you something.* I sit at an old man's knee. I don't know who he is, and I am shy and uncomfortable at first; but there is delight in his eyes, and I see that he loves me. There are many people in the arbor; everyone listens. *Cohn', do you see the moon?* The full, white moon has receded into the southeast; it is a speckled moon; through the arbor screen it shimmers in the far reaches of the night. *Well, do you see?—there is a man in the moon. This is how it happened: Saynday was hungry. Oh, everyone was hungry then; the buffalo were keeping away, you know. Then Saynday's wife said to him, "Saynday, tomorrow the men are going on a hunt. You must go with them and bring back buffalo meat." "Well, yes," said Saynday. And the next day he went out on the hunt. Everyone found buffalo, except Saynday. Saynday could find no buffalo, and so he brought some tomatoes home to his wife. She was angry, but she said to him, "Saynday, tomorrow the men are going hunting again. Now I tell you that you must go with them, and you must bring back buffalo meat." "Well, yes," said Saynday. And again he went on the hunt. Everyone found buffalo, except Saynday. He could find no buffalo, and so he brought tomatoes home to his wife again. She was very angry, but she said to him, "Saynday, tomorrow the men are going hunting again. You must go with them, and you must bring back buffalo meat." "Well, yes," said Saynday. And Saynday went out on the hunt for the third time. And it was just the same: everyone found Buffalo, except Saynday. Saynday could find no buffalo, and so he brought tomatoes home to his wife again. She was so angry that she began to beat him with a broom. Saynday ran, but she ran after him, beating him with the broom. He ran faster and faster, until he got away, and then he wanted to hide. He hid in the moon. There he is now in the moon, and he will not come down because he is afraid of his wife.* My people laugh with me; I am created in the old man's story, in his delight. There is a black bank and lightning in the north, the moon higher and holding off, the Big Dipper on a nail at the center of the sky. I lie down on the wide bench at my grandmother's back. The prayer meeting goes on, the singing of Christian hymns in Kiowa, now and then a gourd dance song.

There would be old men and old women in my life.

I invented history. In April's thin white light, in the white landscape of the Staked Plains, I looked for tracks among the tufts of coarse, brittle grass, amid the stones, beside the tangle of dusty hedges. When I look back upon those days—days of infinite promise and steady adventure and the certain sanctity of childhood—I see how much was there in the balance. The past and the future were simply the large contingencies of a given moment; they bore upon the present and gave it shape. One does not pass through time, but time enters upon him, in his place. As a child, I knew this surely, as a matter of fact; I am not wise to doubt it now. Notions of the past and future are essentially notions of the present. In the same way an idea of one's ancestry and posterity is really an idea of the self. About this time I was formulating an idea of myself.

Miss Johnson said Mayre not Mary why doesn't she talk the way she's supposed to and that Tommy the dirty rat I'll knock his block off and not care if he tells he tells everything and the time Billy Don and I got spanked because we were throwing snowballs and broke a window the one on the side not the driver's side and the lady was smiling until that happened driving slowly and smiling and the glass went crack it was only cracked and then she got mad not really mad but oh oh now we have to do something about that this and that you'll never know just how much I love you I didn't want to go to Mrs. Powell's because she has all those nice things in her house and you have to sit still and she watches you and one time she wouldn't even let me eat an orange in her car it smells she said and your fingers get sticky she said and I don't like her crummy cactus garden either well I like it but there are a lot of better cactuses over by Billy Don's dad's place I wonder who that girl was the soldier's girl on the library lawn and they were having their picture taken and the soldier was trying to touch her down there and she was giggling and I heard the twins laughing about it and I wanted to laugh too but the girl was pretty and I thought she should not have let him do that she's really good and decent probably maybe she was ashamed and didn't know what to do but laugh that's the way I am sometimes oh my gosh mom and dad heard me yesterday and I was singing You're in the army now you're not behind the plow you'll never get rich you son of a bitch and they heard me and weren't mad but said not to sing that even if all the other kids were singing it I think dad wasn't sure and said he said son of a bee didn't he and mom said yes he did and I did but I didn't know it I really didn't know it and one time in the arbor Lucius told me I said some bad words and Aunt Clara heard me and I didn't know I had said them how could I just forget like that Lucius and Marland and Justin Lee and Ponzi we used to play around the arbor and the outhouse and tell jokes and smoke why did Burt tell me he was smoking oak leaves and that was all right well he's a lot older but I bet that wasn't oak leaves maybe it was anyway John was in the shower and I was playing at the sink in the kitchen and I wasn't trying to make the water hot but he thought I was well what's today Wednesday or Thursday no Saturday Saturday at the show when the crook came out on the porch and he started to smoke a cigarette and everyone thought Bob had got killed I didn't though the crook fell then and we all yelled like crazy next time old Bob will get in trouble again and Hopalong Cassidy is coming to the Reel Fred Jackson is a sergeant is he yes but he got busted someone said for fighting for hitting his commanding officer he's pretty okay to me why does he like those records Glenn Miller and Tommy Dorsey and Harry James Sleepy lagoon mom and dad too dad likes that music I think maybe at the Avalon When the lights go on again all over the world oh Billy Don and Burleigh those dumb guys this morning no yesterday no this morning I had to keep them quiet because mom was sleeping she loves to sleep late I don't like it though I like to get up but I had breakfast in bed I made it eggs and toast and jam and I took it to my bed and ate it in bed well I don't do it all the time I pledge allegiance to the flag indivisible My country 'tis of thee sweet land of liberty oh gosh Guadalcanal it isn't so bad to get shot I guess if it's a flesh wound get the medic but they strafe the beach John says the Zeros are more maneuverable but a lot slower than the P-39s and the Mustangs what do they call the P-38s they're so awful fast I'm in a Bell P-39 okay no a Flying Tiger okay sons of the rising sun this is for my kid brother ha gotcha oh oh there's a Zero on my tail eeeeeoooooooooooow lost him in the clouds just dropped down and let him go over me and climbed up oh he can't believe it he's in my sights cross hairs there Tojo that's for the Sullivans well Chuck you can paint four more Zeros on old Sally here no I'm okay thanks honorable colonel we must stop Momaday he comes from nowhere from the sun I tell you he's not human they say he's an Indian that he wears an eagle feather has the eyes the heart of an eagle he must be stopped there son of the rising sun that's for Major Anderson eeeeeeeeeoooooooooow what oh another medal oh it was nothing sir it was for my kid brother sir he got his over Burma it was for the Sullivan boys and Major Anderson what lead the eagle squadron yessir thank you sir it's a great honor

I don't want to see Louise again not since I made that lemonade and she was the only one who bought some shoot for a nickel it was and she came across the street and said it was good and cold and thanked me I hate Henry Aldridge too what was that really neat program The Monkey's Paw The Most Dangerous Game The Mollé Mystery Theatre.

I asked Billy Don if his mom and dad told him stories when he went to bed and he laughed once upon a time there were three pigs Rootie and Tootie and Pootie and Mickey Mouse and Minnie Mouse Scotty had a brand-new red car and it was snowing outside Billy Don began to laugh he got so tickled and we were all surprised because gosh it was right there in school what is it Billy Don the teacher said and he said oh nothing you wouldn't understand I was just thinking and we all laughed like heck it was so funny Ida was sent out of the room and I felt funny about that that she was sent outside and knew that we were all talking about her gee and Miss Marshall said you must not be cruel some people do not have as much as you do and Ida can't help it her clothes are old and dirty I found her crying in the bathroom and you must not be cruel you must make her feel that you are all her friends and then we all went out of our way to be friendly even Charles you're an Indian Charles said and I said yes Indians are no good he said and I said you're a liar he can't stand to be called that gosh anything but that and he's so tough so I took it back

Grandma I miss you I feel sorry for you when I come to see you and see you and go away I know you're lonely I like to see you I love to see you in the arbor cooking and talking to us you goot boy you say Scotty you goot boy and you used to carry me on your back in your shawl and hold me in your lap and I came to sleep with you and you're so soft and warm and I like the smell of you your hair is so thick and heavy it is so black except for the gray here and there you buy me candy corn and candy orange slices jellybeans animal crackers I like to watch you sew and make beadwork let's go to town grandma to the store you have so much money always Uncle Jimmy has money sometimes he buys me something down by Lonewolf his land everyone says he's going to give me some land someday oh yes Miss Marshall my dad's people the Kiowas they have a lot of land in Oklahoma my uncle is going to give me some land quite a lot of it someday no ma'am he's not a farmer but he owns farmland yes ma'am it's very strange well yes ma'am I'm a Kiowa yes ma'am I'm sure it's not Keeowa no ma'am I can't say the Lord's Prayer in Kiowa I can't say much of anything really my dad can yes ma'am I *am* proud to be so American I know it ma'am Lay that pistol down babe

Oh I feel so dumb I can't answer all those questions I don't know how to be a Kiowa Indian my grandmother lives in a house it's like your house Miss Marshall or Billy Don's house only it doesn't have lights and light switches and the toilet is outside and you have to carry wood in from the woodpile and water from the well but that isn't what makes it Indian its my grandma the way she is the way she looks her hair in braids the clothes somehow yes the way she talks she doesn't speak English so well Scotty you goot boy she says wait I know why it's an Indian house because there are pictures of Indians on the walls photographs of people with long braids and buckskin clothes dresses and shirts and moccasins and necklaces and beadwork yes that's it and there is Indian stuff all around blankets and shawls bows and arrows everyone there acts like an Indian everyone even me and my dad when we're there we eat meat and everyone talks Kiowa and the old people wear Indian clothes well those dresses dark blue and braids and hats and there is laughing Indians laugh a lot and they sing oh yes they love to sing sometimes when an old man comes to visit he sits in the living room and pretty soon he just begins to sing loud with his eyes closed but really loud and his head nodding and in the arbor there are sometimes pretty often a lot of people and lots to eat and everyone sings and sometimes there are drums too and it goes on through the night *that's* Indian my dad sets out poles on the river and we eat catfish *that's* Indian and grandma goes to

Rainy Mountain Baptist Church *that's* Indian and my granddad Mammedaty is buried at Rainy Mountain and some of the stones there have peyote pictures on them and you can hear bobwhites there and see terrapins and scissortails and that's Indian too

I gave mom Evening in Paris perfume and a little handkerchief and she was thrilled said so Mother's Day but when I was just a kid last year two years ago I can't remember I went on an Easter egg hunt at school no the park and I got some Easter eggs but I ate them and brought home nothing and was ashamed forever

I'll have a sweetheart in the war and she will look like Faye Emerson when I was at grandma's I had a picture of Faye Emerson it was in a magazine I think and she was my sweetheart and I talked to her all the time I love you darling don't worry oh I know it's tough war is heck but though there's one motor gone we will still carry on Faye yes Faye Emerson Montclair New Jersey if anything happens to me Billy Don see that she gets this letter we were going to be married and live in a little bungalow out west hear that Billy Don that's it time to go thumbs up buddy old pal take care of things take care of that leg pal I'll miss you Oh don't sit under the apple tree with anyone else but me anyone else but me anyone else but me I'm gonna dance with the dolly with the hole in her stocking while her knees keep a knocking while her toes keep a rocking hi'ya Hitler here's one for Major Jordan okay Billy Don you take the ball see and lateral to me and then run out straight sure I can throw it that far can you run that far they won't know what hit them there's a game tonight isn't there oh I love the games the air is cold and full of music and shouting the field is so green under the lights and the stripes are so white so much excitement I heard one of the high-schoolers say the Cavemen were going to win that if they couldn't win on the field they were sure as heck going to beat them off the field everything depends on the game this game the Eagles and the Cavemen I got as close as I could I could see how hard they were playing playing so hard they were crying some of them their arms and legs bandaged and blood showing through cussing at each other I was kind of scared and the quarterback called the signals and the ball was in the air and the helmets and pads cracked together oh it was grand I love football nothing could be better than to be a great football player a back a quarterback or a fullback I told the Canons that I was a tailback but I don't know what that is

Maybe I'll go to Kirby's house but I don't like him well he's all right but he's funny his folks are funny like that time I knocked on the door and no one answered and in the yard I picked up a piece of wood black wood a little block nailed to a big block and I was looking at it it looked like a German subma-rine and Kirby yelled out the window and everyone was there inside and told me to put it down it was his or what was I doing with it anyway but I wasn't going to take it steal it but it felt just like I was stealing it the way they spied on me I didn't know what to do but they were watching me all the time hiding there in the house why don't they answer the door Kirby's dad was in the army a long time ago the First World War and he was gassed Kirby said and there was a gas mask in the closet there I had never seen one a real one before and Kirby and I when we were little used to play war and our rations were always mustard sandwiches I don't know why but they were always mustard sandwiches the bread got dry and the mustard too and darker funny color like sometimes the sand like the canyons at Chinle yeah it's Begay sir he comes from Chinle Arizona I knew him yessir eeeeeeeoooooow puh uh uh uh uh uh uh there you son of the rising sun that's for Corporal Begay the nurse sir oh her name is Faye yessir her father is Doctor Emerson of Montclair New Jersey very rich oh that time at Chinle Jimmy King mom said Jimmy King dressed up like Santa Claus and woke me up I was so excited scared I guess I didn't know what to do I couldn't say anything I just sat up in bed and my eyes were big mom said Jimmy was a boxer mom said a terrific boxer dad said Golden Gloves and he could beat guys twice his size or was it Shiprock Jimmy King came from Shiprock there was Sylvia oh gosh I was little then just a kid but I remember Sylvia's birthday party and I took a crummy present a coloring book maybe was it raining it was dark then Faye came over and we did that thing on the bed standing up she asked me if I knew how sure I said Ponzi and Justin Lee told me mom came in and said what are you doing and Faye told her said that word and mom told me not to do it again she told me later when everyone had gone but dad was there and he said what what did he do and never mind mom said gosh I was just a kid then Onward Christian soldiers the Canons kidnapped Chiquita and left a note for mom pay fifty dollars or you'll never see this dog again earlier I was throwing Chiquita up in the air letting her fall on the bed she didn't like it but I did dad teases her and she gets mad and growls and snaps at him she's so smart mom says and she doesn't like anyone the way she likes mom and those dogs Billy Don's dogs got married and we watched and Billy Don got really scared and went yelling they're stuck they're stuck and JJ turned the hose on them

That really old woman across the creek what's her name Keahdinekeah the way she looks gray hair so thin wrinkled skin scary eyes gray eyes and can't see the way she smells and she cries she reaches out and her hands are so little and soft and her voice is so high and crying like a baby's voice eh neh neh neh neh then she cries yes that's Indian dad says his.dad used to take him in a wagon to Anadarko and they would stop eat watermelons in the shade that's Indian my dad's a great artist he's painting that picture of a war dancer maybe a buffalo hunt and somebody's going to win it at school or the PTA I don't know only I said he would do it so he has to do it dad says grandma's getting old and she likes for all of us to come home and she hugs me and says eh neh neh neh neh Scotty you goot boy and sometimes I sleep in the arbor it's cool out there and Jimmy and Ralph sleep out there the benches are hard but grandma puts lots of covers on the benches and the covers are cool and the moonlight comes in but grandma has prayer meetings in the arbor and they go on and I get so sleepy but first it's fun because there are kids there and the kids don't want to stay in the arbor and sing and talk we run around outside oh but when aunt Clara and uncle Dick and Marland and Lucius are there it's good it's fun they always bring lots of food candy and cookies Kool-Aid toys too surprises I love to go to get the ice it's so cold in the icehouse it feels so good because it's so hot outside and I get so thirsty we get a big block of ice fifty pounds I guess and take it home to the icebox in the arbor and then ice in everything tea and soda pop and we can have ice cream and the icebox is full all the time she cooks all the time and the wind blows there are berries down there pecans by the river so dark there

Maybe I will see Mammedaty he will be there just appear not in a dream but really a vision like mom's mother the way she came beside the bed and she was an angel and was just there who are you maybe I will say but I will know who it is maybe he will look like that picture in the same clothes holding the feathers not smiling but looking just so calm hello are you in heaven grandpa yes I am in heaven well how is it there it is all right but it isn't what everyone says it is what everyone thinks is it beautiful grandpa no not beautiful but it is very quiet very still are there others there grandpa are your mom and dad there no those old people they did not come here but it is all right can you leave yes sometimes if someone wants you needs you I need you don't I grandpa well yes and I wanted to talk to you it is good that we talk together how many Indians are in heaven grandpa I don't know oh grandpa I love you I want you to tell me stories the stories you used to tell my dad I told him many stories he will tell you will he tell me everything no not everything not even all he knows but it is all right it is all right will you tell me about your grandmother the one who was captured is she there no she is not here I have not seen her is Jesus there grandpa I have not seen him but I believe that he is here will I go to heaven grandpa I don't know but it is all right you must not be afraid were you afraid to die no because I saw many things and you will see many things are you going will you come again no I will not come again but if I need you if you need me

Well I have a granddad Theodore Scott his big dog Chief horse Prince once he had a mule and I rode that mule through the barn door but there wasn't room to go through not enough room to go through that door I don't know how we got inside I told everyone mom and dad and granddad and no one could understand how it happened I could have been killed I guess when I get a horse he will have eyes like Prince beautiful eyes granddad was a sheriff too and he shot someone I think and a lot of people tried to shoot him he was too good for them he wasn't afraid mom says he's not afraid but he sleeps with a gun under his pillow Burleigh doesn't believe it so don't I don't care it's true I've seen the gun there I have seen it dad says not to be afraid I don't think that guy will take my football again he grabbed my football I was walking through the yard the high school yard and he grabbed my football and knocked my ice cream down it fell in the dirt and he threw the football to another guy and they played with it keep away and I couldn't get it back didn't know what to do finally they got tired I guess and gave it to me but I was so late dad and I went to the high school to the principal's office and they brought that big guy in and he said he wasn't afraid of my dad but of course he was and I guess he was mad because I told on him and I hope I don't see him anymore and I hope Kathleen didn't see me when they took my ball well girls don't understand they just don't understand like that time at Louise's house when we were playing games and then we sang and I kept turning around to see that pretty big girl older and really pretty and I just wanted to look at her only pretty soon she started crying and everyone wanted to know what was wrong and Mr. Roth tried to make her stop calm her down and said Marie what's wrong and she was crying and said oh they all look at me like I had horns and it was me all my fault and I thought I had done something bad terrible but it was just a misunderstanding I thought she was really pretty that's all

And that pretty girl next door Priscilla she's so dumb and Alvin her brother he's so dumb all he does is talk about God and the Bible and church and that time he kept asking me about prayers my prayers and I said he descended into hell and on the third day he arose again from the dead and he ascended into heaven and Alvin said what you mean Jesus went to hell and I didn't know so I said yeah I guess so and he told his sister and his mom and dad and I wanted him to shut up but he told everybody that I said Jesus went to hell and I didn't know what to do that time either

Well I might go to West Point I told mom that I was probably going to West Point and she said well we'll see you can probably go to West Point if you really want to I want to but maybe my eyes aren't good enough Tommy said you have to have really good eyes my eyes are pretty bad I guess the doctor said I would have to wear glasses how long I asked him and he said well you'll probably have to wear them all your life the Indians didn't wear glasses not the Kiowas how can you hunt buffalo with glasses on I broke my glasses where is West Point anyway They died with their boots on Custer was at West Point and he liked onions Taking a chance on love

Miss Johnson said Mayre not Mary and she says mary not merry mary Christmas Christmas I got boxing gloves and a football and a really good pen once I got a train I got boxing gloves real ones then everybody wanted to box with my gloves we had a tournament and I knocked Earl out well he didn't fall down but he acted really funny knocked out I hit him pretty hard I guess the twins are always fighting each other and they both have a lot of scars they're tough and they get in a lot of trouble after school last week they got in a big fight and Seldon was on top of Meldon hitting him hard in the face Meldon was crying but he was talking really dirty calling Seldon terrible names and blood was all over the place and we were all watching it was so terrible and Seldon better kill Meldon while he's on top and then a lady drove by and stopped and she was really upset and she bawled us all out and said she was going straight to the principal and Norman said aw ma'am they're brothers Billy Don told me the twins used to hit each other over the head with milk bottles the Mollé Mystery Theatre Amos 'n' Andy how *do* you do Mom said she heard me telling those guys Billy Don and Burleigh to be quiet mom's sleeping and that was sweet she said she really thought that was great of me and dad's always saying that's great sometimes he goes to Midland or Odessa I wish I could go we used to go out in a pickup at Chinle with Blackie in the back and the Navajo kids would see us and Blackie barked like crazy oh but that time at San Carlos when that crazy guy on the white horse chased me and mom and mom was scared and I guess I was really scared too but I can't remember so well but mom talks about it a lot and dad wasn't there and the guy was drunk and crazy and really mean and we ran to the trading post and it was closed and mom pounded on the door and finally the trader opened up and let us in and said it was a good thing he was there oh those Apaches they have beautiful horses one day I went to Mr. Patayama's house there and he was taking a nap and Mrs. Patayama told me to be quiet

and mom was mad at me because I had bothered those dumb
people I was in a program at the school there and I said I only
regret that I have but one life to give for my country Nathan
Hale Joe Louis beat Buddy Baer in the first round A Tree Grows
in Brooklyn

My name that's Indian my names Tsotohah Tsoai-talee Kiowa George gave me that name Kiowa George Poolaw on his
gravestone at Rainy Mountain Pohd-lohk those funny names
Pohd-lohk Kau-au-ointy that's Indian Mammedaty Huan-toa
and mom Natachee too that's Indian the round dance holding
hands moving round sideways singing the dresses swaying those
beautiful shawls and moccasins beadwork the war dancers
feather bustles bells quills we went somewhere Carnegie or
Anadarko or Hobart that time there was a dance and give-away
oh it was fine all the colors everyone was wearing such fine
clothes the dancers had fans and rattles there was one big drum
those men four or five were beating that drum like making
thunder the ground seemed to shake and the dancers their feet
seemed to make the thunder how do they do it keep time that
way so perfectly that's Indian and when they stopped the give-
away those women put lots of things down on the ground heck
anybody could just go out there and take them blankets and
stuff money too but sometimes they call out the names Indian
names and those people come out and get gifts dad got a blanket
Pendleton blanket plaid red and blue and green mom got a shawl
black with red flowers that old man gave me some money two
dollars two dollar bills they were new they were folded once
the long way like paper airplanes and Jimmy and Lester gave
me money too they always give me money that's Indian that
give-away it's funny it takes such a long time you get bored
well I get bored if you don't get anything and have to watch
just sit there talking maybe resting and the boy the water boy
comes around with a bucket of water and a dipper and the
dancers drink it's so hot and all the names are called out Goombi
Poolaw Tsoodle Tonamah Poorbuffalo Whitehorse those funny
names Marland told me someone's name was Chester Meat and
he got so tickled it was somehow it was really funny like Billy
Don that time and we all laughed Chester Meat and we all really
laughed that's Indian Chester Meat you'd be so nice to come

home to dad said one time Mammedaty got a horse at the give-away a black horse really a good one well I guess it was the best horse in the world it was black dad said and it had a red blanket on its back and it pranced and danced around and there were feathers in its hair its mane and tail and that time too a girl dad said a beautiful girl in a buckskin dress beautiful beadwork white buckskin she had hair so black and black eyes dad said she was given a name at the give-away and it was good dad said a good thing to be given a name there and the girl was very beautiful and everyone was honored everyone honored her because of that maybe I would have married her if I had been there did she look like Faye Emerson no Minnehaha that's Indian hey when was that I was in Roswell I went to a show it was a good show all about was it Billy the Kid there was a Mexican his name was Jose I hadn't heard that name Jose before and it sounded good to me and I kept saying it over and over again Jose Jose Jose Jose Jose I liked it and mom said she visited Mrs. Garrett Elizabeth I think and her dad Mrs. Garrett's dad killed Billy the Kid well yes I killed the little varmint of course yes he came in you see the room was dark very dark you couldn't see really but he said who is it or who's here or there or something like that I squeezed the trigger there was a flash in the room I saw him he fell oh yeah well listen here Garrett go for your gun Garrett gun Garrett gun Garrett I'll give you the chance you never gave poor Billy Garrett go for it what you're not afraid are you Garrett oh call me Jose just say that I'm a friend of the man you shot down in cold blood *pough* that's for Billy *pough* that's for Billy's girl Faye *pough* that's for Billy's mom that gray-haired little woman back in Silver City *pough* that's for Billy and me Billy and me we rode the range together

All right Angelo look we can do it we're only behind by six points I can get clear look I know I can get clear look just watch me I'll go right down the sideline get the ball to me okay on three oh yes I've got it here they come I stiff-arm one get the knees high high pour it on now you're fast fast ladies and gentlemen this is incredible it looked like a run all the way but Bertelli hid the ball and at the last moment flipped a pass to Momaday in the flat and now the chief has it on his own thirty-five he stiff-arms one man slides off another my lord how did he get out of that there were four blue jerseys he was completely boxed in five six seven men had a shot at him oh now he's reversing his field the stands are going wild two more tacklers get their hands on him but he gets away simply incredible I don't believe my eyes he's at the fifty the forty-five the forty the thirty-five only one man now between him and the goal the thirty the twenty-five he feints he spins he side-steps the lone defender is helpless ladies and gentlemen tied in a knot Momaday trots now walks the ball across the goal line touchdown Notre Dame ladies and gentlemen that play covered ninety-seven yards from scrimmage the fans are wild the most brilliant bit of broken-field running this announcer has ever seen

The dog Wahnookie at Shiprock German shepherd would not let anyone come near me stood between me and anyone else anyone she didn't know well I was just a baby then learning to walk I guess once I went to sleep outside under the slide in the playground and dad came looking for me with a switch and I was afraid but I said hi dad and before he could get mad he said hi and everything was all right oh that geography Sacramento is the capital of California Olympia is the capital of Washington Pierre is the capital of South Dakota is it I think so Albany is the capital of New York arithmetic I hate it what I do sometimes is draw in the books move the pencil down through the words not through the words but around the words well among the words not touching them oh make believe I'm running with the football the words are tacklers move the pencil real fast if you touch a word you're tackled I showed Billy Don now he does it too maybe I'll spend the night at Billy Don's house but last time I got homesick in the night and went home and mom was up sitting at her dresser and she was glad to see me and missed me too and did we whip cream stiff with sugar JJ sings those dirty songs but they are funny tells jokes daddy what's that that's my roll of bills mama what's that that's my purse daddy will you put your roll of bills in mama's purse and the girls of France

Last summer I had that little dagger that Mexican dagger from Mrs. Ball's shop I think and I practiced and practiced throwing it holding the point very lightly between my finger and thumb how was it the dagger felt just right balanced just

232

easily there and finally I could stick it in the ground almost every time then there was the horny toad on the ground and I just saw it and just automatically I flipped the dagger down and it went right through the horny toad I didn't mean to do it it just happened gosh the horny toad wasn't dead but it had the dagger sticking through it and it seemed just the same looking around and I had to get my dagger back but I didn't like to touch it then but I did and I threw the horny toad off and it didn't die or act hurt even but I was a little bit sick I think then afterwards I thought it was pretty neat and I told Billy Don and all the kids you don't want to make any sudden moves when I've got that Mexican dagger it just flicks out like the tongue of a snake partner oh yes like the time this dumb kid jumped on me from behind we were on the playground at lunchtime or recess and this dumb kid jumped on my back and I threw him over my shoulder and he fell on his head and started to cry and I was scared he was hurt and I wanted to say I'm sorry but there were these girls watching and one of them said gee he must be tough and I really liked that so I didn't apologize heck it wasn't my fault the dumb jerk that will teach him to sneak attack it was just a reflex action like throwing the Mexican dagger and that time I threw Leroy Woodley into the lockers it wasn't all that hard but it made a terrific bang like a bomb or something and it scared everybody me too but he wasn't hurt I am tough I guess really tough but Billy Don is tougher

Oh I have had a toothache don't tell me about toothaches there's nothing worse I had a bad toothache I was lying on the divan crying and mom and dad were trying to make me feel better but I just kept crying softly I think bravely and dad asked me what would make me feel better an official Boy Scout hatchet I said and he said okay I could have it

Last night driving along the sky was so red and streaked and everything so still the ground big and black my dad singing Indian songs my mom talking to him and laughing talking to me and laughing and Chiquita on her lap and the flare out there in the fields the smell of the place but going on driving on out and away from Hobbs towards Jal Caprock the ground so big and black the air so cool after the hot hot afternoon the sound of the wind rushing by star star shining bright first star I've seen tonight I wish I may I wish I might have the wish I wish tonight oh please I wish

Miss Johnson said Mayre not Mary and if Jeanine doesn't come to school on Monday I'll put one of those rubber mice or snakes in her desk the sky so red really red and beautiful it was then it was dark all around the headlights jumping around and I put my hand out the window and felt the wind so cool so hard on my hand I guess we were going fast and other stars were around all around there were so many and so close sometimes you see shooting stars the stars were so close last night when we got so far from town that there was no light on the sky no light but the stars on the sky and we stopped dad stopped the car and mom and dad and I and Chiquita got out and looked at the stars there were so many you couldn't begin to count them and some of them were so close together they were like water on a window when you move rain around on the window with your hand I wanted to rub my hand across the sky to see the stars move and run and spread out on the sky the sky was so black so purple but there were so many stars and the stars were so bright the black was closed out almost there was the sky full of stars and made you shiver to see them to feel the cold to hear that the stars were so quiet

But I was yet a child, and I lay low at Hobbs, feeling for the years in which I should find my whole self. And I had the strong, deceptive patience of a child, had not to learn it as patience but only to persist in it. Patience is what children have; it is especially theirs to have. I grew tall, and I entered into the seventh grade. I sat looking into books; there were birds on the lawn, chirping. Girls ambled in the dark corridors in white socks and saddle oxfords, and there were round, sweet syllables on their tongues. Time receded into Genesis on an autumn day in 1946.

West of Jemez Pueblo there is a great red mesa, and in the folds of the earth at its base there is a canyon, the dark red walls of which are sheer and shadow-stained; they rise vertically to a remarkable height. You do not suspect that the canyon is there, but you turn a corner and the walls contain you; you look into a corridor of geologic time. When I went into that place I left my horse outside, for there was a strange light and quiet upon the walls, and the shadows closed upon me. I looked up, straight up, to the serpentine strip of the sky. It was clear and deep, like a river running across the top of the world. The sand in which I stood was deep, and I could feel the cold of it through the soles of my shoes. And when I walked out, the light and heat of the day struck me so hard that I nearly fell. On the side of a hill in the plain of the Hissar I saw my horse grazing among sheep. The land inclined into the distance, to the Pamirs, to the Fedchenko Glacier. The river which I had seen near the sun had run out into the endless ether above the Karakoram range and the Plateau of Tibet.

NOTES OF A TRANSLATOR'S SON

Joseph Bruchac

In this moving essay, Joseph Bruchac describes his own "cycle of becoming" amid racism and the ridicule of his schoolmates. Raised by a beloved Abenaki grandfather who felt compelled by history and circumstance to deny his Indian blood, Bruchac describes how he transformed his grandfather's shame into a personal celebration and reclaimed his Native American identity.

Joseph Bruchac was born in the Adirondacks in 1942 of Abenaki, Slovak, and French ancestry. As a storyteller, fiction writer, and poet, he has published numerous books, including Keepers of the Earth: Native American Stories and Environmental Activities for Children. *Two of his best-known books of poetry are* Indian Mountain and Other Poems *and* Walking with My Son. *He has been awarded a Rockefeller Foundation Humanities Fellowship and the PEN Syndicated Fiction Award.*

THE BEST TEACHERS HAVE SHOWED ME THAT THINGS HAVE TO BE done bit by bit. Nothing that means anything happens quickly—we only think it does. The motion of drawing back a bow and sending an arrow straight into a target takes only a split second, but it is a skill many years in the making. So it is with a life, anyone's life. I may list things that might be described as my accomplishments in these few pages, but they are only shadows of the larger truth, fragments separated from the whole cycle of becoming. And if I can tell an old-time story now about a man who is walking about, *waudjoset ndatlokugan*, a forest lodge man, *alesakamigwi udlagwedewugan*, it is because I spent many years walking about myself, listening to voices that came not just from the people but from animals and trees and stones.

Who am I? My name is Joseph Bruchac. The given name is that of a Christian saint—in the best Catholic tradition. The surname is from my father's people. It was shortened from *Bruchacek*—"big belly" in Slovak. Yet my identity has been affected less by middle European ancestry and Christian teachings (good as they are in their seldom-seen practice) than by that small part of my blood which is American Indian and which comes to me from a grandfather who raised me and a mother who was almost a stranger to me. I have other names, as well. One of those names is Quiet Bear. Another, given me by Dewasentah, Clan Mother at Onondaga, is *Gah-neh-go-he-yo*. It means "the Good Mind." There are stories connected to those names, stories for another time.

What do I look like? The features of my face are big: a beaked nose, lips that are too sensitive, and sand-brown eyes and dark eyebrows that lift one at a time like the wings of a bird, a low forehead that looks higher because of receding brown hair, an Adam's apple like a broken bone, two ears that were normal before wrestling flattened one of them. Unlike my grandfather's, my skin is not brown throughout the seasons but sallow in the winter months, though it tans dark and quickly when the sun's warmth returns. It is, as you might gather, a face I did not used to love. Today I look at it in the mirror and say, *Bruchac, you're ugly and I like you*. The face nods back at me and we laugh together.

The rest of me? At forty-two I still stand 6′ 2″ tall and weigh the 195 pounds I weighed when I was a heavyweight wrestler at Cornell University. My arms and hands are strong, as strong as those of anyone I've met, though my two sons—Jim who is sixteen and 6′ 4″, and Jesse who is thirteen and close to 6′— smile when I say that. When they were little their games included "Knock Papa Down." Each year they've found it a little easier to do. My physical strength, in part, is from my grandfather, who was never beaten in a fight. Like his, the fingers of my hands are short and thick. I hold them out and see the bulges in the knuckles, the way both my index fingers are skewed slightly and cannot completely straighten. A legacy of ten years of studying martial arts.

Do we make ourselves into what we become or is it built into our genes, into the fate spun for us by whatever shapes events? I was a small child, often alone and often bullied. I was different—raised by old people who babied me, bookish, writing poetry in grade school, talking about animals as if they were people. My grandfather joked when he called me a "mongrel," a mixture of English and Slovak and "French," but others said such things without joking. When I was seven I decided I would grow up to be so big and strong that no one would ever beat me up again. It took me nine years to do it. ("Be careful what you really want," a Tai Chi master told me. "If you really want it, you'll get it.") My junior year in high school I was still the strange kid who dressed in weird clothes, had no social graces, was picked on by the other boys, scored the highest grades in English and biology and almost failed Latin and algebra. That winter of my junior year my grandmother died. My grandfather and I were left alone in the old house. That summer I grew six inches in height. In my senior year, though clothing and social graces showed little evolution, I became a championship wrestler, won a Regents' scholarship, and was accepted by Cornell University to study wildlife conservation.

How can I now, in only a few pages, cover the next twenty-five years? How can I adequately describe five years at Cornell and the year at Syracuse University, where I held a creative writing fellowship? At Syracuse, told by an expatriate South African writing instructor that my prose was too poetic, I smashed my typewriter in frustration and burned everything I had written. (Carol, my wife of a year, looked out the window of our small rented student housing bungalow and wondered what kind of bear she had married.) What about the Vietnam protests and the Civil Rights movement, the march on Washington and that long walk in Mississippi where James Meredith and Martin Luther King, Stokeley Carmichael and Marlon Brando took water from canteens I lugged up and down the line while state troopers with shiny insect eyes took our photographs with Polaroid cameras, waiting for the night when their eyes would look out from under white Klan hoods? And what about three years spent in Ghana, West Africa, where I taught in a school by the Gulf of Guinea? The Thunder Cult's drum rumbled at night in the next compound and a mad old man asked me to join him in a visit to Mammy Water under the waves of the man-eating sea. It was in Ghana that our son James raised his arms to the brightness in the night sky and spoke his first word, *Moon!* (I fictionalized my Africa experience in a novel completed in the 1980s. In it a half-breed American teacher discovers himself and his own country through life in a foreign culture—which he finds less foreign than his white expatriate colleagues. It is called *No Telephone to Heaven.*) Then came ten years of teaching in American prisons, and a decade and a half of editing and publishing multicultural writing: my introduction to *How to Start and Sustain a Literary Magazine* (Provision House Press, 1980) is a brief autobiography of my life as an editor. And all of that was made richer and more complicated by twenty years of marriage and sixteen years of learning from two sons—whose accomplishments bring me more pride than anything I've ever done. There isn't space enough here for more than the mention of all those things.

I can only go onward by going back to where my memories begin. I was not a black belt in pentjak-silat then, not a Ph.D. in Comparative Literature, a Rockefeller Fellow, a published poet, a "well-known Native American writer," as articles about me usually begin. (Thoreau might have written his famous "simplify, simplify" for the average newspaper journalist. How easily a few ill-chosen words can be used to encapsulate an entire human life!) Then I was only a child, with few experiences and fewer scars. All that I had in common with the person I am now is a confused heritage and the house I lived in then and still live in today. It is an old house with grey shingles, built by my grandfather on the foundation of a house owned by his wife's parents before it was burned down in a feud. It sits on Splinterville Hill, named for the ashwood baskets once made here. Just to the north of us, the Adirondack Mountains of upstate New York begin. I look out the window of the bedroom where

Carol and I sleep and see, below the blue spruce trees my grand-father planted, the yard where I used to play.

How many memories of my childhood are my own and not those someone else had of me and told me about when I was older? I know that the image of a fence taller than my hands can reach is my own. I can still feel the chill, slightly rusted surface of its wire mesh against my face, my tongue almost freezing to its surface as I taste it on a day when the frost has glazed its red weave to the shimmer of a mirror. Is that my first memory or does the litter of puppies in Truman Middlebrooks' barn come before it? A warm milk smell of small animals, the sharpness of their teeth, the gentle insistence of their mother's muzzle nudged between me and them, pushing me away to roll on my back in the straw while someone's adult voice laughs. I know I am not being laughed at, so it is my grandfather's laughter that I hear. I never heard my father or my mother laugh when I was a child, and somehow life seemed too serious to my grandmother for her to indulge in much humor, even though she won her battle to keep me from my parents—that battle which I cannot re-member but which has been replayed for me from the reluctant memories of those older than I. My grandfather, though, was often joking, often teasing. When he was serious it was a seri-ousness that no one laughed at.

The memory of me climbing the ladder, unafraid and right behind the old man, all the way to the roof forty feet up when I was only two, was my grandfather's. But it was recited about me so often that it became inseparably associated with my thoughts of my childhood. I know that I always dreamed of flight. I still do fly in my dreams. Its secret is simple—just lift your legs when you're falling and you'll never touch the ground until you're ready. To this day I don't understand why I can't continue to do it in the seconds after I wake from such dreams. But I have faith that eventually I will solve that problem one way or another and float away, with my body or without it. And though I've had some spectacular falls—at least one of which I should never have survived—I still love high places, cliffs and trees and resounding waterfalls. I inherited that fear-lessness about high places and dying from my grandfather, just as I inherited certain stories. Here is one of them which is as much a part of my own fabric as if I had been there when that day was being woven:

> *I only went to school until I was in 3rd grade.*
> *What happened then, Grampa?*
> *I jumped out the window of the school and never came back.*
> *Why?*
> *I got in a fight with a boy who called me an Indian.*

My grandparents raised me. I grew up only a quarter of a mile away from my mother and father's home on what we always called "The Farm," a plot of ninety acres with several outbuildings, which had been the home of my grandparents when they were first married. My grandfather gave The Farm to them after they'd been married a few years and were still living with my grandparents. The room where I type this was my parents' room when I was a baby. They moved to The Farm with my younger sister, and I stayed "for a while" with my grandparents. I sat with my grandfather in the wooden chairs he had made and painted blue and placed in front of his general store: Bowman's Store. I was wearing shorts and my toes couldn't touch the concrete as I dangled them down, using a stick to keep my balance as I stayed in the chair. There was a shadow in front of me. My parents. My grandmother took my hand and led me back into the house. "Get to your room, Sonny."

There my memory is replaced by that of my other grandmother, the Slovak one who lived three miles away up the South Greenfield road.

> *Your fader, he was ready to leave your mother. Dere vere so many tears, such crying about you. Ah. Den your fader and mother they come and say they vill take you back, now. Dat is ven your grandfather Bowman, he goes out of the room. Ven he come back it is vith the shotgun. And he hold it to his head and say take him you vill never see me alive again.*

Though I did not hear that story until after I was married, I knew that I was important to my grandfather. I realize now I must have been, in part, a replacement for my mother's older brother, who died at birth. I was always close to my grandfather. He delighted in telling how I was his shadow, how I carried my stick just like a spear and followed him everywhere. But, close as I was, he would never speak of the Indian blood which showed so strongly in him. I have a tape recording we made soon after we returned to live with him, back from three years in West Africa to the old house on Splinterville Hill with our new son, his great-grandchild, whose life would start the healing of wounds I had caused by simply being wanted.

> *Are you Indian, Grampa?*
> *No.*
> *Then why is your skin so dark?*
> *Cause I'm French. Us French is always dark.*

Yet I was conscious of the difference, of the way people looked at me when I was with my grandfather. When I was a freshman at Cornell University he came to visit, bringing two of my friends from high school, David Phillips and Tom Furlong. They spent two nights in the dorm, all of them sleeping in my room. My grandfather told everyone that David was my younger brother. They looked at my grandfather and then, more slowly, at me. David was black. When they asked me if it was true, I said, "What do you think?" When the fraternity rushing week came later that semester, I was on more than one "black list."

> *O my God, Joe, that's Grampa sitting there by the coffin!*

I looked at the old man sitting in the front row in Burke's Funeral Home, right next to my grandfather's casket, and my own heart clenched its fist. Then the man looked at us. His face was younger and slightly less dark than that of his last surviving older brother. It was Jack Bowman. Though he lived in Lake George, the home of a more or less underground community of Abenaki Indian people even today, we had never met him before. In the year we had to get to know Jack before his own heart found a weak aorta less strong than his love for the land and his wife of fifty years, we heard more stories about my grandfather and his family. We also heard some of the denials of Indian ancestry, even though Jack offered no more of an explanation than his brother had for my grandfather's cutting himself off from his own side of the family after he married my grandmother, a woman of high education with degrees from Skidmore and Albany Law School, whose marriage to a semiilliterate and dark-skinned hired man of her father's sparked scandalized comment in Greenfield and Saratoga. In the face of those denials I felt, at times, like one who looks into a mirror and sees a blur over part of his own face. No matter how he shifts, changes the light, cleans the glass, that area which cannot be clearly seen remains. And its very uncertainty becomes more important than that which is clear and defined in his vision.

After Jack's death his wife Katherine fessed up. Yes, she said, Jack and Jesse were Indian. Everyone knew the Bowmans were Indian. She put it into writing and signed her name. It is the closest thing to a tribal registration that I will ever have. But it is enough, for I want to claim no land, no allotments, only part of myself.

There are many people who could claim and learn from their Indian ancestry, but because of the fear their parents and grandparents knew, because of past and present prejudice against Indian people, that part of their heritage is clouded or denied. Had I been raised on other soil or by other people, my Indian ancestry might have been less important, less shaping. But I was not raised in Czechoslovakia or England. I was raised in the foothills of the Adirondack Mountains near a town whose spring waters were regarded as sacred and healing by the Iroquois and Abenaki alike. This is my dreaming place. Only my death will separate it from my flesh.

I've avoided calling myself "Indian" most of my life, even when I have felt that identification most strongly, even when people have called me an "Indian." Unlike my grandfather, I have never seen that name as an insult, but there is another term I like to use. I heard it first in Lakota and it refers to a person

244

of mixed blood, a *metis*. In English it becomes "Translator's Son." It is not an insult, like *half-breed*. It means that you are able to understand the language of both sides, to help them understand each other.

In my late teens I began to meet other Indian people and learn from them. It seemed a natural thing to do and I found that there was often something familiar about them. In part it was a physical thing—just as when I opened Frederick John Pratson's book *Land of Four Directions* and saw that the Passamaquoddy man on page 45 was an absolute double of photographs of Jesse Bowman. It was not just looks, though. It was a walk and a way of talking, a way of seeing and an easy relationship to land and the natural world and animals. *Wasn't no man,* Jack Bowman said, *ever better with animals than Jess. Why he could make a horse do most anything.* I saw, too, the way children were treated with great tolerance and gentleness and realized that that, too, was true of my grandfather. He'd learned that from his father, he said.

Whenever I done something wrong, my father would never hit me. He never would hit a child. He said it jes wasn't right. But he would just talk to me. Sometimes I wisht he'd just of hit me. I hated it when he had to talk to me.

The process of such learning and sharing deserves more space than I can give it now. It involves many hours of sitting around kitchen tables and hearing stories others were too busy to listen to, and even more hours of helping out when help was needed. It comes from travels to places such as the Abenaki community of Swanton, Vermont, and the still-beating heart of the Iroquois League, Onondaga, and from realizing—as Simon Ortiz puts it so simply and so well—that "Indians are everywhere." If you are ready to listen, you'll meet someone who is ready to talk.

This short sketch of my early years, which I shall end here, represents only the beginning of a long apprenticeship I've been serving (*forever,* it seems). I seem to have an unending capacity for making mistakes just as my teachers seem to have an unerring ability to turn my mistakes into lessons. But the patience, the listening that has made it possible for me to learn more than I ever dreamed as a boy, is also the lesson I've begun to learn.

The most widely anthologized of my poems describes one lesson I was taught in the way most good lessons come to you—when you least expect them. Let it represent that part of my life which has come from continual contact with Native American people over more than two decades. Because of that contact my own sons have grown up taking such things as sweat lodges and powwows and pride in Indian ancestry for granted. The small amount that I have learned I've tried, when it is right to do so, to share with others.

BIRDFOOT'S GRAMPA

The old man
must have stopped our car
two dozen times to climb out
and gather into his hands
the small toads blinded
by our lights and leaping,
live drops of rain.

The rain was falling,
a mist about his white hair
and I kept saying
you can't save them all
accept it, get back in
we've got places to go.

But, leathery hands full
of wet brown life
knee deep in the summer
roadside grass,
he just smiled and said
they have places to go to
too

(from *Entering Onondaga,*
Cold Mountain Press, 1978)

TURBULENT CHILDHOOD
Lee Maracle

N*ative American women have always been at the forefront of
indigenous struggles against colonialism and genocide. Lee Maracle's*
Bobbi Lee: Indian Rebel *exemplifies the ongoing tradition of
Native American women's resistance and invalidates the stereotype
of the submissive Indian woman. It is a rough, sometimes
humorous, and often brutal tale of one Metis woman's lifelong battle
against oppression.*

*This section of Maracle's autobiography brings to life a childhood
fraught with poverty, abuse, and racism—a childhood where good
times are few and far between. Against this backdrop, a young
Bobbi Lee begins to question the poverty and injustice that is her life
and learns to fight back in whatever ways she can.*

*Lee Maracle (Metis) is a poet, writer, scholar, and activist for
her people. She is the author of* I Am Woman *and numerous
poems, articles, and essays.*

I WAS BORN IN VANCOUVER ON JULY 2ND 1950 AND RAISED ON THE
North Shore mud flats about two miles east of Second Narrows
Bridge. My first memory is of something that happened when
I was about two years old. My brother Roger and I were playing
down on the flats, catching wee little crabs and putting them in
a quart-sized jar—which seemed huge to us because we were
so small. Suddenly, I knocked over the jar and all the crabs
went scurrying away. Roger yelled "Babe!"—they all called me
"Babe" then—"Go and get them!" Well, I ran behind a log

where they had headed and got stuck in some deep mud. Roger was scared. He thought I was in real trouble and bolted up the trail from the beach to get mom and dad. Dad came down, picked me up out of the mud and patted me; he was so strong it seemed he was spanking me and I wondered why.

My mother, born in a large Métis community in Lac Labiche, Alberta, is the child of a Frenchman and an Indian woman. She grew up on a farm and at nineteen travelled to Edmonton, where she found work as a domestic for a rich Jewish family. Father was born on a small farm in Goodsoil, Saskatchewan, and grew up during the drought and depression of the '30s. People had a hard time then just staying alive, especially those who depended solely on their crops. In addition to the bad times, my grandfather was old and had arthritis, so it was very difficult for him to tend the farm.

As a young boy, my dad trapped animals to support the family. At fifteen he was out on his own, hopping boxcars, travelling around trying to find work. At twenty he joined the army and was sent to train in Edmonton, where he met my mother. Then he was transferred to Jericho, Vancouver. He wrote my mom many letters and finally he asked her to come to the coast and marry him. He was 22 and she was a year younger. They hadn't really known each other very well, mainly through letters, and it wasn't long before they started fighting and getting on badly.

Three years after they were married they had a son, Nelson, but he died at eleven months. A second son, Ed, was born when mom was 27 and he's still alive. In two-and-a-half years there was Roger, and I came along eleven months later. My two sisters, Joan and Joyce were twins; they were born on 12 June 1952. Gordon was born in May 1954, and George in November 1959.

The house we lived in had originally been an RCMP boatshed; my dad nailed hardboard sections (rooms) into the top part where we lived and worked on building and repairing boats in the shed below it. There was no electricity—no heating, hot water or other luxuries like television. We didn't get electricity till 1953, but even then the place was always cold and damp.

Until I was three I spent most of my time with my dad's father. Then later, when dad was around more, he would paddle us out in his rowboat to shoot ducks, which we learned to do quite young. I remember the first time clearly. I was standing in the skiff aiming intently at some ducks, but when I pulled the trigger it was too much for me—the jolt knocked me back right into the water. Dad grabbed at his gun and when I popped out of the water he was angry at me for almost getting it wet.

Later, dad started fishing off the docks in Steveston, which was about twenty miles from home. I helped the other kids gut the fish he caught. Sometimes mom left the babies at home with granddad and came along with my two older brothers to help.

When I was three years old I still didn't talk. My parents were worried about it and took me to see a doctor—several, in fact. I found out later they were psychiatrists. My folks were always arguing about me. I was often left with a woman named Eileen Dunster—whom I called "Aunt Eileen"—because dad kept beating me up and mom didn't like it.

Though I didn't talk, I remember watching things and thinking a lot. I don't know why, but I was a very serious kid. Once mom came in and said "It's raining cats 'n' dogs outside!" I ran to the window to see, but was disappointed to find only the usual rain drops coming down. I wondered for a long time why she had lied like that.

My silence lasted another year. Then one day mom caught me talking to Roger, with whom I was very close, and after that the jig was up. I started talking a little with my parents, but not very much; I didn't like big people. I thought they were interesting, but not people I wanted to talk to.

My parents fought a lot—nearly all the time. When they had parties—which was almost every week—dad got drunk and made us kids drink beer too. He would then make us dance and do other stupid things—which I really hated. I remember the first time I thought I hated my dad. My sister and I had this game: we would both run into the house and the first to touch the toilet seat got to use the bathroom first. Once my sister pushed me away from the toilet seat when I clearly had her beat. In retaliation I pulled her off the toilet and she peed on the floor.

She was crying and told dad. He ran in and slapped me hard in the face. I didn't cry; I just stared coldly at him. He then turned and left the house. I was four years old.

Around that time things got really bad in the family. The old man was always beating up on Ed, my oldest brother. He'd throw him against the wall and sometimes end up hurting him pretty badly. Dad started being gone a lot of the time, but when he came home we would all run away. Ed started staying away for days. Once, when he was 13 and I was 9, he was gone for almost a week. Mom got real worried and kicked dad out of the house, knowing Ed wouldn't return as long as he was there. We kids knew where Ed was but didn't say anything. Dad and Ed came back together the next morning and I was surprised to see that dad wasn't angry; in fact, he seemed to be proud of the spunk Ed had shown in running away.

Our family was very poor at this time. Dad built boats and was apprenticing for carpenter papers. But when I was five, he just upped and left us, going north to fish. After that, he rarely came home and never sent mom any money. So things got even worse than before. With their marriage practically broken off, mom had to earn a living for all of us. Granddad helped mom with the crab shack business she ran with my dad. Ed and granddad caught the crabs at night and watched us kids while mom pounded them during the day. She would then go around selling them, and that's how we managed to get a little money.

It wasn't long, however, before my younger brother Gordon was born. Mom couldn't work for a time after that, and by the time she could, granddad was too old to trap. So mom did both jobs, working night and day, trapping and pounding. But after a while this got to be too much for her and she had to stop. We kids were getting older and started helping out. Ed got a paper route and made about eight dollars a month when he was only eight. When Roger reached that age they started caddying at Capilano Golf Course. Both boys went caddying on Saturdays and Sundays and usually brought in ten or twelve dollars a week. When I turned seven I started taking in washing and ironing for Whites in the neighbourhood.

Sometimes we went to the nearby Indian Reserve and played with the kids there . . . but not often because we usually had so much work to do at home. Every summer mom planted a garden. We all worked in it and some of the vegetables lasted us into the fall.

There was always a lot of talk in the neighbourhood about my mom—how she used to run around and all that. Only Ed and my youngest brother are dad's kids. When dad was gone, people were always trying to break into the house. I remember one night when a guy broke in; mom had a wood chopping axe and was standing by the window telling him to get out or she would chop his head off. He finally left, but I dreamed that night that mom had killed him. I woke up in a sweat.

The community we lived in was really very strange . . . weird things were always happening. An uncle of ours lived about a mile away. Time and again he came over and stole our skiff and sold it to a man named Sebastian. Whenever it happened, mom walked over to Sebastian's place about two miles away and got it back. But they always argued fiercely. Once mom went over with an axe: she was bent on really fixing him for buying the skiff again, which he knew was ours. Actually, the skiff was over at his place a lot.

When Sebastian saw her steaming down the trail with an axe he panicked and called the police. When mom got there he backed off yellin' that the police were coming. She just took the skiff and went home. She locked up the house and we all hid in closets. Sure enough, the police came and banged loudly on the door. We didn't answer. They then broke into the house and looked around, but didn't find us. I remember being really scared that mom would be taken away to jail.

Most of the people we knew lived on the Indian Reserve. The people outside the Reserve in our neighbourhood were mainly squatters, living on houseboats or shacks on the mud flats. There were a few large families like ours, but most were smaller. Some of the men worked as longshoremen and others collected welfare—about half and half. Then there was one man who worked as an electrician and another who repaired radios. Both families had two kids, but for a very long time they didn't let them play with us. I guess it was because of mom's reputation.

Six families, most on welfare, lived in boathouses built up on stilts. The dredger's house was on stilts too, but it was really nice. He was from South Africa and his wife was mulatto. She talked a lot about the racism back home—about how they'd had to leave because her husband, a white, had married a coloured woman. They moved into the neighbourhood when I was four and I played a lot with their son, Brian. I didn't know what Blacks were then; I just knew they were different, much friendlier to us.

Another family lived between our house and the Reserve. The father worked until they discovered he had a tumour in his head. Once it was removed he couldn't balance himself well, so the family was forced to go on welfare.

Then there were the Reids, who owned the local store. They were really mean to all the neighbourhood kids. Sometimes when we walked into the store Mrs Reid would throw us into a big barrel filled with lizards. Her life was miserable—always mean and fighting with her husband. They were always drinking and getting into car accidents. Once they even drove through our woodpile and smashed into the house.

There was also a Canadian Indian-Mexican family nearby. Gracie Flores, the daughter, spent some time looking after us kids when mom went away for a few days. Then there was Jimmy Waddel. His family lived above the store and his father worked at McKenzie Barge and Derrick, a boat-building outfit. Jimmy and the older Korris boy down the street always picked on my brother and the younger kids from the Reserve. Whenever we played they tried to bully us around. So one day we decided we'd had enough. It was quite funny. Ten of us little kids were making faces at Jimmy from around the corner of a house, calling him "dirty old man," "whitey," "white boy," and things like that. We had this huge chain from a logging boom with us and when he chased after us we all hid behind a tree. He could see us, of course, but when he ran up we wrestled him to the ground. Then we took a big padlock from dad's boatshed and chained and locked him to the tree. The chain was real heavy, so he couldn't get away. We just left him there crying.

That night Mrs Waddel came over to tell my mother that Jimmy was lost. She was weeping. Jimmy was only eleven. I didn't think much more about it until the police came. Suddenly

I wondered if anyone had unlocked him. I was only five and didn't have the key. All of us kids kept quiet. Ed didn't know. He was older and we knew he would tell on us. Next morning they finally found Jimmy. He was still crying and told them the whole story—except who had done it. After that he never bothered us little kids again.

When I turned seven I had my first birthday party. I got a skipping rope and remember really enjoying it. We didn't skip with it much, though. We would have fun tying it around Roger, me and my little sister, Joan, who was very small for her age, five, about the size of a three-year old. Bound together, we would run down the hill as fast as we could. Joan couldn't keep up and usually ended up being dragged along. Once she got caught in the bushes and got scratched. She was usually screaming about something, so we didn't pay any attention; just kept yelling back, "Come on Joan! Keep running!" Finally we realized how hard it was becoming to pull. Looking back we saw we'd been pulling little Joan through the thick brambles. She was covered with cuts and bruises and crying loudly. We promised her all sorts of favours and she promised not to tell mom. At home she said she'd fallen into the bushes, but mom didn't believe her. It was the first time I got a spanking from my mom.

The next came when I lost a new pair of shoes that the Campbell family had given me. We were playing in the old sawdust pits, jumping into them from a high crumbling wall. Joan put my shoes down and they disappeared into this little hole. We dug for them, but the walls of the hole kept caving in. Then we got a shovel and held Joan upside down by the feet while she dug deeper and deeper. But we couldn't find them and almost dropped Joan on her head. Finally we gave in and told mom. She spanked us good, mainly because she didn't want us down at the sawdust mill. She got so angry, she sprained a finger. It swelled up so bad she couldn't spank Joan, but Roger and I spanked her good because we figured she was the cause of our problem and deserved a good one.

Soon after this incident, mom became very ill—or at least it seemed so to me. I was very worried. I thought it was my dad's fault that she was dying because he wouldn't take her to the hospital. I decided I would shoot him . . . he was just no good, I thought. All he could say was that he didn't have enough money to take mom in, but we knew it wasn't true because he was a pretty good fisherman. I knew about death because we had done a lot of duck hunting and fishing. I thought it wouldn't be difficult to shoot dad. I told Roger my plan—he was eight then—and he talked me out of it, saying "If mom dies, shoot him. But let's wait and see—otherwise it's just stupid." Well, I agreed—somewhat afraid to go ahead with my plan anyway— and mom got better in a couple of weeks. You have to understand that I really loved mom, and I hated my dad—especially when I was a young kid.

For a long time, dad had only been coming home occasionally, then one day he moved back in and said to us kids that he was going to stay around awhile. Actually, he started being quite nice to us. My earlier hatred melted and I even began to like him a little. He got a job with Sterling Shipyards and continued to fish, taking Ed along with him. He wanted to take Roger too, but he was only eight and couldn't pass for twelve, which was the minimum legal age for fishing.

One day when Roger and I were down at the waterfront, he said: "Babe let's take the skiff and go see dad; he's fishing down at Rivers Inlet." I said "Okay," and he ran to the crab shack to get the oars. It was locked, but we were determined to go by now and "borrowed" a pike pole and paddle from Allen George's canoe on the beach. We knew what we were doing was wrong. Mom and dad had both told us not to play around the water. We'd taken the boat out without asking several times—sometimes for hours—and mom and dad would worry, telling us how dangerous it was when we finally returned. Nevertheless, we pushed the heavy skiff over some barnacles down to the shore. We didn't know it, but we'd scraped up a few small holes in the bottom. Paddling and poling, we headed up the coast and out toward the ocean, bailing water all the time. After travelling about five miles, we found ourselves at the mouth of the inlet near Lion's Gate Bridge. We couldn't paddle beyond the point no matter how hard we tried. Finally, the ocean current settled us onto the shore. Long hours of paddling and poling had convinced us it was time to go home. But how were we going to get the skiff back? We sat there a long time trying to figure it out: "Should we leave the skiff and walk back? Or try to make it back against the current, tired as we were?" As we talked it over, an RCMP patrol boat pulled up. The police asked us a few questions, then towed us home. Mom was worried finding us missing and the boat gone and had phoned the RCMP after a few hours. At home Roger just kept crying, saying he'd really wanted to visit dad up at Rivers Inlet. Mom told him we'd only gone five miles and it was another 300 to Rivers Inlet. But Roger was still too young to understand much about miles, so the tears kept falling. I was tired and didn't care anymore about Rivers Inlet, just wanting to lie down and rest.

In 1959, when mom became pregnant again with my younger brother, dad left home for good. He yelled at mom, saying she was whoring around with other men, havin' kids that weren't his, and so on. Maybe he was right, but he fooled around plenty too. Since 1947 he would be leaving her for six months to a year at a time. Sometimes she talked to us about how bad it was being without a man in the house, and what it was like when they had no kids. She said Nelson died because dad refused to take him to the hospital—and she would never forgive him for that. Then when he was home they argued and fought a lot about Nelson, Ed and me. Dad just didn't like Ed and kept complaining that I wasn't even his kid. He accused mom of telling us stories when he was gone, trying to make us hate him. But in fact, mom remained loyal to him until long after he'd left her, always telling us he was a good man who just had too many troubles.

Around this time a girl named Karen Thomas—we called her "Toni"—came to live with us. She'd been working in the canneries but was continually being laid off because of strikes or shortages of fish. So she decided to look after us kids while mom worked. She became like an older sister. We would often sit around in the evening and have long discussions—mainly mom and Toni. Sometimes they'd talk about politics. You see, when I was seven mom joined the Communist Party. Two years later there were lots of conflicts and she dropped out. I never found out why, except her saying the communists were real creepy, but since then she's been anti-communist.

With dad gone, we began working after school and didn't have much chance to play. When I was nine I started taking care of my baby brother in the summer while mom worked at the Army & Navy Department Store. She'd always been at home before and now we felt lost without her. We just couldn't understand why she had to go off to work every day and I remember our telling her in childish anguish that we would all work harder if she stayed at home. I was taking in ironing and doing a little baby-sitting outside, but we couldn't make enough to live on. She had a deeply held ethic, handed down from both her family and dad's father, that people ought to work. Government was always trying to put Indians on welfare, but they didn't want it. Government said they were going to take away Indian trapping and fishing rights and put them on welfare—the Indians resisted. Our grandparents had been involved in many anti-welfare struggles.

With mom, it was partly a matter of pride; she didn't want her folks to come out and see her living like that . . . on government handouts. She would sometimes cry and talk to me, saying she couldn't understand how it was we could work so hard and yet be so poor . . . and grumbling under her breath that she would never accept their dirty welfare money. So we all worked very hard at the crab shack and various other jobs. Mom was nearly forty and was having a very difficult time carrying George. Once she had been crying and sick for about two days. I cried too. We were very close then. She asked over and over, "Why are we so poor when we work so hard?" She was just talking out loud, but I felt she was asking me and I didn't have an answer. I just wondered alone with her how it was that no matter how hard we worked—my brothers caddying or doing other odd jobs, me ironing, etc.—we never seemed to have anything to eat but the fruit and vegetables we canned. We almost never bought anything. I never wore a regular pair of shoes till I was ten—only runners—and we never had any heat in the house. I also began wondering why most people—white people—didn't like Indians and treated us badly, like we weren't as good as they were. And soon I began to wonder if, or how, we could change the situation we found ourselves in. We seemed

to be caught in the same rut all the time . . . always runnin'
around in the same miserable rut. But I was still far too young
and inexperienced to understand the social and class nature of
our oppression.

A couple of years later, when I was eleven, mom bought
another house. She was one of the few people in the neighbourhood who owned their own place. We got $15,000 for the old
house and lot—and I was really happy to leave the mud flats. I
always seemed to be sick in that house, with no protection
against the cold, wet winters and the wind which constantly
whipped in off the ocean. Things got a lot better when we
moved into the new place. It had a furnace and central heating.
Some of our friends from the Reserve helped us move, but we
girls did most of the work as the boys were out fishing.

Then my mother began to change . . . for the worse, I
thought. She quit drinking, stopped running around with men
and became very moralistic. But what was bad was that she
stopped being the easy-going person we all loved and enjoyed
being around. Actually, we thought she was going a bit crazy.
She sat and stared a lot, talking to herself and acting in other
strange ways. A certain tension filled the house and it scared all
of us.

Because mom wanted me to, I started studying the Bible . . .
but I didn't like it. It was full of unbelievable fantasies. As a kid,
I thought a lot, but never daydreamed or fantasized. My dreams
were mostly of conversations I'd had; I'd remember things that
happened and try to figure them out. I was always trying to
understand things—why there was air, how we breathed, and
so forth. There was something in me that made me conscious
of all the little things that happened.

Three months after I entered school I became aware that I
was an Indian and that white people didn't like me because of
the colour of my skin. I talked about it with kids on the Reserve
but they would just say "We don't like whites either." Even the
older people didn't like whites. Many worked in the white
communities, around white people, but they had no white
friends. Like most of the kids, when some white called me a
name or abused me, I fought back. But otherwise I just ignored

them like everyone else, fighting their contempt with silence. Of course, my situation wasn't simple because my old man was white. But when he got drunk and angry with mom he called her a "dirty old squaw."

By the time I was nine I didn't want anything to do with whites. There were many in my school, but I had no friends and asked no questions in class. When a teacher called on me I just refused to answer. As time went on I became very nervous and uncomfortable at school; I just wanted to be completely away from white people in my daily life. A talent I had in art added to my misfortune. I once made a clay bear and glazed it black, but it came out gray. I tried again, but still it came out gray. My teacher was nice to me and sympathetic. He took my bear around to the other classes and talked about how well it was done. The kids took notice and some told me they really liked it. Of course, I remained passive. I didn't want their compliments, or even to be noticed. I wanted only to be left alone, ignored. Their attention just embarrassed me, and my hatred of that bear grew monstrous in comparison to its size. Because of it I was drawn into the Whiteman's spotlight—a place I wanted to avoid. But I silently accepted the situation—their tolerance, their racism.

After we moved, I went to a new school in Lynn Valley. I remembered that standing up and being introduced to my new class was—after the bear incident—the second most humiliating incident in my life to that point. The teacher then appointed a girl to show me around the school. I really needed it too; I'd become completely introverted, keeping all to myself and rarely talking. My problem was complicated because it was around this time that mom started talking to herself, flying off the handle at nothing, and forgetting things all the time. I thought a lot about it and decided that I didn't ever want to become like her. In fact, I'd reached a point of not wanting anything more to do with either mom or dad. We'd been very close before, mom and me, but now we seemed very far apart.

There was another new girl in my school, named Gertrude. I'd known her in grade two. When I was little I always wanted hair like hers, long and very blonde. Sometimes she teased me saying, "Don't you wish you had long pretty hair like mine?" It made me very sad and angry. Then one day I was playing with her hair; she'd let me do it because it flattered her. We were in school. Then, as I braided the long blonde strands, I added some of dad's boat glue, which I kept in my desk. I worked it carefully into the braids and by recess they had become hard as a rock. When Gertrude jumped up to flaunt her pony-tail, it swung around and hit her like a stick right in the face. She screamed, then started crying. I was taken to the principal, who gave me a hard strapping. They told mom, but she didn't get angry; in fact she thought it was funny and laughed. "Maybe that'll teach her not to bug you anymore," she said. By grade six, Gertrude had become a really vain and mean person, but she never bothered me again.

After a time in the new school I started to change a bit. I became a little more relaxed around white people. One of my teachers was a pretty nice guy. I remember reading about various religions and talking to him about why people believed in these strange ideas. He had been to the Soviet Union in 1956 and was a liberal—not at all anti-Russian. I decided that I would like to go visit Russia too. When mom was in the Communist Party she'd subscribed to a magazine called "Soviet Union," published in Moscow. Sometimes all of us kids would sit around and talk about what we saw and thought. I remember liking the photographs very much—especially the ones of Eskimo dwellings. The idea that they were all alike fascinated me.

This Mr. Cleamens was also my music teacher. He asked why I never sang with the rest of the kids in the chorus. When I didn't reply, he said that if I didn't start singing he would have me stand up in front of the entire class and practice so I would overcome my shyness. But I remained silent in the chorus. Finally, he told me to stand and sing before the class. I don't remember if I uttered a few notes or not; just that I started crying and didn't go to school for the next three weeks. I've never been able to sing . . . can't even carry a tune. After I returned he allowed me to remain silent. Strangely enough, our choir won several prizes that year.

In grade six my marks improved for the first time. I was a

straight "A" student that year and the next. I also became good friends with a Jewish classmate named Maria von Strassen. Once I even went to synagogue with her. But I decided I didn't want to become Jewish—or any other religion for that matter.

Maria, however, was a very nice girl, and very quiet. Everyone used to pick on her because of her being Jewish, quiet and a good student . . . I guess. Anyway, I often walked to school with her even though the other girls didn't want anyone to play with or talk to her. Once a gang of them came down on me as I walked to school. They started calling me names and beating up on me. I became furious and ferocious, screaming that if they didn't stop I'd kill them all, one by one. "I'll get every last one of you! No matter how long it takes me! I'll kill you all!" I yelled. But that just made them madder. They sat on me and punched my arm and stomach very hard. I was sick for a couple of days after and wore sweaters so mom and the others wouldn't find out what happened.

A few days later we were playing softball at school. The biggest girl, the one who started the fight with me, was pitching. When I came to bat I really whacked the ball and it hit her right smack in the stomach. She fell down, unconscious, while all her friends came rushing in to beat me up again, yelling that I'd done it on purpose. "You're bloody right," I yelled back, "and if you come closer I'll smash you with this bat!" As they moved in, I swung the bat around and nearly hit one of the girls in the head. Someone ran in to get the principal while one of the girls who hadn't been involved in the matter said, "No one is going to hurt you Bobbi. Why don't you give me the bat and let's forget it?" "Get away," I said, "or I'll knock your head off too!"

The tension was building, but nothing else happened. The girls just drifted away, knowing I was very serious. Then the principal came out and talked to us. From then on, whenever there were parties, the girls made sure to tell me I wasn't invited . . . and when our class went on biology field trips, or to the zoo and so on, nobody would walk with me. The other girls started easing off her and she even made some new friends. This really made me cynical. It was the first time in my life I'd been open to friendship with white girls, and now their contempt and ostracism forced me to conclude that all whites were the same: creepy, cruel racists that I wanted nothing more to do with.

As far as school was concerned, I didn't even want to go anymore. I would often drink mustard with water, getting a bit sick in order to stay home. Mostly, I just left the house and, instead of going to school, took long walks down the canyon or out in Stanley Park. Even in winter I went up to the swamp and hiked—sometimes with my brother, sometimes alone. At times we hiked into the water shed and guards would come and chase us off. Then we sometimes saw bears and ran away. Around our new house the bears were really strange; sometimes they came right into the yards looking for food. Once there was a knock on our door and mom hollered, "Come in! Come in!" but no one entered. Then more knocks and more "Come in's." Finally though we rarely ever opened our door personally for visitors, mom went and pulled it open with a swish of frustration. Standing there on his hind legs was a huge bear. I wanted to laugh and scream at the same time. Mom was so frightened she just stood there for an instant, her mouth open; then she slammed the door and ran around locking all the doors and windows . . . as if the bear was bound and determined to come in. Instead, he just ran away . . . probably as scared as we were.

Later, we had other troubles with bears. My younger brother, George, was three and often went to play in a nearby fruit orchard. One day I walked down through the trees looking for him. Suddenly, I found him playing peacefully with two small bear cubs. I'd heard how fierce mother bears became in defense of their cubs and ran home as fast as I could to tell mom. She told me to get him immediately. Luckily, there was no sign of the mother bear yet and I grabbed George and pulled him all the way back to the house. When more people moved in, the bears slowly left the area. But that was much later.

Squirrels were more fun. We kept them around the house by feeding them . . . almost like pets. We also had a racoon, but he was pretty wild.

Sometimes dad came to visit us and often paid the house bills. There'd be a lot of tension in the atmosphere, but no serious trouble that I can remember. My negative feelings toward him eased off, but there was still little emotion in our relationship. In the wintertime he stayed at the house and slept downstairs. Mom slept upstairs with us kids. They didn't live together; just shared the same house. We would put up with him, more or less, till he left again for who knew how long.

THE TALKING THAT TREES DOES

Geary Hobson

T aken from a novel in progress entitled Daughters of Lot, *this story of kinship and memory reads like an annotated genealogy of people and place, and illuminates a relationship between land, people, and identity that is at the center of the lives of many Native American people. In the midst of displacement and land loss, a young man learns that no matter where life and circumstances may lead, he carries his identity in his mind, in his heart, in his very flesh and bone.*

Geary Hobson is a Cherokee, Chickasaw, and Quapaw poet, writer, and essayist. He was born in 1941 in Chicot County, Arkansas. He edited The Remembered Earth: An Anthology of Contemporary Native American Literature *and was a contributor as well. He has recently published a book of poetry entitled* Deer Hunting and Other Poems. *He teaches in the English Department at University of Oklahoma at Norman.*

BEFORE I COMMENCE, I JUST WANT TO SAY THIS: I TAKE A LONG time telling you all about these kin—these aunts and uncles and grandparents and great-grandparents and cousins and all—and the land hereabouts and its shapes and looks back then and all its changes and all its going-ons . . .

All that land you see across the bayou yonder and some of it on this side, counting where we're sitting right now, used to belong to our folks. All along Emory Bayou, clear down to where it cuts and runs into Muddy Bayou, and then on north a ways nearly to Black Bayou, and then on due west some almost to Coldstream, nearly all the land that Eustace Tanner claims title to now and rents on shares to people like the Hewitts and Renfros and Wades—that whole portion, which is a shade-bit more than a section, used to be held in the name of our people. Back then, at the time I'm going to tell you about, Uncle Andrew Thompson held title to it but it wudn't just his. What I mean is, he didn't own it all to hisself. The way we all looked at it, it was more Aunt Minnie's and Aunt Velma's and even to say that ain't entirely correct neither. What I mean to say is, it belonged to us all, not to one, or even two, but to *all*. All of us that was kinfolks and lived on it and spent our time on it and knowed it as ours. In them days there was a whole slew of little cabins and clapboard houses belonging to Thompson and Squirrel kin scattered throughout the section and it was mostly woods then. It was ours and it was like an island surrounded by a whole sea of newcomers who moved in and built their houses and started their farms and set up stores and cotton gins and churches and such-like all around us. The way we looked at it, that was alright, long as we was left by ourselves. And for a long time that was the way it was.

I was born out west around Simms Bayou, over where some of your mother's folks are still living. Matter of fact, a whole lot of that land out there used to be ours too. Some kinfolks out there still own some of that land, but what they got left ain't much. It's all just a turnip patch now, upside what it used to be. Same as it is over here. I don't remember my mama any. She died of the typhoid fever when I was two and I never knowed my daddy neither, except that he was a white man. Don't ask me how I know that or why it's even important, if it is, even. I might get around to telling that but I doubt it, since I think it's a separate story all to itself. I was took and raised by Mama's folks, my Grandma and Grandpa Sanford, until they up and died too. First it was Grandma that died and then a few months after that, Grandpa passed on too. They lived right by Grandma's folks, the Lamleys, on a dirt road that run alongside Simms Bayou pert-near all the way to Bayou Bartholomew. When Grandpa passed away or went, as he used to say, "back into the earth," I was took and raised by my Uncle Achan. He was one of Grandma's brothers.

There was four of them in Uncle Achan's house on Simms Bayou, not counting me, and they was all old folks and Uncle Achan's bachelor or widowed brothers and sister. There was Uncle Achan, who was sixty-something and head of the place, and his younger brothers, Joe and Zeno, and there was their older sister, my Aunt Gustine, who was in her seventies. They all talked French to each other, but I never picked up none of it. They come from around Arkansas Post and sometimes they would talk about all the property their mama and daddy had had over there long before Arkansas became a state. Quapaw they was mostly, even if you wouldn't of thought it of them because of that French they talked and the way it looked to me like they tried to act when other folks not kin to them or me come around to visit. I'll give you some for instances. Aunt Gustine used to set a real pretty tea set out for evening visitors, and this to folks who wouldn't of been able to tell the difference between store-bought tea and stumpwater. She never done this to put on airs, I don't 'spect, but just to try and keep up some kind of sign of what their folks' ways had been like at the Post when they was all little kids growing up there. And there was Uncle Zeno and his realfine five-dollar gold watch that he was proud as all git out of. Five dollars for a gold watch was some big doings in them days. He used to carry it around in a little homemade watchpocket that Aunt Gustine had fixed up for him on his britches, even when he hunted and fished or chopped corn or cotton. They was a stand-offish bunch that generally kept to theirselves, in a whole lot of ways like my Aunt Minnie and Aunt Velma that I'm going to tell you about directly.

I never minded living with them even if I did have to do a right fair amount of fetching and toting for them—as Uncle Andrew one time said about it—and never got to be around any kids my own age. Except for some corn, Uncle Achan and them didn't farm any. They had some horses and hogs, but like us when I lived with Uncle Andrew, they let their stock run loose in the woods until they needed them. Uncle Achan and my other uncles just hunted and fished mostly, just like our granddaddy Jed used to do. Of course, Jed was directly descended from them and he had the same kinds of ways they had.

I stayed with them for two years and I learned a lot about fishing and hunting. I also learned most of my American from them because I couldn't talk it very good when I was littler and living with Grandma and Grandpa Sanford. Grandpa Sanford talked Cherokee to me and to Grandma too. She learned it during all them years she lived with Grandpa. Uncle Andrew used to come over there from time to time to see how us all was doing. Mainly, though, I think he came just to see me. Finally, one time when he come over, he talked to Uncle Achan and Aunt Gustine about me coming back over here and going to school. Why I was pert-near twelve years old and wouldn't of knowed anything about schooling even if it was to of snuck up on me and bit me in the butt. Uncle Andrew told about how his daughter Letty was learning to read and write real good and that I ought to learn it too. Me, I was all for it. He said they had a surveyor feller with the new railroad that was running by Coldstream who was teaching the younguns thereabouts their ABCs and stuff. Said the man wanted to git out of railroad work because he hated traveling around and that he wanted to set up a full-scale school at Coldstream. So, anyway, it was decided by Uncle Achan and Aunt Gustine and Uncle Andrew and them other Lamley uncles that I ought to come over here and live with Uncle Andrew and Aunt Elvira and learn my ABCs with my cousins and the other kids. And that was how I come to live over here and here I been ever since.

Well, that schooling part went okay for a few months and then that surveyor feller, Mr. Bailey, was up and transferred out by the railroad to somewhere else and that was the end of my schooling. But at least I had my ABCs by then and could read a smidgin and figure some figures and from then on out I went on and learned more by my own self after I growed up.

That great-big cypress over there, where the bayou starts to turn this way? Well, up that rise from it, that's where Uncle Andrew's house used to be, and from where we're sitting now you couldn't of seen it in them days for all the trees. That house was pretty big even for them days. It was log-built with four

266

rooms connected by a dog-trot to four more rooms. It had a wide front porch and a little bitty back porch and the whole thing was set high up on cypress blocks and covered on the outside with cypress shingles. There was a lot of out buildings too, a barn, a cow shed, a corncrib, and a pigpen. Now you can't hardly see a single sign of none of it, for shore none of the oak and gumball trees that covered the whole place. But if you look close from here, you can see a couple of apple trees that's gone wild mixed in that thicket that runs alongside that ditch going into the bayou. That's all that's left of the fruit orchard Uncle Andrew had in his backyard. One time about ten years ago, I walked around up there, looking at the plowed ground, and I picked up a handful of them old-timey square nails. They was all bent and eat up with rust and not good for nothing anymore. But I still got them in a coffee can that I keep on my bedstand.

Now this bayou here, I spent many a day in there when I was little, getting my tail end wet frogging after crawdads and shiners, and when I got bigger I trapped and fished and hunted all up and down it, clean down to Muddy. I have took many a coon and possum and rabbit out of them bayou woods and snagged many a bass and cat and buffalo with my trapboxes and trotlines. Now you look out there and what do you see? Nothing but a handful of cypress and a soybean field that stays too damp most of the year-round for that fool Eustace Tanner to get much more than a sorry crop out of. That Tanner. He's a sight. Like most of his kin, he's a man that's so stingy and selfish and shifty that he has to lock his tools up every night so he won't steal them off of hisself. It was all a sight better when it was all bayou woods down there.

Uncle Andrew was looked on as our chief around here when I was a boy, but we never called him that. I mean we never made a point of just flat out calling him chief. He just was. He was your great-great granddaddy, and he wudn't actually my uncle at all. What he was, he was a cousin. But I called him uncle all the same and even sort of looked up to him like the daddy I never had. He farmed quite a bit of cotton and corn and had some livestock that run wild in the woods until we needed some beef or ham or a horse to ride. People used to say that he was better at farming than most of the white farmers around here even, and you might not believe it but that's saying something for shore since it's been my notice that white people always act like they invented farming and things like that. Uncle Andrew was married to Elvira Squirrel, who was Quapaw Indian and close kin to Lamley and Tyrell folks. Uncle Andrew, as you know, was close to being a full-blood Indian hisself. He was almost half-Chickasaw and full half-Cherokee. Him and Aunt Elvira had two girls. There was Letty, who was eight when I came over here to live with them, and there was Marandy, who was already a grown woman and married and with a family of her own. Marandy and her husband lived further off down the bayou a ways, but still in yelling distance of our house. Uncle Andrew and Aunt Elvira had a boy too, I think I heard one time, but he died when he was little and so I never knowed him.

This was all Thompson land that Uncle Andrew farmed. It belonged to his and Aunt Minnie's and Aunt Velma's daddy, and they say that just before he died, he—old Alluk, their daddy—put it all in Uncle Andrew's name because in them days women couldn't hold title to land. Matter of fact, Indians wudn't suppose to neither. I heard it told that old Alluk got around that prejudice by his out and out oneryness and by out-whiting the whites. He donated money to both the Coldstream Baptist Church and the Coldstream Cumberland Presbyterian one that has long since gone out of business, and he never even set foot in neither one of them. This was before the Methodist one come along that Aunt Elvira and Marandy joined up with. Old Alluk bought this section sometime back in the 1840's and moved here from Bonaparte. It was after he died and Uncle Andrew and Aunt Elvira got married and started their family that all the assorted Squirrel and Tyrell kin started moving in over here.

But even if all the outside folks counted Uncle Andrew as our leader, it was really my two aunts, Aunt Minnie and Aunt Velma, who was the real head of our folks. Since Arkansas law in them days had it that no woman—not even two women together—could own land in their own name, it was all in Uncle Andrew's name. Them aunts was old women even when I was a boy and they lived off down hereabouts on the bayou, off to theirselves. Two old-maid aunts they was, always good to me and passable pleasant to most other folks around here, but still at the same time they kept off by theirselves mostly. When I first came over here to live, they was medicine women and they did midwifing and stuff like that for all the folks around here. Over at Simms Bayou, Aunt Gustine and Uncle Achan was medicine people too, but they wudn't educated to it like Aunt Minnie and Aunt Velma was. And that wasn't all. Aunt Minnie and Aunt Velma was makers of spells and fixers of bones, what they used to call "putter-inners" and "taker-outers." This meant they was in a special kind of class as healers and was looked up to by mostly everybody around. And it wudn't just our folks that come to them for doctoring either. Sometimes white folks and niggers come to see them, too, when they needed help.

Back then, there wudn't no doctors—school trained white doctors I mean—around here like there is now. Some of the plantations started hiring doctors a little later on, but when I first come over here there wudn't none. The closest white doctor I knowed anything about was over at Delta City and he was a half-blind old drunk who was just as apt to saw you in two as to cut your britches leg off if you was to go see him to have him do something about your bad leg. They tell a story about how he doctored a cow with a whole mess of calomel when he got called out to somebody's house one time. I don't remember whose house and whose cow it was. The story goes that when that doctor got there and asked where the patient was, the man whose house he was at said, "She's on back there in that-ter back room, Doc," and so when the doc went on back he made a wrong turn or something and instead of going into the bedroom he winded up at a kind of lean-to shed they had there—a milk stall I 'spect it was—that was built on the back of the house. "She," so the doc must of thought, was the white-face cow they had tied back there and not the man's wife who was in the bedroom the whole time. Well, the doc guessed that the cow's belly was a little too swole up so he dosed her up real good with some calomel. They say that for a whole week that cow shit like a tied coon. And they also say that he never did git around to doctoring that sick woman.

So there was no doctors to speak of in these parts. Not unless a person wanted to go to a cow-doctoring old drunk over on the river at Delta City and that about twelve miles away. That, or travel sixty mile by train to Pine Bluff, but even then to go by train to Pine Bluff, you would of had to go clear out to Monticello to catch the train. Or if a boat was handy, and I guess this would of been the most likely thing to do, you could go down and then cross the river to Greenville where two or three school trained white doctors was. But folks around here in them days wudn't likely to do things that way. They was all—white, colored, Indian—pretty hard-working folks, farmers and loggers and hunters and fishermen, folks not known to have much in the way of cash on them or a whole lot of time on their hands for traveling. So when it come to patching up torn-up bodies and dosing whooping cough and such-like, why they had to make do with what they had. My two aunts was Indian medicine-makers, taught by their own aunt who was, so I been told, a full-blood Deer Clan Cherokee woman who come into these parts from the old country back east when the government started pushing Indians off of their lands, and they knowed a heap about doctoring and so folks just naturally come to them for help.

Aunt Minnie and Aunt Velma was Cherokee. Well, they was and they wudn't. What I mean is their mama was Cherokee, Deer Clan, like that older medicine-maker sister of hers whose name I never knowed except that I remember that an older cousin of mine sometime just called her Deer Woman and that she was a Sendforth. Their granddaddy, Aunt Minnie's and Aunt Velma's, was an Indian who somehow got his name listed on the government enrolling census as Sendforth because I 'spect he likely considered hisself and his family too as them that was sent forth from their homeland. Anyhow, that's where my name come from. My granddaddy, the son of the Sendforth I'm talking about, he changed it to Sandford, and according to Uncle Andrew, it was my mama who spelled it Sanford, dropping one of the "d's." I guess maybe I'm expected to change it up some too, since it seems like that's what the tradition calls for. Only I won't. I'm satisfied with it just the way it is. Always remember this: we ain't the people our granddaddies and grandmas was. I know that real good and so I guess I just don't have the gumption to change my name any like they done.

As I done said, Aunt Minnie and Aunt Velma's daddy was old Alluk Thompson. He was a Chickasaw man from Mississippi and he come into these parts about the time Arkansas become a territory, settling down first at Bonaparte, then over at Simms Bayou, and then finally over here. Now Bonaparte, in case you don't know it, was a pretty good-sized river town back then, like Delta City is now, only even bigger, and it was knowed far and wide for its saloons and bawdy houses and gambling dens. It was kind of like the way the south side of Pine Bluff is these days, except that it would of made Pine Bluff look like a Sunday School class if the two was to be put upside each other and looked at. Bonaparte is long gone. When I was still just a little-bitty squirt, it was washed away. I can still remember when it happened. There come a big flood and it was entirely washed off the face of the land. All its buildings and streets and stores and pest-houses and filth and meanness was swept clean away by the Mississippi. I 'spect Bonaparte might be found somewheres down in the Gulf of Mexico now, mayored over and sheriffed over by big catfishes talking Mexican. Wouldn't faze me a bit to hear it.

Now, old Alluk's wife died while they was still living in Bonaparte, a long time before the flood come, and when she did, he come up and moved to Simms Bayou where there was other Indian folks living, taking with him when he moved Aunt Minnie and Aunt Velma, who was just little girls then, and a whole passel of assorted kinfolks. Old Alluk stayed at Simms Bayou just about a year, long enough to sell off his holdings in and around Bonaparte. Then he up and moved over here, buying this section when there wudn't no more than a handful of people in the whole township. That old aunt come with them, too, and she was by that time a kind of substitute mama to Aunt Minnie and Aunt Velma as well as their medicine teacher. The story goes that she hated old Alluk like rat poison, but that she come along on the move to help bring up the girls and Uncle Andrew, too, who was just a little-bitty kid then, and even then she wouldn't live in the same house with him. She lived off by herself in the woods a ways and, as I heard it, would never set foot in Alluk's house as long as he was around and would never talk nothing but Cherokee to them girls and Uncle Andrew, or for that matter to other folks neither when she even bothered to talk to other people at all. I can just barely remember that older aunt, who I calculate would of been my great-great aunt. She was always a shadowy person to me, just like my memory of her is now, and I remember her as the oldest person I think I ever seen or even knowed about. So even if Aunt Minnie and Aunt Velma was almost half-Chickasaw as well as being half-Cherokee, they was really more Cherokee in their ways because of that older aunt's influence on them. That woman just straight out took them girls away from their daddy, but like some older folks was in the habit of saying when I was a boy, that had been the best thing that could of happened to them. There had been some talk, all a long, long time before I was even borned, that my aunts had been wayward and wild some before they moved away from Bonaparte and Simms Bayou and come over here, especially with that white-trash element there was around at Bonaparte. Whatever the story was, that old aunt took over care of them and brung them up proper in a good Indian way. She, who had spent just about all her whole life taking care of them or some other Thompson or other kin and never getting married to nobody, just like her nieces in their time would never wed nobody either, left her impression on them girls just as sure and certain as a candle mold does when you go and pour a dab of hot wax on it.

. . . because I believe that all this forever afterwards will be the key to who you going to be and what you make out of yourself to be. It ain't no real never-mind at all whether you stay living around here the rest of your life, or whether you move off to somewheres else. You this place and this place is you. Don't ever forgit it, son.

WATER WITCH

Louis Owens

According to Choctaw and Cherokee traditions, rivers are *sacred, living beings with destinies of their own. In this personal essay, Louis Owens remembers his father, a man who knew rivers and their secret hiding places deep within the earth. Owens shares his childhood memories of California's Salinas River, whose presence captured his imagination.*

Louis Owens, of Choctaw, Cherokee, and Irish ancestry, is a professor of literature at the University of California, Santa Cruz. His novel The Sharpest Sight *is also set in the Salinas Valley. He has recently published a critical work entitled* Other Destinies: Understanding the American Indian Novel.

FOR A WHILE, WHEN I WAS VERY YOUNG, MY FATHER WAS A WATER witch. He took us with him sometimes, my older brother and me, and we walked those burned-up central California ranches, wherever there was a low spot that a crop-and-cattle desperate rancher could associate with a dream of wetness. The dusty windmills with their tin blades like pale flowers would be turning tiredly or just creaking windward now and then, and the ranch dogs—always long-haired, brown and black with friendly eyes—would sweep their tails around from a respectful distance. The ranches, scattered near places like Creston, Pozo, San Miguel, and San Ardo, stretched across burnt gold hills, the little ranch houses bent into themselves beneath a few dried up cottonwoods or sycamores, some white oaks if the rancher's grand-

273

father had settled early enough to choose his spot. Usually there would be kids, three or four ranging from diapers to hotrod pickups, and like the friendly ranch dogs they'd keep their distance. The cattle would hang close to the fences, eyeing the house and gray barn. In the sky, red-tailed hawks wheeled against a washed-out sun while ground squirrels whistled warnings from the grain stubble.

He'd walk, steps measured as if the earth demanded measure, the willow fork held in both hands before him pointed at the ground like some kind of offering. We'd follow a few yards behind with measured paces. And nearly always the wand would finally tremble, dip and dance toward the dead wild oats, and he would stop to drive a stick into the ground or pile a few rock-dry clods in a cairn.

A displaced Mississippi Choctaw, half-breed, squat and reddish, blind in one eye, he'd spit tobacco juice at the stick or cairn and turn back toward the house, feeling maybe the stirring of Yazoo mud from the river of his birth as if the water he never merely discovered, but drew all that way from a darker, damper world. Within a few days he'd be back with his boss and they'd drill a well at the spot he'd marked. Not once did the water fail, but always it was hidden and secret, for that was the way of water in our part of California.

When I think now of growing up in that country, the southern end of the Salinas Valley, a single mountain range from the ocean, I remember first the great hidden water, the Salinas River which ran out of the Santa Lucias and disappeared where the coastal mountains bent inland near San Luis Obispo. Dammed at its headwaters into a large reservoir where we caught bluegill and catfish, the river never had a chance. Past the spillway gorge, it sank into itself and became the largest subterranean river on the continent, a half-mile-wide swath of brush and sand and cottonwoods with a current you could feel down there beneath your feet when you hunted the river bottom, as if a water witch yourself, you swayed at every step toward the stream below.

We lived first in withdrawn canyons in the Santa Lucias, miles up dirt roads into the creases of the Coast Range where we kids squirmed through buck brush and plotted long hunts to the ocean. But there were no trails and the manzanita would turn us back with what we thought must be the scent of the sea in our nostrils. Rattlesnakes, bears and mountain lions lived back there. And stories of mythic wild boars drifted down from ranches to the north. In the spring the hills would shine with new grass and the dry creeks would run for a few brief weeks. We'd hike across a ridge to ride wild horses belonging to a man who never knew that the kids rode them. In summer the grasses burned brown and the clumps of live oaks on the hillsides formed dark places in the distance.

Later we lived down in the valley on the caving banks of the river. At six and eight years we had hunted with slingshots in the mountains, but at ten and twelve we owned rifles, .22s, and we stalked the dry river brush for quail and cottontails and the little brush rabbits that, like the pack rats, were everywhere. Now and then a deer would break ahead of us, crashing thickets like the bear himself. Great horned owls lived there and called in drumming voices, vague warnings of death somewhere. From the river bottom we pinged .22 slugs off new farm equipment gliding past on the flatcars of the Southern Pacific.

Once in a while, we'd return to Mississippi, as if my father's mixed blood sought a balance never found. Seven kids, a dog or two, canvas water bags swaying from fender and radiator, we drove into what I remember as the darkness of the Natchez Trace. In our two-room Mississippi cabin, daddy longlegs crawled across the tar papered walls, and cotton fields surged close on three sides. Across the rutted road through a tangle of tree, brush, and vine, fragrant of rot and death, was the Yazoo River, a thick current cutting us off from the swamps that boomed and cracked all night from the other shore.

From the Yazoo we must have learned to feel water as a presence, a constant, a secret source of both dream and nightmare, perhaps as my father's Choctaw ancestors had. I remember it as I remember night. Always we'd return to California after a few months, as much as a year. And it would be an emergence, for the Salinas was a daylight world of hot, white sand and bone-dry brush, where in the fall, red and gold leaves covered the sand, and frost made silver lines from earth to sky. Here, death and decay seemed unrelated things. And here, I imagined the water as a clear, cold stream through white sand beneath my feet.

Only in the winter did the Salinas change. When the rains came pounding down out of the Coast Range, the river would rise from its bed to become a half-mile-wide terror, sweeping away chicken coops and misplaced barns; whatever had crept too near. Tricked each year into death, steelhead trout would dash upstream from the ocean, and almost immediately the flooding river would recede to a thin stream at the heart of the dry bed, then a few pools marked by the tracks of coons, then only sand again and the tails and bones of big fish.

When I think of growing up in California, I think always of the river. It seemed then that all life referred to the one hundred and twenty miles of sand and brush that twisted its way north-ward, an upside-down, backwards river that emptied into the Pacific near Monterey, a place I didn't see till I was grown. As teenagers, my brother and I bought our own rifles, a .30-.30 and an ought-six, and we followed our father into the Coast Range after deer and wild boar. We acquired shotguns and walked the high coastal ridges for bandtail pigeon. We drove to fish the headwaters of the Nacimiento and San Antonio rivers. And from every ridge top we saw, if not the river itself, then the long, slow course of the valley it had carved, the Salinas. Far across were the rolling Gabilan Mountains, more hawk hills than mountains, and on the valley bottom, ranches made squares of green and gold with flashing windmills and tin roofs.

After school and during summers we worked on the ranches, hoeing sugar beets, building fences, bucking hay, working cattle (dehorning, castrating, branding, ear-clipping, innoculating, all in what must have seemed a single horrific moment for the bawling calf). We'd cross the river to drive at dawn through the dry country watching the clumps of live oak separate from the graying hillsides. Moving shadows would become deer that drifted from dark to dark. Years later, coming home from an-other state, I would time my drive so that I reached that country at daybreak to watch the oaks rise out of night and to smell the damp dead grasses.

Snaking its way down through our little town was a creek. Dipping out of the Coast Range, sliding past chicken farms and country stores, it pooled in long, shadowed clefts beneath the shoulders of hills and dug its own miniature canyon as it passed by the high school, beneath U.S. 101, around the flanks of the county hospital and on to the river where it gathered in a final welling before sinking into the sand. Enroute it picked up the sweat and stink of a small town, the flotsam and jetsam of stunted aspirations, and along its course in tree shadow and root tangle, under cutbank and log, it hid small, dark trout we caught with hook and handline. From the creek came also steelhead trapped by a vanished river, and great blimp-bellied suckers which hunkered close to the bottom, even a single outraged bull-head which I returned to its solitary pool. At the place where the chicken-processing plant disgorged a yellow stream into the creek, the trout grew fat and sluggish, easily caught. We learned every shading and wrinkle of the creek, not knowing then that it was on the edge already, its years numbered. I more than anyone, fisher of tainted trout, kept what I thought of as a pact with the dying creek: as long as the water flows and the grass grows.

Up on Pine Mountain, not so much looming as leaning over the town of my younger years, a well-kept cemetery casts a wide shadow. From this cemetery, one fine summer evening, a local youth exhumed his grandmother to drive about town with her draped across the hood of his car, an act so shocking no punishment could be brought to bear. Later, when I asked him why, he looked at me in wonder. "Didn't you ever want to do that?" he asked. That fall, after a bitter football loss, members of the high-school letterman's club kidnapped a bus full of rooters from a rival school, holding them briefly at gunpoint with threats of execution. The summer before, an acquaintance of mine had stolen a small plane and dive-bombed the town's hamburger stand with empty beer bottles. The town laughed. Later, he caught a Greyhound bus to Oregon, bought a shotgun in a small town, and killed himself. It was that kind of place also. Stagnant between Coast Range and river, the town, too, had subterranean currents, a hot-in-summer, cold-in-winter kind of submerged violence that rippled the surface again and again. Desires to exhume and punish grew strong. Escape was just around a corner.

Behind the cemetery, deep in a wrinkle of the mountain, was an older burial ground, the town's original graveyard, tumbled and hidden in long grasses and falling oaks. Parting the gray oat stalks to read the ancient stone, I felt back then as astonished as a Japanese soldier must have when he first heard the words of a Navajo code talker. Here was a language that pricked through time, millenia perhaps, with painful familiarity but one that remained inexorably remote.

A year ago, I drove back to the house nine of us had lived in on the banks of the river. The house was gone, and behind the empty lot the river had changed. Where there had been a wilderness of brush and cottonwoods was now only a wide, empty channel gleaming like bone. Alfalfa fields swept coolly up from the opposite bank toward a modern ranch house. "Flood control" someone in the new Denny's restaurant told me later that afternoon. "Cleaned her out clear to San Miguel," he said.

GRACE

Vicki L. Sears

For many Native American children in the foster care system, incidents of physical abuse are often compounded by psychological assaults of racial and cultural bigotry. Vicki Sears's short story, "Grace," demonstrates that the Trail of Tears is not yet over for Native American people. The personal suffering endured by nine-year-old Jody Ann and her younger brother acts as a mirror for the historical and contemporary abuse, disruption, and dislocation of Native American people in North America.

Vickie L. Sears (Cherokee) is a writer, storyteller, and psychotherapist. She currently lives and works in Seattle, Washington.

I THOUGHT WE WERE GOING TO ANOTHER FARM BECAUSE IT WAS time for spring planting. But the lady, she said we were going to be her children. You know how it is grownups talk. You can't trust them for nothing. I just kept telling my brother that we best keep thinking of ourselves as orphans. Our parents got a divorce and we don't know where they are, so we need to keep our thinking straight and not get fooled by this lady. I don't care if her skin is brown just like us, that don't mean nothing.

I hear my brother dozing off to sleep and I want to shake him, wake up, but these people are driving this truck and they can hear everything I say anyhow, so I just let him sleep.

This is the second time we've been riding in this old beat-up green pickup. The first time they came and got us from the children's home they took us down to Pioneer Square. I could see right away they was farm people by the truck having straw in the back and them not having real good clothes, like they wear in the city. City people talk more too. These people were real quiet right off. They answered the questions the orphanage people asked them but they didn't tell them much of anything. I guess I liked that some, but I wasn't going to tell them nothing about me. Who knew what they'd do? We never went nowheres before with brown people.

The man, he had on bluejeans and a flannel shirt and a jean jacket. His hat was all sweaty and beat up like his long skinny face. His boots was old, too. I guessed they didn't have much money and were needing to get some kids to help them with their work. Probably we'd stay with them until harvest time and then go back to the orphanage. That happened before, so it didn't matter much anyhow.

The woman was old and skinny. She had hands what was all chewed up and fat at the knuckles and she kept rubbing them all the time. She had white hair with little bits of black ones popping out like they was sorry to be in there by themselves. She had a big nose like our daddy has, if he still is alive, that is. She and the man was brown and talked like my daddy's mother, Grandmother, she talks kind of slow and not so much in English. These people, though, they talked English. They just didn't talk much.

When they said they was going to take us downtown I thought they was going to take us to a tavern because that's where the orphanage lady took me real late one night, to show me where all the Indian women was and what kind of people they are, always being drunk and laying up with men. That woman said that is all us Indian girls like to do and I will be just like that too, so I thought that's where these people would take us, but they didn't. They took us to dinner at this real nice place and let us have soda pop and even bought us a dessert. Me and Brother both got us apple pie, with ice cream, all to ourselves. I started thinking maybe these people are okay, but a part inside of me told me I best not get myself fooled. So I told them they wouldn't want us to live with them because my brother is a sissy and I'm a tomboy. But the lady said, "We like tomboys and Billie Jim looks like he is a strong boy. You both look just fine to us." Then they took us to walk in the square and we stopped by this totem pole. The orphanage lady told me that pole was a pretend God and that was wrong because God was up in heaven and the Indian people was bad who made the pole. This lady, though, she said that the totem pole was to make a song about the dead people and animals and that it was a good and beautiful thing. She had Brother and me feel the inside of the pole. Like listening to its belly. I don't know what she meant by that, but the wood was nice. I liked better what she said about the pole.

We walked around for a while and then they took us back to the orphanage. The lady said they would come back, when all the paper work was done, to get Brother and me, but I thought she was just talking big, so I said "Sure," and me and Brother went inside. We watched them drive away. I didn't think they would come back, but I thought about them being brown just like my daddy and aunts and uncles and Brother and me. They were more brown than us, but I wondered if they were Indian. They didn't drink, though, so maybe not.

We didn't see those people for a long time. Brother and me went to a big house to help clean for spring coming. I don't see why you clean a house so good just because the seasons change, but we done that anyway and then went back to the orphanage. I kept thinking on how nice those farmers were and how they might be Indians, but I didn't want to ask anybody about them. Maybe, if it was for real that they were going to come back for us, it would spoil it to ask about them. Seems like you don't ever get things just because you want them so it's better not to ask.

Then, one day, one of the matrons comes to tell me to find Billie Jim because there are some people come to visit.

My brother was up in a tree hiding from some of the big boys. First, I had to beat up Joey so's he would let Billie Jim come out the tree. We rolled in the dirt fighting and I knew I was going to be in trouble because I was all dirty and there was blood on my face. I thought I would get whomped too for getting in a fight. I spit on my hand to try to clean up my face,

but I could see by the scowl on the matron's face that I didn't
look so good. I pushed Brother in front of me because he was
clean and maybe the people wouldn't see me so much. We went
into the visiting room and I saw it was those farmers whose
names I didn't remember. They asked the boss man of the home
if they could take us now. He said, "Yes. It's so nice to place
these 'special' children. I hope they'll be everything you want."

The man reached out his hand and the farmer brought his
long arm out his sleeve. The orphanage man pumped his arm
up and down, but the farmer just held his still. It was funny to
see. The woman, she just barely touched the hand of the man.
She was not smiling. I thought something was wrong, but I
knew we were going with these people anyhow. I never cared
much about where I went, long as the people didn't beat on us
with sticks and big belts.

We didn't have to do nothing to get ready because we found
our suitcases in the hall by the bottom of the stairs. The boss
man gave Brother and me our coats and said, "You be good
children and perhaps we won't have to see you here again."

I wanted to tell him I didn't like him, but I just took Brother's
hand and we went out the door.

The people went to lots of stores downtown and then we
went to lunch again.

I asked them, "Do you use a stick or strap for spanking?"

The man said, "We don't believe in spanking."

Before I could say anything, Billie Jim pinched me under the
table and I knew he had to go bathroom. So I said, "Excuse
us," and we got up to leave. The lady, she asked Billie Jim,
"Do you have to go to the bathroom?"

Brother just shook his head and the woman said, "Paul, you
take him."

They left and I worried about Paul messing with Billie Jim.
My stomach felt all like throw up. When they came back, I
asked Billie Jim, in our secret way, if something happened and
he whispered no.

I wondered if these people were going to be all right, but I
kept on guard because grownups do weird things all the time,
when you never know they're going to.

After we ate, we walked and stopped at this drinking fountain what is a statue of Chief Sealth. Paul, he told us what a great man Sealth was and Billie Jim asked, "You know him?"

Both Paul and the woman laughed and Paul said, "No. He lived a long time ago. He's a stranger with a good heart."

Then the woman reached down to take my hand, but I didn't want her to get me, so I told her I had to take care of my brother and took Billie Jim's hand.

So then we were riding in this truck going to some place I never heard of, called Walla Walla. Grace, that's the lady's name, said they lived on a farm with chickens, pigs, a horse, and lots of things growing. She said we can have a place all our very own to grow things. When I sat down next to her, she let me ride by the window. I seen how my legs didn't touch the floor and how long hers were. She wasn't as long as her husband, but way bigger than me. She put my brother in her lap where he went to sleep, with his chubby fingers in her hand, but I stood guard just in case things got weird. Paul said I should help him drive home by looking at the map so he'd know the roads he was going on. I thought that was dumb because I knew he came to the city lots and must know how to get hisself home. I went along with him though, because he seemed to be nice and it was easy for me. I can read real good cause I'm nine years old. I told him that and see that Grace is smiling. She's got wrinkles that come out the corners of her eyes and more that go down her cheeks. She has on a smelly powder that reminds me of cookies. She says that there are lots of other children in neighbors' farms and that they have grandchildren who visit them lots. I guessed I would have to do lots of babysitting.

It's a long long ways to where they live and I couldn't stay awake the whole time. I woke up when Grace said, "Come on, sleepy heads. It's time to go to bed."

She gave my brother to Paul to carry, but I walked by myself, up one step into the house. We went through the kitchen, up some stairs, to the second floor with four bedrooms and a bathroom. She asked me if I have to go to the bathroom and I said yes. She showed me it and then closed the door. That's funny because she didn't stay. After a while, she came to knock and say, "There's a nightgown on your bed. I'll show you where you will sleep."

She took me to a room with only one bed with nobody else in it. I asked her, "Where's Brother going to sleep?"

Grace tried to take my hand to go with her, but I put it behind my back and followed her. She led me down the hall to a room where Billie Jim was already in a bed, all by hisself, sound asleep. Then we went to a room Grace said was for her and Paul and said I could come there if I'm scared or having a bad dream.

I told her, "I don't never have bad dreams and can take care of myself."

She asked me, "May I help you with your nightgown?"

Then I knew she was going to do bad things like the orphanage woman and I wanted to grab Billie Jim and run, but I didn't know where I was. I started to back down to where she said to sleep and she said, "It's all right if you don't want any help. Have a good sleep."

She went into her room and I watched until she closed the door. There was a lamp beside the bed and I slept with it on.

The first thing I did the next morning was check on Billie Jim. I asked him if they messed with him and he said no again. Nobody came into the room I was in either. We got dressed together and then went downstairs. Already Paul and Grace were up and at the breakfast table.

Grace asked, "What would you like for breakfast? Pancakes or bacon and eggs?"

Billie Jim said, "We can pick?"

"Sure," Grace said, "all you have to do is to wash your face and hands before coming to table. Can't have you start the day with a dirty face."

We looked on each other and saw we was dirty.

Grace said, "There's a pump here, if you want, or you can go upstairs to the bathroom."

We wanted to use that red pump with the very high handle. I tried to make it give water, but Grace thought she had to help push it down. She put her hand over mine but I moved mine. She smiled though, so I let her pump the water into a tin basin and give me a big brown bar of soap. She said she made it out of pig fat. It smelled icky but it made lots of bubbles.

After we ate, Paul said, "Come on, kids. I'll introduce you to our animal friends."

He put on his hat and opened the green screen door. There wasn't no grass nowhere. Just dirt, except where there was tall stuff growing. Paul told us it was alfalfa and wheat and that it got really high before you cut it. He took us into the barn to show us Henry, who was this old horse what lived there forever.

Out back of the barn was a pen with big fat pigs and a mommy one with some babies. I didn't like them much, but Billie Jim asked if he can touch them and Paul said, "Sure," so Billie Jim went into the pen and one of them pigs ran after him so Billie Jim screamed and the pig pushed him up against the barn wall so Paul had to chase the pig away. Billie Jim done good though and didn't even cry.

Paul walked us to the chicken house and showed us Rhode Island Reds and bantams. He taught us how to fill a basket with eggs by taking them out from under the chickens. I thought the chickens was mean, though, because they tried to bite us. Paul laughed and said as how it will get easier to do. Then we met the cows and Paul tried to teach us to milk them. I couldn't make nothing come out, though Billie Jim got a little. The warm milk tasked icky. We walked all over the place that morning and then we got to ride on a tractor with Paul for a long time.

I was sleepy, but Billie Jim wanted to do more things, so we went down to this wooden bridge which went over this river that Paul showed to us. He said we should be very careful to not fall into the river because it was very fast and we would be drownded.

Down to the bridge, I layed on my tummy and Billie Jim was on his and we poked at knotholes in the wood. The water was so fast it went around and around while it was going all wavery at the same time. When we put sticks through the knotholes, the water would just pull them right away like it was never going get fed another stick. We did that a long time until we heard Grace calling us to lunch.

At the lunch table I asked, "When will we start doing the work we came to do?"

Paul and Grace looked on each other as though I had asked something stupid and then they smiled.

Paul said, "You came to live with us to be just like one of our children. You will have lots of time to play and go to school. You'll have some chores because everybody on a farm has to work. One of you will help feed the chickens. One of you can care for the pigs. You can both help with Henry, and there'll be times when you can ride Henry, all by yourselves, into the woods or across the fields, after you learn to ride him. Other times we will all go to town or picnics or pow-wows or rodeos. Everybody has to have time to play. That's the way it is."

Then Grace said, "I'll teach you how to sew and can and cook, Jodi Ann. You and I will go on special walks and plant a garden together. You too, Billie Jim, if you want. I want us to be friends and happy together."

I heard everything they had to say, but I was waiting, too, for the strange things I was sure they would do. I meant to keep my ears and eyes open just in case we needed to run somewheres.

About three days after going to her house, Grace tells us at breakfast table that, "Today is a good day to plant the garden. What would you like to grow, Billie Jim?"

"Potatoes an' rhubarb!" he says, all excited.

Then she asks me and I said, "Carrots and string beans, ma'am, because they're red and green. It'd be pretty."

She patted my shoulder and said, "Yes, it would be lovely. That's nice you can see that, Jodi."

I put my head down so she wouldn't see me smile.

Grace got this basket with lots of little envelopes and told us, "Come on."

We went outside, round to the side of the house. Paul was waiting, sitting on his tractor. He said, "It's all turned over for you."

Grace said, "Thank you, Paul," to him, and to us she said, "Here's two places for each of you. I'll go down to the other end."

She moved to her place and went down to the ground on knees and hands. Billie Jim and me just stood there because we never planted nothing before. She gave us some envelopes which shook with stuff, but they didn't mean nothing to us. Grace saw us standing and asked, "Have you children ever planted things?"

We shook our heads no so she came over and give us little shovels, like spoons, and took hers and made a little hole and put in a seed and covered it over with dirt. Then she put water on the place. She said, "You just do it like that, all in rows. Then you put the envelope on a stick here at the back of where you're planting. Then we wait for the rain and sunshine to help them grow."

She patted Brother on the hand and went back to where she was working.

We spent a long time doing gardening. The dirt felt good, like stored-up rain smells. We ate lunch by the garden and Grace said, "I think we deserve a walk. Let's go down by the river, kids."

Down to the river, Grace showed us different plants and birds. She knew a lot about birds. She told us the songs by making whistles through her teeth. She tried to show us how to do whistles with grass between her thumbs, but I think my teeth weren't big enough. Billie Jim didn't have a tooth in front, so he couldn't do it either. She showed us these grasses, too, that she said made baskets and we picked some. When we got back to her house, she put them in a big round pan, like for taking baths, and filled it up with water. That night she bit some grass apart with her teeth and showed me how to weave them in a basket. She thought I didn't know how to do this, but my grandmother already showed me before. I forgot some though, so my basket wasn't so good. She said, "You'll get better."

Grace read a story to us, then Billie Jim and me went to bed. When I was going to sleep, I thought on her telling about the birds.

One morning time I woke up extra early. The house was all quiet and I thought to go see some birds. I got dressed and went, real soft, down the stairs. I stopped on hearing noises in the kitchen. I crept up to the door and saw Grace putting water in the coffee pot, then poking embers in the stove. She went back to the sink and stood in the new sun coming in the window. She took one hand in the other and she rubbed on her swollen-up knuckles and all up and down her fingers. She put some stuff, what smelled like Vicks, all over her hands and slow rubbed her knuckles. Then she opened and closed her hands lots of times and rubbed more. She looked out the window the whole time, making a little smile all the time she was rubbing on her fingers. It looked like she done that lots of times before, so I stood still, so she didn't see me because the sun is so nice on her skin and shining in her hair, kind of like baby rainbows. I just wanted to watch. I did that for a long time and then made sounds like I was just coming down the stairs.

Grace said, "You're up very early, Jodi."

I said, "I wanted to go see birds and stuff."

She said, "If you want to come with me, I'll show you something magic."

She reached out her hand, but I put both arms behind my back and took hold of my own hands. She smiled and opened the door.

"We'll just take a walk over to alfalfa. I want to show you some colors."

We walked between the wheat and alfalfa, the air all swollen up with their sweetness. Grace pulled down a piece of alfalfa and said, "Smell."

It was all sharp and tickled inside my nose, kind of like medicine. It got dew on it and it landed on my cheek. Grace got some on her nose. I wanted to touch it, but didn't.

Grace said, "See the different colors?"

She ran a finger down the alfalfa and I saw there was places where it was real dark then lighter then sort of like limes are colored. I always thought it was all one color, but I was fooled. Grace did the same thing with the wheat and said, "And here's something else that's wonderful. Look what happens when the sun comes to the plants."

Grace moved them different ways and I saw the light changes the colors, too. It's almost like you can look right through them.

She said, "If we come back at lunch and suppertime, when

the sun is in a different place in the sky, they'll be different again. Do you want to?"

"Yeah!" I answered.

"Okay," she said. "It's just for you and me, though, Jodi."

Grace told me about the red-winged blackbird, what I never saw before, while we went back to the house.

Later, Grace called me and we went to see the colors again. They were changed. This time I saw, too, the little hairs each one had, what makes a wheat kernel, all full of lines and different parts just like people.

Then Grace said we had to go get a chicken for dinner. In the chicken yard, there was chickens scratching at the ground and picking in it for bugs. Their heads bobbed up and down and jerked from side to side. It was funny to watch them. Then, all of a sudden, they all ran to the coop. I didn't see no reason for it, but Grace pointed up in the sky and told me, "They see the shadow of the hawk. They're afraid, so they hide because they know hawks like to eat chickens."

The hawk circled awhile but went away and the chickens came back into the yard, scratching and clucking like nothing ever happened. Grace walked around in the yard, looking at all the birds, and finally spied one she liked. She chased it until she caught both the wings flat, with the chicken squawking the whole time we was walking to the clearing between the barn and house, to a stump where I had seen Paul split the kindling. Grace said, "You hold the chicken by the feet and give it a quick clean cut with the ax. Do you want to try it?"

I didn't never think on killing nothing to eat and didn't want to do it. I remembered the wild kitten I made friends with out in the tall grass back at the orphanage. I thought about how one of the orphanage matrons killed the kitten and hung it round my neck and told everybody I killed it. All day I had to wear the kitty, but I didn't cry. I just pretended like the kitty never was important. Now Grace wanted me to kill the chicken and I didn't want to, so I tried to back away, only she said, "I know you are strong enough to do this, Jodi."

She stuck out the handle to the hatchet, but I couldn't take it. I shook my head no and said, real quiet, "I don't want to, ma'am."

I backed up more and she said, "Well, we need supper. You watch and perhaps you'll be able to do it the next time."

Grace took that chicken and held it on the chopping block and chopped off the head so quick I almost didn't see her do it. I jumped back when the blood went flying everywhere, all hot-smelling in the sun, and making dark plops in the pale dust. She let the chicken go and picked up the head and threw it in the garbage. There wasn't no noise except chicken toenails making little scratches in the dry hard dirt and wings trying to fly when the chicken ran around and around. I didn't want to see it do that, but it was hard to stop looking. It ran in circles whole bunches of times and then just fell down, sort of jerking, till it stopped. That's when its eyes looked just like Popsickle kitty and my stomach felt like throw up and I wanted to run. Grace pulled out a big piece of string from her apron pocket and I knew it was going to be just like before, when she said, "Jodi, come on over. We'll string the chicken upside down and take off the feathers."

But I couldn't go near her. I yelled, "No!" and ran into the barn. I climbed the ladder and went behind some hay and pulled it all over me till nobody could see me and stayed real quiet. I sucked in air and didn't give it back. Grace came and called out, "Jodi, I'm sorry if I scared you. It's all right if you don't want to help. Jodi? You don't have to hide. It's all right."

But I was thinking on how I told a grown-up no and didn't do what she said. I knew I was going to get whipped. Paul and Grace would send me and Brother back because I was bad. Billie Jim was going to be all mad with me because we had to leave. Didn't nobody want to keep us if I'm bad and Brother and me most always went to places together.

I stayed in the hayloft a long time. Then I heard Paul and Brother calling me. They was yelling it was suppertime like nothing was wrong. I peeked through the slats of the door to the hayloft and saw Grace standing in the kitchen doorway. She didn't look mad. Paul and Billie Jim was holding hands, walking toward the fields, calling my name. Grace looked up to the barn like she knew I was there and started out to the barn.

I heard her shoes scrape on the rocks in the barn doorway,

when she stopped walking. She said, "Hello, old Henry. You need some water, friend?"

The bucket handle squeaked and there was walking. The yard pump handle went crank crank crank and then water gushed into the bucket. Footsteps came back and there was horse tongue slurping, like Henry was real thirsty.

Grace said, "You know, Henry, when I was little, I used to do some of my best thinking sitting in the grass up on a hill behind my house. I guess the best place now would be up in the hayloft. It's the most like a grassy hill right around here."

Then I heard the dry snaps of weighted wood as Grace bent the ladder steps coming up. She was puffing a little when she came to the loft ledge and climbed over. I peeked out the hay and saw her dangling her legs and making a hum.

"Yes sir, Henry, old friend," says Grace, "this feels almost like my hill. If I were little and scared, this might be just the place to come think. I guess I'd know I was in just about the safest place in the world. Everything would be all right up here. After I had things all sorted out, I could come down and run on home to Momma and know she loved me, no matter what."

That was the most I ever heard Grace say in one mouthful of talking. I still didn't make noise, though. She was talking big, but she was still a grown-up. She sat there awhile, swinging her legs and humming. Then she said, "Well, Henry, guess I'll go into the house. I'm getting cold and hungry."

Grace climbed down and I saw her go to the screen door. She stopped and called out, in a loud voice, "Jo-o-o-d-d-i-i!" She waited a little bit then went in the house.

I wanted to think nothing was going to happen, but I knew I was going to get whomped. I had been spending most of the day in the barn but couldn't think on nothing to do, except face the punishment. I went down the ladder and out the barn. I peeked around the corner of the parlor window. Billie Jim was listening to Charlie McCarthy on the radio. He was sitting in Paul's lap while Paul read the paper. Grace was rocking in her chair, knitting. She looked like my real grandmother except my grandmother is short. I missed my grandmother only thinking on her won't do no good so I went around to the back door and slammed it real loud, when I came into the house, and marched right to the living room. Billie Jim jumped up and ran to me and said, "You made us real worried. Where was you?"

He grabbed my arm, but I pulled away and said, "I don't know why you were worried. I was only up to the top of this grassy hill, what I found, thinking about things."

Grace put down her knitting and looked at me. I felt my heart running fast when she looked at Paul. He looked back on her for a little then said, "Was it a nice hill, Jodi?"

I knew I couldn't say no more lies without making spit in my mouth because my throat was all dried up and my tongue would stick and not make words, so I just shrugged a shoulder. Grace stood up and started coming toward me. I figured to just stay where I was to take the hit so I was getting ready. Instead, she said, "I'm glad you're home so we can eat supper. I hope you had a nice adventure too."

She reached me and my body was stiff with waiting, but her arms was out like she was going to hug me. I didn't back down and she closed her arms around me and hugged. I just stood there, still stiff, and she bent down to whisper in my ear. "You've got straw in your hair, Jodi." Then she patted me on the shoulder and we went to the kitchen.

While she was putting food on the platters, Grace said, "Jodi told me she doesn't like fried chicken much, so she doesn't have to eat any if she doesn't want. We even have two nice pork chops here, with mint jelly, just in case Jodi would rather not eat the chicken."

She turned around with a platter filled up with chicken and on the end was the pork chops. They tasted good with jelly. We never got that in the orphanage.

I watched Grace real good the rest of the time before bed, but she never said nothing about the chicken or me not being good. She never said nothing about it ever again.

The April we came in, turned into July with everybody just doing their work and playing too.

We met Jim and Sara and Crystal, Paul and Grace's kids. Between them three, they had twelve kids and, sometimes, everybody came over at once and cousins and other people too. Lots of times we cooked outside and sometimes we ate things we growed in the garden. It was just like at our Daddy's house a long time before, except there weren't no grandparents because Grace and Paul were the grandmother and grandfather. Their parents was dead.

We did lots of things together. Paul taught Brother to fish and both of us to swim. When Brother and him went away for fishing, Grace and me did beading. She showed me how to do beads in a circle. We made lots of things to take to pow-wows. I sold one I made, but Grace sold lots. I made two baskets I liked, but I kept them. We went to a pow-wow over to the reservation and one at White Swan and down to Oregon. Everybody in the family went, in all the trucks, lined up on the highways and we all stopped together to eat.

One day, Paul said to Grace. "Their hair is long enough now. I guess it's time."

Billie Jim looked at me across the table and motioned at me to come with him. He took his short legs up the stairs, as fast as he could, to the bathroom and said, "Hurry up, Jodi."

He only left the door barely open enough for me to squeeze after him and slammed and locked it.

He whisper-yells, "They're gonna cut our hair, Jodi! Don't let 'em do it! Please make 'em not do it, Jodi!"

I asked him, "How come you think they're going to do that, Billie Jim? This ain't the orphanage. They won't cut it off like there. Grace and Paul and everybody, almost, gots long hair."

"But Jodi Ann, didn't you listen when Paul said it was long enough? It means a cutting!"

I started to say more, but Paul called us to, "Come on downstairs, kids, and meet us outside."

We went downstairs and out the door and walked slow to where Grace was standing. She had her hands behind her back. Paul was rolling a big log from the woodpile toward where the chopping block was. Paul set the log up like the block and said, "Okay, kids, we have a surprise for you. Take your seats and face each other."

My stomach was sick and I started to think Billie Jim might be right. When we sat down, I looked on Billie Jim and knew how much of a little kid he was and how I was supposed to take care of him, but it felt like the best thing was to just run away.

Grace stood by me and Paul was by Billie Jim. Paul said, "Okay, Grace, count with me. Ready? One, two, three, now! Surprise!"

When they yelled surprise, all their arms go up and I jumped and grabbed Billie Jim, pulling him off the log, and we ran backwards.

Grace said, "Wait, Jodi! Look!"

In each of their hands were ribbons, streaming out in the breeze.

Paul said, "It's time to teach you how to braid your hair. Come on over."

We walked over, still holding hands, and Paul said, "Okay, now Jodi, you watch me while I do Billie Jim. Then Billie Jim can watch Grace and you."

They slow weaved the ribbons in the shiny black of our hair. In and out go hair and ribbon until the end, when there was just enough to tie the braid tight. We did it to each other until we was real good at it and sometimes Paul and Grace let us braid their hair. We all went to the next family picnic with ribbon braids.

Paul showed us how to ride and take care of Henry, too. We went lots of places all by ourselves on Henry. He never went too fast, but sometimes he tried to scrape us off on trees. Sometimes he liked to go through the barn door with the top part closed. One time he knocked me off and I didn't want to ride no more, but Grace said I got to because Henry would think he won something and wouldn't let me ever ride him again, so we got the box for me to stand on and I got back up.

I got to spend lots of time with Grace. Many mornings I watched her doing her finger rubs while seeing the morning coming, by peeking around the doorway. We went on walks together all the time. She taught me lots about flowers and birds. Most of the time just her and me went, but sometimes we let Brother come. I let her hold my hand sometimes too because it seemed like the bumps in her fingers felt better. Least she always smiled when I let her. She didn't squeeze my hand or put it in her tee-tee. She didn't never put her fingers in mine or play with Billie Jim's pee-pee. Neither did Paul. Brother and me both like that.

One day, Billie Jim and me was brushing Henry when Grace yelled, "Oh, Jodi and Billie Jim! Come see what Pickles is doing!"

We ran to the other side of the barn by the door, where hay was stacked. There was a big pile not in a bale, so Billie Jim and me could feed the cows and Henry, and there, in the middle of the pile, was Pickles, the cat. She was laying on Paul's bathrobe, sort of all crookedy on her side and making funny noises. Rufus the dog was sitting by her and sometimes Pickles hissed at him when he stuck his nose near her. That was funny to see cause they were friends.

I asked Grace, "What's the matter with Pickles?"

Billie Jim said, "She's sick, you dummy!"

I wanted to pinch him, but Grace took our hands, pulling us into the straw. She said, "You watch and something amazing is going to happen. Pickles is having babies."

We sat forever, but nothing happened except Grace talked real slow and stroked Pickles. Pickles made funny noises and her stomach swelled up and down and moved and she licked her bottom, but that's all. The screen door banged and Billie Jim jumped up, yelling, "I'm gonna get Paul!"

When he was gone, Grace asked, "What are you thinking, Jodi?"

I said, "I don't see how Pickles can make babies and, besides, it's boring."

Grace pulled me up to her lap and told me about how the babies got inside and growed and I thought it was icky and she said, "It takes a long time and lots of hard work to make something as special as a baby. Someday you might want to do it. Here, you pet Pickles too."

It felt good in Grace's lap and we stuck our arms out at the same time to pet Pickles.

Just about that time we heard a squishy noise with a grunt from Pickles. Then this icky stuff came squirting out and then Pickles acted like she couldn't get no air and was panting and then this kitten popped out in a white sack and Pickles bit it open and ate it up and licked the sticky stuff off the kitten. I heard what Grace said, but was thinking on not having no babies if I have to do that.

Billie Jim came back with Paul and Paul said, "Aa-a-y, that's where my bathrobe went. I couldn't find it this morning. You're doing a nice job, Pickles."

He pats her head and she meows to him.

Grace said, "Paul, you take Billie Jim for a walk and tell him some things."

Paul said, "We did that before we came out, Grace."

He put his arm on Billie Jim's shoulder and my brother was smiling like he was full up with something nobody ever knew before.

Paul said, "Let's all sit down together here."

All of us watched Pickles have two more kittens and then Grace said, "Well, it's time to give our new momma a rest. Billie Jim, you bring her some water. Jodi, you run get an egg and put it into a bowl. Rufus, you come inside with me before you get your nose scratched."

Billie Jim and me went lots of times to see Pickles that night. The kittens were all crawling on Pickles' tummy and pushing for milk and making soft cries while Pickles was licking their fur all soft clean. Grace was right that they were beautiful.

In August, everybody in the family came around every day for the harvest. It was real hard work. Brother and me helped too, but mostly the grown-ups did it. Grace and Sara and me cooked lots. Outside the air was all pale green and sort of fuzzy with little pieces of the cutted stuff filling the wind. It smelled real clean and wet even though it was hot days. I liked it except it made me sneeze. Grace said, "It's best if you stay inside, Jodi, and help with cooking. You can make your biscuits."

I made good biscuits. We all worked really hard.

One harvest day, it was after a big rain in the night, Billie Jim and me were playing Huckleberry Finn on these boards we made into a raft, in a pond in the bend of the road. All of a sudden, there was this high screaming sound and a long white ambulance coming down our road. It ran fast by us making mud fly all over. We ran after it, up to the house. Jim said, "Stay back kids. Give them room."

Some men went into the house and came back with Paul

sleeping in this bed they carried. Paul had a thing on his face with a bag going in and out like wind. Grace came behind him and she looked like she was going to throw up. They speeded away. Everybody else got in the green truck and we went to the hospital where we sat in a hall. Then came a medicine man who sang songs with his rattle, but the nurse people made him sit in the hall too. He didn't care though because he still sang real soft and, whenever there wasn't no nurse around, he went back in the room. After a long time, a doctor came to say, "Each of you can go in, two at a time." Then he went away.

Sara took me in and I see Grace was looking really sad so I look on Paul and knew he was dead. His skin felt all cold and he didn't have no smile. I couldn't think on what it meant. I wanted Grace to make it not be, but she just patted my hand. I wanted to hold hers, but she didn't do nothing but pat me.

A long time later, we went back to the house with Sara. Grace didn't come home for three days. When she saw Brother and me, she said, "Come into the living room, children. I need to talk with you."

Me and Billie Jean went in and Sara and Jim and Crystal were there too. Everybody was all quiet.

Grace said, "In a little while the county car will be here to pick you up because you are going back to the orphanage. They say I'm too old to keep you children by myself. I told them we would be just fine together, but they tell me a woman alone isn't enough. So you have to go."

Billie Jim asked, "Didn't we do enough work?"

I pinched him and he yelped so Grace took my hand and Billie Jim's too, then she said, "You're wonderful children, but they just won't let you stay. But you be strong an' make us all proud of you."

I wanted to run, but I didn't know how come.

Then Grace said, "Let Sara and Crystal help you while I rest here."

Nobody said nothing while we packed up. I saw a car coming what had writing on it. It was the kind that most always takes and gets us from foster homes. It stopped and the driver started honking. Billie Jim and me didn't walk too fast going downstairs, but didn't no one say we were bad because we were slow.

Everybody walked by us to say a goodbye except Grace. She took our hands to go out the back door. She knelt down and said "Ouch."

I asked her, "You hurt?"

She just said, "I knelt on a little rock, but it's okay. You be good children. Listen to the Creator like Paul told you and you'll stay strong."

Grace took Billie Jim in a hug and kissed him too. He squeezed her neck and I saw he was crying, but he didn't make no noise. Then she took both my hands. I looked on her big brown knuckles and didn't want to leave watching her in the sun. She hugged me real hard an' I hugged her too. We didn't say nothing and she stood up really slow.

The county man put us in the back seat and started to drive, right away. We both began to get up on our knees, to see out the back window, but the man yelled to us, "Sit down," so we did and we couldn't see nobody until we went over the bridge and turned onto the highway. Then we saw Grace, still standing still by the door, waving. Billie Jim and me held hands to wave too.

And that's the way it was.

Uncle Tony's Goat

Leslie Marmon Silko

In the matrilineal society of Laguna Pueblo, young boys are traditionally taught proper conduct, and corrected when they fall short of it, by their mother's brothers. In the following story, a young, mischievous boy learns some important lessons from his uncle about respect for animals, responsibility, love, and the interconnectedness of all life.

Best-selling author, poet, and essayist, Leslie Marmon Silko (Laguna) was born in 1948 and grew up at Laguna Pueblo in New Mexico. Of herself she writes, "I am of mixed-blood ancestry, but what I know is Laguna." Though Silko is perhaps best known for her widely acclaimed novel, Ceremony, she is also the author of Laguna Woman, a collection of poems, and Storyteller, a collection of fiction and poetry. She received a MacArthur Foundation award in 1981. Her most recent novel is Almanac of the Dead.

WE HAD A HARD TIME FINDING THE RIGHT KIND OF STRING TO USE. We knew we needed gut to string our bows the way the men did, but we were little kids and we didn't know how to get any. So Kenny went to his house and brought back a ball of white cotton string that his mother used to string red chili with. It was thick and soft and it didn't make very good bowstring. As soon as we got the bows made we sat down again on the sand bank above the stream and started skinning willow twigs for arrows. It was past noon, and the tall willows behind us made cool shade. There were lots of little minnows that day, flashing in the shallow water, swimming back and forth wildly like they weren't sure if they really wanted to go up or down the stream; it was a day for minnows that we were always hoping for—we could have filled our rusty coffee cans and old pickle jars full. But this was the first time for making bows and arrows, and the minnows weren't much different from the sand or the rocks now. The secret is the arrows. The ones we made were crooked, and when we shot them they didn't go straight—they flew around in arcs and curves; so we crawled through the leaves and branches, deep into the willow groves, looking for the best, the straightest willow branches. But even after we skinned the sticky wet bark from them and whittled the knobs off, they still weren't straight. Finally we went ahead and made notches at the end of each arrow to hook in the bowstring, and we started practicing, thinking maybe we could learn to shoot the crooked arrows straight.

We left the river, each of us with a handful of damp, yellow arrows and our fresh-skinned willow bows. We walked slowly and shot arrows at bushes, big rocks, and the juniper tree that grows by Pino's sheep pen. They were working better just like we had figured; they still didn't fly straight, but now we could compensate for that by the way we aimed them. We were going up to the church to shoot at the cats old Sister Julian kept outside the cloister. We didn't want to hurt anything, just to have new kinds of things to shoot at.

But before we got to the church we went past the grassy hill where my uncle Tony's goats were grazing. A few of them were lying down chewing their cud peacefully, and they didn't seem to notice us. The billy goat was lying down, but he was watching us closely like he already knew about little kids. He yellow goat eyes didn't blink, and he stared with a wide, hostile look. The grazing goats made good deer for our bows. We shot all our arrows at the nanny goats and their kids; they skipped away from the careening arrows and never lost the rhythm of their greedy chewing as they continued to nibble the weeds and grass on the hillside. The billy goat was lying there watching us and taking us into his memory. As we ran down the road toward the church and Sister Julian's cats, I looked back, and my uncle Tony's billy goat was still watching me.

My uncle and my father were sitting on the bench outside the house when we walked by. It was September now, and the farming was almost over, except for bringing home the melons and a few pumpkins. They were mending ropes and bridles and feeling the afternoon sun. We held our bows and arrows out in front of us so they could see them. My father smiled and kept braiding the strips of leather in his hands, but my uncle Tony put down the bridle and pieces of scrap leather he was working on and looked at each of us kids slowly. He was old, getting some white hair—he was my mother's oldest brother, the one that scolded us when we told lies or broke things.

"You'd better not be shooting at things," he said, "only at rocks or trees. Something will get hurt. Maybe even one of you."

We all nodded in agreement and tried to hold the bows and arrows less conspicuously down at our sides; when he turned back to his work we hurried away before he took the bows away from us like he did the time we made the slingshot. He caught us shooting rocks at an old wrecked car; its windows were all busted out anyway, but he took the slingshot away. I always wondered what he did with it and with the knives we made ourselves out of tin cans. When I was much older I asked my mother, "What did he ever do with those knives and sling-shots he took away from us?" She was kneading bread on the kitchen table at the time and was probably busy thinking about the fire in the oven outside. "I don't know," she said; "you ought to ask him yourself." But I never did. I thought about it lots of times, but I never did. It would have been like getting caught all over again.

The goats were valuable. We got milk and meat from them. My uncle was careful to see that all the goats were treated properly; the worst scolding my older sister ever got was when my mother caught her and some of her friends chasing the newborn kids. My mother kept saying over and over again, "It's a good thing I saw you; what if your uncle had seen you?" and even though we kids were very young then, we understood very well what she meant.

The billy goat never forgot the bows and arrows, even after the bows had cracked and split and the crooked, whittled arrows were all lost. This goat was big and black and important to my uncle Tony because he'd paid a lot to get him and because he wasn't an ordinary goat. Uncle Tony had bought him from a white man, and then he'd hauled him in the back of the pickup all the way from Quemado. And my uncle was the only person who could touch this goat. If a stranger or one of us kids got too near him, the mane on the billy goat's neck would stand on end and the goat would rear up on his hind legs and dance forward trying to reach the person with his long, spiral horns. This billy goat smelled bad, and none of us cared if we couldn't pet him. But my uncle took good care of this goat. The goat would let Uncle Tony brush him with the horse brush and scratch him around the base of his horns. Uncle Tony talked to the billy goat—in the morning when he unpenned the goats and in the evening when he gave them their hay and closed the gate for the night. I never paid too much attention to what he said to the billy goat; usually it was something like "Get up, big goat! You've slept long enough," or "Move over, big goat, and let the others have something to eat." And I think Uncle Tony was proud of the way the billy goat mounted the nannies, powerful and erect with the great black testicles swinging in rhythm between his hind legs.

We all had chores to do around home. My sister helped out around the house mostly, and I was supposed to carry water from the hydrant and bring in kindling. I helped my father look after the horses and pigs, and Uncle Tony milked the goats and fed them. One morning near the end of September I was out feeding the pigs their table scraps and pig mash; I'd given the pigs their food, and I was watching them squeal and snap at each other as they crowded into the feed trough. Behind me I could hear the milk squirting into the eight-pound lard pail that Uncle Tony used for milking.

When he finished milking he noticed me standing there; he motioned toward the goats still inside the pen. "Run the rest of them out," he said as he untied the two milk goats and carried the milk to the house.

I was seven years old, and I understood that everyone, including my uncle, expected me to handle more chores; so I hurried over to the goat pen and swung the tall wire gate open. The does and kids came prancing out. They trotted daintily past the pigpen and scattered out, intent on finding leaves and grass to eat. It wasn't until then I noticed that the billy goat hadn't come out of the little wooden shed inside the goat pen. I stood outside the pen and tried to look inside the wooden shelter, but it was still early and the morning sun left the inside of the shelter in deep shadow. I stood there for a while, hoping that he would come out by himself, but I realized that he'd recognized me and that he wouldn't come out. I understood right away what was happening and my fear of him was in my bowels and down my neck; I was shaking.

Finally my uncle came out of the house; it was time for breakfast. "What's wrong?" he called out from the door.

"The billy goat won't come out," I yelled back, hoping he would look disgusted and come do it himself.

"Get in there and get him out," he said as he went back into the house.

I looked around quickly for a stick or broom handle, or even a big rock, but I couldn't find anything. I walked into the pen slowly, concentrating on the darkness beyond the shed door; I circled to the back of the shed and kicked at the boards, hoping to make the billy goat run out. I put my eye up to a crack between the boards, and I could see he was standing up now and that his yellow eyes were on mine.

My mother was yelling at me to hurry up, and Uncle Tony was watching. I stepped around into the low doorway, and the goat charged toward me, feet first. I had dirt in my mouth and up my nose and there was blood running past my eye; my head ached. Uncle Tony carried me to the house; his face was stiff with anger, and I remembered what he'd always told us about animals: they won't bother you unless you bother them first. I didn't start to cry until my mother hugged me close and wiped my face with a damp wash rag. It was only a little cut above my eyebrow, and she sent me to school anyway with a Band-Aid on my forehead.

Uncle Tony locked the billy goat in the pen. He didn't say what he was going to do with the goat, but when he left with my father to haul firewood, he made sure the gate to the pen was wired tightly shut. He looked at the goat quietly and with sadness; he said something to the goat, but the yellow eyes stared past him.

"What's he going to do with the goat?" I asked my mother before I went to catch the school bus.

"He ought to get rid of it," she said. "We can't have that goat knocking people down for no good reason."

I didn't feel good at school. The teacher sent me to the nurse's office and the nurse made me lie down. Whenever I closed my eyes I could see the goat and my uncle, and I felt a stiffness in my throat and chest. I got off the school bus slowly, so the other kids would go ahead without me. I walked slowly and wished I could be away from home for a while. I could go over to Grandma's house, but she would ask me if my mother knew where I was and I would have to say no, and she would make me go home first to ask. So I walked very slowly, because I didn't want to see the black goat's hide hanging over the corral fence.

When I got to the house I didn't see a goat hide or the goat, but Uncle Tony was on his horse and my mother was standing beside the horse holding a canteen and a flour sack bundle tied with brown string. I was frightened at what this meant. My uncle looked down at me from the saddle.

"The goat ran away," he said. "Jumped out of the pen somehow. I saw him just as he went over the hill beyond the river. He stopped at the top of the hill and he looked back this way."

Uncle Tony nodded at my mother and me and then he left; we watched his old roan gelding splash across the stream and labor up the steep path beyond the river. Then they were over the top of the hill and gone.

Uncle Tony was gone for three days. He came home early on the morning of the fourth day, before we had eaten breakfast or fed the animals. He was glad to be home, he said, because he was getting too old for such long rides. He called me over and looked closely at the cut above my eye. It had scabbed over good, and I wasn't wearing a Band-Aid any more; he examined it very carefully before he let me go. He stirred some sugar into his coffee.

"That goddamn goat," he said. "I followed him for three days. He was headed south, going straight to Quemado. I never could catch up to him." My uncle shook his head. "The first time I saw him he was already in the piñon forest, halfway into the mountains already. I could see him most of the time, off in the distance a mile or two. He would stop sometimes and look back." Uncle Tony paused and drank some more coffee. "I stopped at night. I had to. He stopped too, and in the morning we would start out again. The trail just gets higher and steeper. Yesterday morning there was frost on top of the blanket when I woke up and we were in the big pines and red oak leaves. I couldn't see him any more because the forest is too thick. So I turned around." Tony finished the cup of coffee. "He's probably in Quemado by now."

I thought his voice sounded strong and happy when he said this, and I looked at him again, standing there by the door, ready to go milk the nanny goats. He smiled at me.

"There wasn't ever a goat like that one," he said, "but if that's the way he's going to act, O.K. then. That damn goat got pissed off too easy anyway."

from *YELLOW RAFT IN BLUE WATER*
Michael Dorris

In his novel, Yellow Raft in Blue Water, *Michael Dorris tells the poignant story of three contemporary Native American women and the family secrets that bind them.*

Life for fifteen-year-old Rayona, the youngest of the novel's three leading characters, is no fairy tale. She's been abandoned without explanation by her mother, kept at arm's length by a grandmother afraid to show love, ridiculed because of her mixed African-American and Native American heritage by her cousin and his friends, and molested by the new assistant pastor.

In this part of the novel, Rayona, aided by a newfound friend, returns home, determined to rebuild her shattered life.

Michael Dorris (Modoc) holds a bachelor's degree in English and classics from Georgetown University and a master's in philosophy from Yale. His best-selling novel, Yellow Raft in Blue Water, *was a Booklist Editor's Choice for 1987 in both the Adult and Young Adult categories. He is also the author of* The Broken Cord, *an account of his adopted son's battle with fetal alcohol syndrome, and the co-author of* The Crown of Columbus. *He lives in New Hampshire with his wife, writer Louise Erdrich, and their children.*

I'M NOT THAT HARD FOR EVELYN TO FIND. I'M STOPPED, HALFWAY down the trail, with my eyes fixed on the empty yellow raft floating in the blue waters of Bearpaw Lake. Somewhere in my mind I've decided that if I stare at it hard enough it will launch me out of my present troubles. If I squint a certain way, it appears to be a lighted trapdoor, flush against a black floor. With my eyes closed almost completely, it becomes a kind of bull's-eye, and I'm an arrow banging into it head-first.

Evelyn has a right to say anything, to call me a liar, to laugh, to demand an explanation, and when I sense her presence behind me, I'm ready for her. She has never seen me angry and I'll surprise her when I turn, lashing out and defiant, making fun of what suckers she and Sky have been. But Evelyn does the worst thing she can do. She doesn't say a word.

It's as if she sends off radiation that tickles the back of my neck and blows against my legs. I know exactly how far away she has positioned herself, right on the edge of my shadow, a smaller, heavier, older, unknown image of myself. I can wait her out. If silence is her plan, she'll have to forget it and go away if I keep quiet.

But she doesn't. We stand like two leafless trees that have grown on the path overnight, and she's the tougher.

"Now you know," I say. It's her move, but not a word. I feel the energy draining, flowing down my limbs and into the ground. If she touches me now I'll crumble. I can't take the suspense. "Say something."

"Oh, Ray," Evelyn says. "I'm so sorry." Her voice is new. Her lungs have cleared of their years of smoke and what comes out her throat is cool as cotton, young. I think it can't be Evelyn after all and twist around to see with my eyes. Evelyn still wears her white dishtowel apron and in her large, strong hands she shapes a ball of creamy dough. Her eyes are different though. Before I've always seen in them a suspicion of the world, a fine edge of disbelief, a glint that says "sure, you bet, uh-huh," and today that's gone. They look back at me like two bright jewels and I'm helpless.

"Now you know," I say again, and she shakes her head no.
"I don't know shit."
"I lied from the beginning." My voice is low, pulled from me.
"It doesn't matter. It's nothing."
I turn back to speak to the raft. "I'll tell you the truth."

"You don't have to," she says. "Sometimes it's better to leave things be. No one else has to know, and I can forget. I'm expert at that."

"Why are you being so nice?" I ask her. It's the tip of the iceberg of what I want to know. We both listen as my words float in the air and slowly break apart. "Why?"

"Don't ask me that," she finally says in her clean voice.

"What then?"

"Tell me if you want to."

So I tell her. We are stuck in a stable distance from each other, magnets connected by the stream of my words. I start my story in the middle and move in both directions. I tell her unimportant things, memories of little events that happened to me, clothes Mom wears and Dad's funny mailman adventures. I tell her Aunt Ida's favorite programs and I tell her about Father Tom and the yellow raft. I tell her yes, Seattle, but the reservation too, and Mom there somewhere with a man named Dayton and all her pills from Charlene. I tell her I wanted to trade places with Ellen. I tell her about my lifetime membership and I tell her about Mom just walking off and leaving. My story pours like water down the drain of a tub, and when the last drops cough out, I stop.

I don't hang for her answer anymore. There's a weight off me. I said it all out loud and the world didn't come to an end. I listened to my story, let loose, running around free in the morning air, and it wasn't as bad as I expected. It didn't even take that long to tell, once I got started.

From the parking lot comes the sound of the early-bird tourists arriving for the holiday, their ice chests full of food and litter. If Evelyn and I stay like this much longer, we'll take root.

"Now I know." Her voice is back to normal, full of gears that need oiling and rough edges. I wonder if I've imagined that it was ever different. "So what are you going to do about it?"

"I don't know."

"Well, figure it out. Nothing good's going to happen as long as you hide here. Your poor aunt is probably worried to death, that damn priest should have his ass kicked, and your mother is off sick somewhere."

I turn, and her words are a lightbulb switching on in my head. Of course Mom's sick. She was in the hospital. She has to take pills. That explains a lot.

"What do I do?" I say, more to myself than to Evelyn, but she answers first.

"Norman and me are driving you home."

"But you have to work," I say. "It's his busy day at the station."

"Don't make excuses. I haven't had a trip in a year and it's about time. It's a holiday. Anybody can cook the crap they'll eat today, and Norman can either close the damn Conoco or find somebody to run it."

"Why are you doing this?"

Evelyn pulls a leaf from the nearest tree and rotates it in her hand. She looks at it long and close enough to memorize the pattern of its veins. "Because somebody should have done it for me," she says. "All right?"

She turns and walks heavy but quick back toward the lodge. She bends forward, adjusting for the slope of the path, and her hips push like pistons as she plants each foot firmly in front of the other. Fueled with her idea, Evelyn looks as though she could march through solid rock to get where she wants to go. I follow in her wake, littering the trail with my unused box of Heftys. While Evelyn gets her keys I run into the equipment cabin and take the one thing I don't want to forget.

Sky does a double take when Evelyn pulls the car in front of the station.

"Be ready to roll when we come back in fifteen minutes," she yells out the window. "We're hitting the road."

Sky gets an expression on his face like he seriously wonders if this is happening. He's interested in all departures from what he expects, and he's sparked at the surprise of Evelyn's announcement.

"Just like that? Just take off?"

Evelyn nods her head, her mouth narrowing to a wide grin.

"Far out," Sky says. "Let me just lock the pumps and I'll be waiting." Before we pull out, he makes a show of taking the sign that hangs on the glass door of the station and reversing it to show CLOSED.

"And you wondered if he wanted to play hooky," Evelyn says to me as we reverse, and then head for the trailer. "He's an overgrown kid." There's color in her cheeks as she lights a cigarette with her Bic and blows out smoke. "Sky," she says to herself like he's beyond her understanding. "He didn't even ask why." She can't conceal her approval. "That's the kind to find yourself someday. You should have met my first husband. Scared of his own crap. The first thing he did when we got married was to open a savings account, but I didn't wait around for the interest to collect."

When we return for Sky and ease onto 2 going east, Evelyn treats him as though he must have known all the facts about me and just forgotten them.

"Ray was *always* leaving after a month," she tells him. "Where's your brain?"

"I don't get it," he says, confused. "Let me get this straight. Your folks have come back from Europe and are meeting you out *here*?" He draws his eyebrows together over his round, fleshy nose and turns to me for enlightenment.

Evelyn cuts in. "Come on. You knew she was pulling your leg. Don't let her see what a clunk I'm married to." She reaches across the gearshift to the other seat where Sky is sitting and slaps his thigh.

"Well, wait a couple or three minutes," Sky says, twisting so he can see me in the backseat. "You mean you *are* a full-blood Indian now?"

"You're the one that's full of it," Evelyn says. "Don't ask so many questions and they will all be answered." She drives us down the flat, straight highway. At the horizon line, miles ahead, the road seems to come to a point and at that place, in the glare of the sun, to merge with the sky.

"It looks like the edge of the world," I say, leaning forward. Next to me on the backseat is Evelyn's old suitcase, full of my things. When she saw me about to leave with my same plastic bag she rummaged in her closet until she found what she called her valise, a hinged box covered in worn, shiny pale green cloth with a strip of tan running like a strap around the middle. I offered to pay her for it but she laughed.

"I should pay you," she said. "I've kept that contraption for fourteen years without using it. It belonged to my mother, and I carried it when I left my first husband, and then again when I came to marry Norman. I'm not likely to be needing it a third time."

I transferred everything from my sack to the case, and on top put my money and the two VCR tapes from Village Video. In all this time they'd never been out of their boxes. I left my park uniform at Evelyn's for her to return, but I wore a B.L.S.P. T-shirt.

We stop for coffee and food at a cafe in Kremlin, fifteen miles west of Havre. The sign says it's the town where you're a stranger only once. Evelyn gives her Western sandwich an extra dose of pepper and asks, "Well, where to?"

I've thought about this. "There's a big Indian rodeo in Havre today," I say. "I think Mom'll come. Anyway it's as good a place as any to look."

After I say this it dawns on me that my return to the reservation isn't my idea but Evelyn's. I've been so caught in her determination that I left off thinking for myself, and now I'm about to be thrust back into the thick of what I escaped. I start hoping we'll have a flat, anything, to delay our arrival and give me a chance to get my bearings. We arrive at Havre, however, without a hitch. At the top of the hill, seeing all the people milling about, all the Indian trucks with "Fry Bread Power" bumper stickers and little moccasins hanging from the rearview mirrors, makes me want to throw the clutch in reverse, rewind back to this morning, and think things over. A clown with a dead flashlight waves us through a gate with a giant fiberglass wagon wheel suspended sideways over the top, and into the Hill County Fairgrounds. We pass the H. Earl Clark Museum, a train caboose, and a sign that warns against loose dogs. I tell myself I'm making too much of things, that I won't see anyone I know. People sometimes leave a rodeo early if things aren't going their way.

The parking lot has a SORRY FULL sign across the entrance. I take a long-shot chance. "Why don't we go up to Canada?" I suggest. "Saskatchewan is less than fifty miles. We can see your old friends."

Sky has an argument with himself about this idea and his face changes back and forth depending which side he's on, but Evelyn pays no attention. She swings the car around a dusty corner and noses into an empty space. The sounds of the crowd surround us as soon as the engine quits, the choppy rumble of conversation, the calls and clapping.

After we pay admission, Sky and Evelyn stick to me like pennies on a Bingo card. They stand close together, shifting their weight, looking in every direction, and making a point to talk loud to me. They act as though I'm their safe conduct, the reason they're allowed in. For just a flash I see them through Aunt Ida's eyes: a skinny middle-aged hippie and a heavyset woman in Bermuda shorts and a yellow nylon shirt with STAFF written in brown thread across her breast, her gray hair short as a man's, and her mouth blazing with bright lipstick for the occasion. Their skin is colorless and loose over their bones. They're nervous, not used to being strangers surrounded by Indians.

But they can relax. They aren't the ones who are about to be challenged.

I'm not five feet inside the gate when I come face to face with the last person I want to see. Foxy Cree is standing in the shade under the bleachers, and is in the process of violating the Absolutely No Alcoholic Beverages rule that is posted at every entrance. His half-closed eyes scan the crowd, pass me once, then zero in. He smiles to himself and moves in my direction.

"Find some good seats," I tell Sky and Evelyn. "You don't want to have to sit in the sun."

At my suggestion, Sky wanders off toward the stands, but not Evelyn. She waves him on when he looks back. "I'll be there, darling," she says, but she's looking at Foxy and knows trouble when she sees it.

"Do you know that one coming?" she asks, punching me in the side.

I have to admit that if you're not acquainted with Foxy he's handsome. He has a thin straight nose, deep-set black eyes, and long hair, divided today into two leather-wrapped braids. Beneath his weathered blue jeans jacket he wears an unbuttoned cowboy shirt. On his head is a black Navajo hat with a bead-work band. He's taller than me by a good three inches and so slim he can slip out of the window of a car without opening the door. But once you know him none of that counts.

"Ray*ona*," he says, all sly. His voice has a lilt to it that usually shows on people about the same time their vision goes blurry and their drinks spill. It's the voice of a person who thinks he's a lot wilier than the one he's talking to. "I saw this dark patch against the wall and I thought, Foxy, either that's the biggest piece of horse shit you've ever seen or it's your fucking cousin Rayona."

Evelyn is on red alert. This scene has no part in her vision of family reunions.

"We thought you was dead," Foxy goes on. "Or gone back to Africa." He says that last word real slow.

"Fuck you," I say.

"Rayona, Rayona, *Rayona*," Foxy sings. It isn't three o'clock and he's loaded already. His dirty cowboy boots stay in one spot but his body revolves as if moved by a breeze. He sways toward Evelyn.

"You here for the show, white lady?" he asks her. "You like dark meat?" He looks her over and stops at her chest. He laughs real low.

"Is this the piece of trash you were telling me about?" Evelyn has forgotten about being a stranger. I see her muscles bunching beneath the thin yellow material.

"No," I tell her. "Don't. Go with Sky."

She doesn't want to leave. She's ready to wipe the floor with Foxy but my look stands in her way. "This is my cousin," I say. "He might know what we came to find out. Let me talk to him."

All this time she's staring Foxy down, telling him with her eyes everything she thinks, and I can see she has penetrated his muscatel. His mouth hangs open as though it has been slapped and his face is full of complaint. He's wounded by the injustice of Evelyn's power, but that will turn to spite once he has me alone.

Without blinking, Evelyn asks if I'm sure, and when I say yes she suddenly takes a step toward Foxy, which makes him jump back.

"Norman and me'll be waiting for you. Don't take any crap." With a last, narrow-eyed warning look at Foxy she turns her back and disappears into the crowd.

I don't wait for him to recover. "Who's here?" I ask.

Foxy's still watching the place where Evelyn was standing and it takes a second for him to swing in my direction. "Holy shit," he says. "Where'd you find her?"

"What are you doing here?" I ask it a different way. This time it gets through.

"I'm here to *ride*, Rayona," he says. My name is ugly in his mouth, just as he means it to be. "I got me entered in the bareback bronc on a hand-picked mount." He reaches into his pocket and draws out a piece of paper with 37 written on it in black Magic Marker.

"You'll never make it," I say and laugh at him before I consider what I'm doing.

His face clouds over. "You think?"

I don't know what to say. He's about to get madder no matter what.

He looks blank and rubs his registration paper between his fingers. I think he might pass out on the spot, but instead he's gathering an idea.

"Are you here with anybody?" I ask him. "You can't compete."

"If I forfeit I'm disqualified for all the fucking rodeos this summer."

"Come on, Foxy. They'll bump you anyway. You'd break your neck. You're drinking."

The bubble of Foxy's plan has popped in his brain and he's ready to deal. He reaches into his pocket for a piece of paper.

"But you're not. Oh no, not Rayona. How's your priest boyfriend?" He balances himself with a hand that weights my shoulder. His fingers dig into me.

I go cold. "Shut up." I push him away and he falls heavily onto the ground. He shakes his head as if to clear it, then climbs to his feet.

"You turd," he says. "You're going to ride for me."

"Don't be dumb. I've never even been to a rodeo before."

"Well, you're here now. All you have to do to keep my qualification is be sober enough to make it through the chute."

"No way."

"Do it for your mom. My horse belongs to the guy she's shacked up with."

Dayton, I think.

I want to hit Foxy, to kick the drunken leer off his face. I close my hands into fists and then I see a knife open in his palm. He holds it loose, ready. His legs seem steadier. His eyes are flat and red and I know he'd cut me without thinking twice.

I take the easiest way out: I surrender. I don't know whether it's that I'm scared or that I'm defeated by the mention of Mom. I don't really believe they'll let me ride in Foxy's place anyway. When they see I'm a girl they'll disqualify me. And, too, the idea is impossible. The only experience I've had with horses was one summer in Seattle when Mom had a boyfriend who took us to a park where they rented saddle rides and I took a few lessons. I liked it all right, but those ponies were tame, trotted along in a line on paths through the trees. I can't imagine myself on a wild bronc, so I agree.

"What time?"

"Now you're talking, cousin," Foxy laughs. He clicks the knife closed in one hand, and focuses his eyes on the form he still holds in the other.

"Three forty-five," he says. "Number thirty-seven. Horse named Babe."

He hands me the registration and then feels into the side of his boot for the long paper bag around the wine held tight against his thin leg. He tips it to his mouth, drinks, then wipes his dripping chin. "I'll be watching, just in case you forget."

He starts to walk bowlegged to the stands, when the drink in his brain splashes the other way and he turns back.

"If they think you're a girl," he says, figuring it out as he goes along, "they won't let you ride." He wrestles with this thought, then slips off his jean jacket and hands it to me. "Put this on and button the front."

It's large for me, but Foxy is pleased with the effect. He walks behind me and tugs on the thick black braid of my hair.

"Now this," he says, and sets the black Navajo on my head. I can't believe Foxy and I have the same size brains, but we must because the hat fits.

"They'll just think I sat out in the sun too long." Foxy breaks down at his own joke. He laughs so hard he loses his breath in wheezes and coughs and finally spits on the ground. "You're a real Indian cowboy," he says.

It's less than a half hour until the event. I don't look for Sky and Evelyn since I have to figure this out for myself. The news that Mom is still on the reservation is sinking in. There's a part of me that's relieved. Ever since this morning, when Evelyn said Mom was sick, I've been worried in some nameless place, and now that relaxes. I wonder if in the weeks I've been gone, Mom has tried to find me, if she and Aunt Ida have made peace and worried together that I disappeared. No. She's still at this Dayton's and I still don't know how to find him. My one path to his door is through his horse. He's got to be around when she's ridden. Maybe Mom's here with him. Wouldn't she be surprised to see me contest? How would she feel if I got thrown on my head?

How will *I* feel? Fear rises in my neck at the thought of actually going through with Foxy's plan. I've seen bronc riding on "Wide World of Sports," and all I can remember is the sound of big men falling hard on the ground, the sight of crazed horses tossing their heads and kicking their hooves.

I've been walking toward the stock pens while I think, looking into the crowd for Mom's face, but instead I see Annabelle, and she's spied me first. She's dressed for the rodeo in tight jeans, a purple Bruce Springsteen T-shirt, long silver earrings, a bunch of turquoise bracelets on each arm, and blue Western boots. Her straight black hair hangs below her shoulders and her skin is tan and smooth. She has circled her eyes with dark liner and her fingernails are long and perfectly red. There's something about her that reminds me of Ellen, but then I realize that it's Ellen who's reminded me of Annabelle. Ellen is dim in comparison.

Annabelle comes up to me and demands, "Why are you wearing Foxy's hat." If she's surprised to see me, she doesn't let on.

"He gave it to me."

"Is he drinking?"

"He's drunk."

"Shit," she says. "He's up in a few minutes. He'll get bumped."

"He wants me to ride for him." I'm unbelieving all over again at the idea.

Annabelle cannot trust her ears. She doesn't know whether to laugh or get mad. She decides to get mad. "That asshole," she says. "I told him to stay straight, at least until after his event. I've had it with him."

No matter how many jeans jackets and hats you put on Annabelle, nobody would ever mistake her for a boy. She opens her purse, shakes out a Virginia Slim, and taps it against her lighter. She seems to notice me for the first time.

"Where have you been?" She's impatient and pissed off, but all the same this is the friendliest she's ever acted. It's the first time she's talked to me directly and not just to make an impression on whoever else is listening.

"Working at Bearpaw Lake State Park." I speak quickly, steeling myself for a mean reply.

"Really?" she says. Her imagination is caught. "God, I should get a job and get out of this place."

Now I know who Annabelle reminds me of. She's like the pictures I found in Aunt Ida's trailer. This is how Mom must have been, young and pretty, when she left, when she met Dad and they got married.

"Well, are you going to?" Annabelle asks.

"To what?"

"To ride for Foxy?"

Annabelle will be impressed if I say yes. I'll be different in her eyes, dumb maybe, but worth knowing. I take her question seriously. I consider what Evelyn would do if this was happening to her.

"Yes," I say.

★ ★ ★

Dayton could be any one of the men clustered around the corral when I come in answer to the announcer's call and hand over my credentials. The starter pins 37 to the back of Foxy's jacket, and like a robot I mount the fence and stand above the trapped brown horse. Lots of cowboys grow their hair long, and a braid is nothing strange. No one looks at me. Maybe they're embarrassed to see the fear in a rider's eyes.

From the instant I lower myself into the stall and onto the mare's broad and sheening back, I buzz with nerves. She inclines her head and regards me with one rolled eye, and I feel her quiver through the inside of my thighs as I grip her high around the shoulders. It's the kind of vibration that comes when you touch a low-voltage electric fence, enough to scare back cows and sheep. Tensing with not even a blanket or saddle between us, her skin seems tight-stretched. With one hand I take the rope that runs from the bit in her mouth and with the other I reach forward to pat her back.

"Hey Babe, hey girl," I say.

It's a game, I want her to know. We're just playing. We don't mean it for real.

She paws her feet, snorts. A cowboy hanging on the fence touches my hat and motions for me to hold it with my free hand. I take it off and am sure that now, at last, they'll get a clear view, realize I'm a girl, see that I don't know how to sit, and call it off. But they still don't see me.

I nod to the gate. I'll never be ready, but now is as good a time as any. There are dangers to staying in the chute too long. If the horse panics she'll heave herself against the sides, crushing my legs. Or worse, one buck in that packed space would throw me to the ground with nowhere to roll away from a kick. It's happened more than once on "Wide World." The announcers talk about the metal plates in riders' skulls.

The sounds of the rodeo around me fade in my concentration. There's a drone in my ears that blocks out everything else, pasts and futures and long-range worries. The horse and I are held in a vise, a wind-up toy that has been turned one twist too many, a spring coiled beyond its limit.

"Now!" I cry, aloud or to myself I don't know. Everything

has boiled down to this instant. There's nothing in the world except the hand of the gate judge, lowering in slow motion to the catch that contains us. I see each of his fingers clearly, separately, as they fold around the lever, I see the muscles in his forearm harden as he begins to push down.

I never expected the music.

Wheeling and spinning, tilting and beating, my breath the song, the horse the dance. Time is gone. All the ordinary ways of things, the gettings from here to there, the one and twos, forgot. The crowd is color, the whirl of a spun top. The noises blend into a waving band that flies around us like a ribbon on a string. Beneath me four feet dance, pounding and leaping and turning and stomping. My legs flap like wings. I sail above, first to one side, then the other, remembering more than feeling the slaps of our bodies together. Things happen faster than understanding, faster than ideas. I'm a bird coasting, shot free into the music, spiraling into a place without bones or weight.

I'm on the ground. Unmoving. The heels of my hands sunk in the dust of the arena. My knees sore. Dizzy. Back in time. I shake sense into my head, listen as the loudspeaker brays.

"Twenty-four seconds for the young cowboy from eastern Montana. Nice try, son. Hoka-hay."

A few claps from the crowd. I know I should move. I've seen riders today limp off when they fall, their heads hung, their mounts kicking two hind legs at the end of the ring until the clowns herd them out.

But Babe is calm. She stands next to me, blowing air through her nostrils, looking cross-eyed and triumphant. She wins the hand. Her sides ripple. It could be laughter, it could be disgust for having been touched. Dayton's horse.

So I don't leave with a wave to the stands. The first toss is warm-up, practice. I grab the rope, throw my arms around her neck and swing aboard. She stiffens, fuses her joints. The broad muscles of her shoulders turn steel under my gripping legs.

And bang! We're off again. This time instead of up and down she bolts straight ahead. The wind whips my braid, blows dust into my eyes till I have to squint them shut. She runs one fast circle around the pen, her body in a low crouch. She's thinking.

When you don't know what to expect, you hang on in every

way you can. I clasp the rope in one hand, her mane in the other. I dig my heels into the hollows behind the place where her forelegs join her ribs. I lean into her neck, and watch the ground rush by on either side of her ears.

Without warning she slows, moves close to the rough plank fence where the Brahmas are milling, and shifts her weight. She stops on a dime and, still clutching her with every part of me, I roll to the left. I'm pinned between Babe and the boards, with my back against the wall. My breath is squeezed out and there's no way I can protect my head, lolling above the pen. Then, without once lightening on the weight she presses against me, Babe walks forward as if to clean herself of me, as if I'm mud on the bottom of a boot.

It works. The next thing I know I'm on the ground again, Foxy's jean jacket ripped and torn across the shoulder seam, the air rushing back into my lungs, tears smeared on my cheeks. My ribs hurt, and behind me the bulls knock on the fence with their horns.

And before me is Babe, her lips drawn over her yellow teeth, her head low and swinging back and forth, her legs planted far apart. She looks astonished, at herself or me I can't tell.

As I stand she begins to retreat, one foot at a time. For an instant, I hear the crowd again, but I can't bother with them. I have Babe in my bead, our eyes in a blinding fix. Our brains lock, and she stops while I grab her mane and hook a leg over her back. Before I'm balanced, she rears. Her front legs climb the air, and I dangle along her back, suspended. When at last she drops, I'm low on her flank, our hips one on top of the other, my body fitted into her length. She rears again, and again there is air between us, yet I hang on. I smell her sweat, feel the warmth of her skin beneath my face and hands. There is nothing in the world but her and I think I can stay up forever.

When she kicks out with her hind legs, though, I slide over her neck, down her long head, and slam into the ground. I concede for the second time today. I'm so winded I can't move, stupid as I must look, my face in the dirt, my ass in the air, and my legs folded beneath me. When my ears stop ringing I hear the loudspeaker again.

". . . give this kid a hand, folks. He may not be much of a

rider but he ain't no quitter! Looks like he damn well wore out that wild mare too, even if he didn't bust her."

There's real clapping this time, a few whistles, but I get strength more from my curiosity about the last thing he said. I open one eye and the world is upside down, but that isn't the strangest thing. Not ten feet from me, sitting like a big dog and nodding her head, slumps Babe. She looks as bad as I feel, and as it turns out, we both need a hand from the clowns in getting out of the ring.

Some of Mom's navy boyfriends in Seattle used to talk about their sea legs and I never knew what they meant. They tried to explain how once you became used to the roll of waves, walking on dry land was never the same again. It felt lifeless.

Now I catch on. I'm back from throwing up behind the pens. I've rinsed the dirt from my face and dusted off my pants and jacket and the black hat someone handed to me as I limped out of the corral. Wild horse riding is the next-to-last event in the rodeo. As I lean back against the announcer's stand, I keep shifting my legs and waiting for something to happen under my feet. My muscles haven't yet set into the hard, stiff ache that lies ahead, but all through me I feel a ticking that hasn't run down.

There's a part of me that wants to submerge and disappear. Everybody that passes has to say something they think is funny about my ride, and I have to laugh at myself with them or be a bad sport. But there's another part of me that would climb back on Babe in a flash, no waiting, if that horse would appear in front of me. People tell me how lucky I am that I didn't break my neck or my back, or at least bust a shoulder, I fell so hard, but when I was riding I was mindless and beyond hurt. I was connected to a power I never knew existed, and without it I'm unplugged. On Babe, I would have burned out my circuits rather than choose safety. Up there, my only worry was gravity.

But on earth, my troubles haven't gone away. I stand, puzzling out what to do next, while the MC reads out the list of winners: Best bull ride. Longest saddle bronc. Fastest hogtie. I can't return to Bearpaw Lake with Sky and Evelyn. At the end of the season, when I would have no choice but to move along, I wouldn't be any closer to knowing what to do than I am now. Already Ellen and Andy and John, even Dave, are as removed and strange, as ancient history, as kids at my schools in Seattle. The ride on Babe is a boundary I can't recross, and I'm stuck on this side for better or worse.

Evelyn and Sky are different because they're here, because they brought me, because even though she doesn't know it, Evelyn got me on that horse and kept putting me back, because Sky closed the Conoco and gave up his Christmas money without asking any questions. But I can't live in the trailer with them any longer. My parents have returned from Switzerland.

Brahma riding. Bareback bronc. The fear comes back.

Annabelle pushes through the crowd and walks to face me. She carries two red paper Coke cups and hands one over. Her dark-rimmed eyes are excited.

"I wouldn't have believed it. I don't believe it," she says. "You're out of your mind. You're a maniac."

This is a compliment from Annabelle. I take a long pull on my Coke and discover it's beer.

"Do they know you're a girl?" Annabelle whispers. "You're insane."

The MC is about to announce the All-Around, the award for the cowboy who has done the best at the most events. It's what everybody waits to hear, and the crowd noise simmers down.

"Before the last prize," he says, "the judges have voted an unscheduled citation, one that's only given on rare occasions."

He holds up something shiny and silver that gathers light from the late afternoon sun and reflects it back in a bright beam.

"It's engraved special," he goes on. "I wish you folks could see it. This buckle shows a bronc and a rider throwed in the air, with genuine coral and jet inlay. One hundred percent nickel silver plate."

I see Evelyn and Sky in the bleachers, straining to hear. Their hands shade their eyes against the afternoon glare, but I'm standing under the judges' box and have my borrowed hat pulled low in front of my face.

"So come on, folks, and give a real Havre hand for the roughest, toughest, *clumsiest* cowboy we've seen around here in many a moon. It gives me genuine pleasure to award the hard-luck buckle, for the amazing feat of being bucked off the same horse three times in less than a minute, to a home-grown Indian boy, number thirty-seven, Kennedy 'Foxy' Cree!"

Some people let out yells and war whoops, and everybody starts pounding me on the back and shoving me forward. Kennedy Cree is Foxy's real name, and this minute it's mine too. Annabelle gives a sharp piercing whistle through her fingers and stomps her blue boot in the sawdust. I fill my lungs with stockyard air. There's no escape.

So I run the steps and reach to shake the MC's hand. He looks close at me this time, then closer. He realizes I'm no cowboy. I pry the buckle from him anyway and hold it to my right and left for the stands to see. Behind me there are surprised, voices talking to each other and when I look down at the other winners assembled nearest to the grandstand I see their eyes are wide too. It's no use pretending. I knock off my hat, undo the rubber band, comb with my fingers, and shake out my braid. With my free hand I unsnap the ruined jacket and shrug it from my shoulders. I thrust out my chest.

At first there's silence. Everyone gapes at me and then at each other and then at me again. The quiet hangs like a Seattle fog as we stand there, facing off in the long afternoon light. And finally from far away, clear and proud, Evelyn shouts: "Rayona!" Annabelle whistles again, loud as a siren. And when I raise the silver buckle high above my head, the rest of the crowd joins in.

THE BALLAD OF PLASTIC FRED

Eric L. Gansworth

When you're four years old, the world seems to be a place of infinite possibilities. And death is something that happens only to flickering people within the make-believe edges of a movie screen.

In this chapter from a novel in progress, Eric Gansworth tells the story of how one young Native American boy learned about death on a summer afternoon. Told with great humor and subtlety, "The Ballad of Plastic Fred" works to explode the stereotype of the wooden—or in this case plastic—Indian, devoid of human feelings. Gansworth shows the effect that stereotypes still have on the lives of Native American people today.

Eric L. Gansworth (Onondaga) was born in 1965 and raised on the Tuscarora Indian Reservation in western New York. He holds a bachelor's degree and master's degree from the State University College at Buffalo. He currently teaches at Niagara County Community College and the State University College at Buffalo. He is an artist as well as a writer, and several of his paintings have been exhibited in a Native American Art Exhibition at Niagara County Community College Gallery.

WE WERE GOING DOWN TO THE CORNER STORE ON THE DAY I learned about death. My sister had just recently gotten her license. Or maybe she hadn't yet. I can't remember. You didn't need a license to drive on the reservation, and the only store on the res was the one we were going to. It would've been just as easy to walk there, since it was only on the end of our road.

But Kay was just beginning to drive, and that made everything exciting. I was only four, and excitement was pretty cheap in those days.

It was summertime, June or July, I think. I knew that I was going to be heading off to school for the first time very shortly. My cousin Innis, who was two years older than me, had already been to school for a while. A lot of new kids had been playing with him since he started school. They would come over and visit, and he would be gone for long periods of time, presumably visiting with them. He lived next door. We used to play together all the time, but not so much anymore. I was left hanging around with his brother Horace, but nobody called him Horace, except for his mom when she was mad. Everyone else called him Ace. Ace was prone to random bursts of violence, and though he was younger than me, he was much larger. I didn't hang around with him without some big person to protect me. Cowardly, but safe.

That morning Innis had actually been home. We had been playing in the mountain. The mountain was this mound of dirt that had been dug out for my aunt's patio, which had never actually gotten built beyond the cinder block foundation. The mountain was on the patch of land between our two houses. It was small, I guess, but to us it seemed like another whole world. We had dug a hole into one of the interior folds of the mountain for later use as a cave for the six-inch plastic Indian figures we all played with. We could never quite figure out who those Indians were. They were all peach-colored and they didn't really look like anyone from our reservation. There was some speculation from my older cousins, those in the fourth or fifth grade, that one of those figures might be of Gary Lou's older brother, who had gone to Hollywood to be a star. We had seen him in some movies on TV, but I could never recognize him. He was killed by the cavalry before he ever got any close-ups. I don't really think anyone else recognized him either, but they all wanted him to be a star so bad that they made themselves see him in "that wild horde of savages."

So one of the figure's names was always Fred, as that was our star's name. It was always the one who was in a running position, crouched with one leg up. His mouth was open wide, in either a war cry or a really big yawn. In the hand that was in front of him, he carried a hatchet, a tomahawk, and he had two feathers sticking out of his hair in the back. All he wore was a loincloth, but when we looked underneath, to the area that wasn't covered, there was nothing there. He was a warrior without any balls. It didn't make sense to us, because we knew Fred had balls. After all, he went to Hollywood to become a star.

But it wasn't really him up there, anyway. Even in the ending credits, we couldn't find his name in the "Indian savages" list. We found out from his mother that he had changed his name. She had married a white man, who had a distinctly white last name. For Hollywood, Fred Howkowski had become Frederick Eagle Cry. Frederick Eagle Cry died daily on some TV somewhere, but Fred Howkowski lived on in California, occasionally sending his mother picture postcards of palm trees and big houses that described to her his most recent death so she could tell us and we'd all go to the movies so we could play Spot the Savage on bargain night.

Plastic Fred was getting a little beat. This was the figure everyone always wanted, and he usually died the most dramatic deaths of all the figures we had. He had to be rejuvenated every so often, and the old Fred would be retired to our version of the ancient burial ground. We would give the Freds to one of Innis's older brothers, Ely, who either used them for target practice, or tied them to firecrackers, or put lighter fluid to them, or in some other way creatively mutilated them. When he was done with them, he would give us back the twisted and blackened plastic which hardly resembled a figure anymore, and we would give them to Ace. It was his job to set them strategically around the mountain for their best dramatic potential. He had quite a knack with that sort of arrangement.

This Fred's days with us were numbered. He was covered with pockmarks from our discovery that we could throw darts at him and that if we were lucky, the darts would stick as he toppled from his ledge and remain stuck as he landed, which was a really cool-looking death. This Fred also had a large hardened glob of Testors model glue on the back of his head with a little sharp spine poking out. We had found a feather that had fallen off of this sparrow that one of our cats had killed and we decided to put it on Fred. Innis stole one of his dad's saws and we hacked the plastic feathers off of the back of Fred's head and glued on the real one with the model glue. The feather lasted about four or five days and then it finally broke off and all we were left with was the mound of glue and the feather's spine. How do birds keep them so long, anyhow?

So it was still pretty early in the morning, probably around eight-thirty or nine, though I hadn't been able to tell time all that well yet. The sun was hot, but not unpleasantly so. We had shoved all the finely sifted dirt we had dug out for the cave. We had shoved it all together to create a small very soft hill in the inner valley of the mountain, and now that the sun had reached over the mountain's edge, the hill was warm. I took my sandals off and patted my toes in the dirt, leaving small circular prints. Innis did the same, but he hadn't had to take his shoes off. He never wore any in the summer. We wrestled toes with each other in the heated earth, stirring up small clouds of dust, which swirled in the sunlight.

We did this for a while. I asked him if Ace were up yet. Just as I asked it, I heard their screen door slam. I waited and listened for the splash that meant it had just been their mother throwing out some dirty wash water, but the sound never came. Ace was coming. He jumped down next to me and stuck his feet in with ours, sneakers and all. Ace had no aversion to shoes in the summertime.

Ace asked me where the Indians were. I told him that they were in the house. He was a little irate over this; he wanted to play right then. Innis said that he'd pee on him if he didn't behave, and this calmed the younger brother down instantly. I guessed that Innis had made good on this threat at some time in the past, though I had nothing to substantiate this. I also told him that we didn't want the dogs to get them and chew them up, which is what would happen if we left them unattended. To pass time, we planned for our impending departure from the mountain.

We were waiting for my sister to get up. She had said the night before that if Mom would give her the keys she would drive us down to Jugg's store to get a new Plastic Fred. Maybe we'd get a bottle of pop too. There was always pop in the fridge, but it wasn't the same as drinking pop while sitting on one of Jugg's high stools that surrounded his lunch counter. People in high school seem to really love sleeping in late.

Kay finally came out of the door. We were pretending not to notice but had been watching the door all morning. She leaned against the porch railing for a minute, adjusting her sandals to conform against her heels. She went to the car and hopped in. I grabbed my sandals as the others ran to line up at the edge of the driveway. After some moments of adjusting the various settings of the car, Kay started it and jerkily drove to the place my cousins were standing, just as I joined them. We all piled in, Innis getting to sit in the front seat since he was older. He turned on the radio and began spinning the dial to find a good song. He found "Daydream Believer" by The Monkees and we were all happy with that, so that was what we listened to as we pulled out of the driveway.

Ace and I couldn't see too much as we were small and the seat backs were high. We entertained ourselves by pretending we were members of The Monkees. The song ended, and we all listened to find out what the next song was going to be. The announcer said that it was going to be something new from The Jefferson Airplane. This was some new group and one of Kay's favorites. I knew that we would be listening to the new song through speakers that vibrated because the volume was turned up so high.

We never did get to hear the new song that day. In her excitement, Kay was more interested in the volume control than the steering wheel. We promptly crashed into Ardra's mailbox just down the road. We hadn't been going very fast, but we did enough damage that we had to stop. We all got out of the car and looked at the uprooted mailbox and the dent in the front end of the car.

Ardra came out of her house, wiping her hands on a dish towel. She watched as Kay picked up the mailbox and tried to stick its post back into the hole we had rammed it out of. It went back in, and actually wasn't damaged. But the hole had been widened by our hit and the mailbox sat lazily at an angle. Ardra looked closely at it, and seeing that neither the box nor its post were any worse for the wear, told us to go along, that Enoch, her husband, would put some rocks in the hole to steady it when he got home. We went.

When we got to the store, Kay told us to stay in the car while she ran in. We started to whine, but not for long. Her mood had changed substantially since our encounter with the mailbox. She was back out in a few seconds. She threw the bag in the backseat, just barely missing me. She slammed the car into reverse and we stirred up a dust cloud in the small gravel parking lot.

We flew down to the picnic grove, just below the hill upon which the store sat. We pulled in, bouncing around in the backseat as she drove over the pitted and rutted path into the grove. She got out and left the door open as she sat down hard on the concrete bandstand. The three of us got out and walked over to where she was sitting. I opened the bag to see what she bought.

I reached in and pulled out some bottles of Pepsi and passed them around. I pulled the plastic Indian from the bag. It wasn't Fred. It was a chief with a headdress and a bow and arrow. How could she mistake this guy for Fred? I mentioned this to my sister; she told me to shut up and snatched the bag away from me. She pulled a pack of cigarettes from the bag and ripped them open. She lit one. I didn't even know she smoked.

We left the grove a couple of minutes later. We were all looking out the windows, studying hard the road and the ditches that bordered the road. We were looking for a dead cat, any dead cat would do. We just needed one. There was a high mortality rate for reservation cats and there were usually some dead ones lying around the sides of one road or another.

Innis had gotten the idea. We had to find some way to explain the new dent in the car. It wasn't as if the car were new or anything, or that it didn't already have some dents in it. This dent, however, would not go unnoticed. It wasn't just the fender that was dented. The mailbox had impacted with the hood and had left its own noticeable mark. We knew that we could get away with this if we had some really good reason for the dent. We also knew that if we said it happened because of the radio, we'd be walking to the store for quite some time to come. We were in this together.

330

My mother loved cats. We had eight of them. When our cat had kittens, my mother just couldn't bear to give them up. The survivors from the second litter were already grown up, and the mother was pregnant again. It appeared we were going to have more. Virtually the entire population of the res knew of my mother's love for cats. Innis thought if we told my mother that we had hit the mailbox while trying to avoid running over a cat, that would be a good enough excuse. We agreed.

He thought he had seen a dead cat along the side of the road as we had headed to the store, but he couldn't remember exactly where. He did say that it was after Ardra's house. He was quite sure of that. He thought if we brought the dead cat home with us, it would be even more convincing. Kay thought this was really gross, but she was a desperate woman. We had to hurry, too. We were only supposed to have gone down the road.

Kay warmed to the idea the closer we got to the house, and the closer she got to not being able to drive for a while. She even told us that she hoped it was a fresh one, and not stiff and loaded with maggots. It was, after all, the middle of summer. A rotting cat would not be too convincing. My mother would probably insist on a burial, and she would most certainly notice the odor of a high-summer dead cat. We hoped along with Kay. None of us really wanted to handle the cat. The anonymous plastic Indian sat casually on the backseat.

I spotted the cat. Innis was right. It was beyond the spot of our collision, but not much. It was in front of the field next to Spicy's house. On the other side of the field was Ardra and Enoch's. As we got out of the car, we could see the lounging mailbox. Enoch apparently hadn't gotten home yet. We walked over to the cat. It was an orange one, the color of Creamsicles, my mother's favorite cat color. It was still alive.

Someone had hit it not long before Innis had seen it the first time. It was lying in the gravel and dirt that edged the road. There was a trail of streaky blood from the place on the road where it must have been hit to the place it now rested. It must have dragged itself. The blood had come from its rear end. Its back legs were bent at impossible angles. It was breathing heavily, panting. Its eyes stared up at us as we surrounded it.

I squatted down to pet it. I didn't know what else to do. Kay yelled at me and pushed me aside before I could reach it. She said that the cat might try to bite. She said that she couldn't do it.

"Sure you can, just do this," Ace said, moving closer to the cat. He was out of reach for any of us. I was still sitting in the weeds. Kay and Innis had already turned and started moving toward the car.

Ace stomped hard once on the cat's neck. The cat made a small squeaking noise and then did not make another. The cat expired under the hot summer sun. We had all seen it go. I wondered who would be putting food out for it tonight, how long those scraps would sit before they knew the cat wasn't coming home.

We started walking back to the car.

"Hey, aren't we takin' this?" Ace was holding the cat by the tail, lifting it out to his right, like a fisherman showing off his prize catch of the day. Innis told him to put it down and to wipe his hands on the weeds. He dropped the cat back to the ground and did as he was told. The cat stirred up a little dust which blew away in a couple of seconds.

My mother didn't ask about the dent. She had been on the phone when we walked into the house. As soon as she finished talking to someone she would dial someone else's number and begin with her one greeting which always meant some serious bad news.

"Did you hear?"

My other sister, Gretchen, told us what had happened. Fred Howkowski had shot himself in Hollywood. The cavalry must have finally come.

My mother glanced at the old clock hanging on the wall near our phone, got off the phone, and rushed out the door. She still had curlers in her hair. She was going to drive Fred's mom and dad to the airport. They were bringing him home to be buried on the reservation. The plastic Indian chief rode in the backseat with Fred's dad.

I wondered why Fred went and did that. Maybe he just couldn't find someone to stomp on his throat.

I asked Kay if we could walk back and bury the cat. She said sure. We buried it in the mountain. We wrapped it up in an old flannel shirt which didn't fit her anymore. We put it in an old cardboard canning jar box. We did this so the dogs wouldn't find it.

We told Mom about the dent when she got home. The plastic Indian chief joined the tribe. We continued to play in the mountain, being careful not to dig where we had buried the cat. Whenever we went to the store the rest of the summer, we walked. We drank a lot of Pepsi. We occasionally bought a Mountain Dew.

We never bought another Plastic Fred.

"The Language We Know" by Simon Ortiz. Reprinted from *I Tell You Now: Autobiographical Essays by Native American Writers,* edited by Brian Swann and Arnold Krupat, by permission of the University of Nebraska Press. Copyright © 1987 by the University of Nebraska Press.

"The Warriors" by Anna Lee Walters from *The Sun Is Not Merciful* by Anna Lee Walters. Reprinted by permission of Firebrand Books, Ithaca, New York 14850. Copyright © 1985 by Anna Lee Walters.

Selection from *Waterlily* by Ella Cara Deloria. Reprinted by permission of the University of Nebraska Press. Copyright © 1988 by the University of Nebraska Press.

Selection from *Life Among the Piutes: Their Wrongs and Claims* by Sara Winnemucca Hopkins. Originally published 1883. Copyright © 1969 by Sierra Media, Inc., Bishop, California. Originally published by G. P. Putnam's Sons.

Selection from *Night Flying Woman: An Ojibwa Narrative* by Ignatia Broker. Reprinted, with permission, from *Night Flying Woman: An Ojibwa Narrative* by Ignatia Broker, copyright © 1983 by the Minnesota Historical Society.

Selection from *Black Elk Speaks* by John G. Neihardt. Copyright 1932, © 1959 by John G. Neihardt. Originally published by William Morrow & Co.

Selection from *My Indian Boyhood* by Luther Standing Bear. Reprinted from *My Indian Boyhood* by permission of the University of Nebraska Press. Copyright 1931 by Luther Standing Bear. Copyright © 1959 by May M. Jones.

Selection from *The Middle Five: Indian Schooldays of the Omaha Tribe.* Reprinted by permission of the University of Wisconsin Press. Originally published in 1900. Copyright © 1963 by the Regents of the University of Wisconsin.

Selection from *Lame Deer: Seeker of Visions* by John Fire/Lame Deer and Richard Erdoes. Copyright © 1972 by John Fire/Lame Deer and Richard Erdoes. Reprinted by permission of Simon & Schuster, Inc.

"Saint Marie" by Louise Erdrich. From *Love Medicine* by Louise Erdrich. Copyright © 1984 by Louise Erdrich. Reprinted by Permission of Henry Holt and Co., Inc.

Selection from *Indian School Days* by Basil Johnston. Reprinted with permission from *Indian School Days* by Basil H. Johnston, published by Key Porter Books Limited, Toronto, Ontario. Copyright © 1988 Basil H. Johnston.

Selection from *Sundown* by John Joseph Mathews. Copyright © 1934 by John Joseph Mathews, assigned 1987 to the University of Oklahoma Press.

Selection from *Mean Spirit* by Linda Hogan. Reprinted with the permission of Atheneum Publishers, an imprint of Macmillan Publishing Company. Copyright © 1990 by Linda Hogan.

Selection from *The Names: A Memoir* by N. Scott Momaday. Reprinted by permission of the author. Copyright © 1976. Published by University of Arizona Press.

"Notes of a Translator's Son" by Joseph Bruchac. Reprinted from *I Tell You Now: Autobiographical Essays By Native American Writers,* edited by Brian Swann and Arnold Krupat, by permission of the University of Nebraska Press. Copyright © 1987 by the University of Nebraska Press.

Selection from *Bobbie Lee: Indian Rebel* by Lee Maracle. Reprinted by the permission of Women's Press, Toronto, Ontario. Copyright © 1990 by Lee Maracle.

"The Talking That Trees Does" by Geary Hobson. Reprinted by permission of the author. Copyright © 1983.

"The Water Witch" by Louis Owens. Reprinted by permission of the author. Copyright © 1988.

"Grace" by Vickie Sears. From *Spider Woman's Grandaughters* by edited Paula Gunn Allen. Reprinted by permission of Beacon press.

"Uncle Tony's Goat" by Leslie Marmon Silko. Reprinted by permission of author. Copyright © 1974.

Selection from *A Yellow Raft in Blue Water* by Michael Dorris. Copyright © 1987 by Michael Dorris. Reprinted by permission of Henry Holt and Co., Inc.

"The Ballad of Plastic Fred" by Eric L. Gansworth. Printed by permission of the author.